First published in 1933
by George Allen & Unwin Ltd.

This edition first published in 2026 by Routledge
4 Park Square, Milton Park, Abingdon, Oxon, OX14 4RN

and by Routledge
605 Third Avenue, New York, NY 10158

Routledge is an imprint of the Taylor & Francis Group, an informa business

Publisher's Note
The publisher has gone to great lengths to ensure the quality of this reprint but points out that some imperfections in the original copies may be apparent.

Disclaimer
The publisher has made every effort to trace copyright holders and welcomes correspondence from those they have been unable to contact.

For Product Safety Concerns and Information please contact our EU representative GPSR@taylorandfrancis.com. Taylor & Francis Verlag GmbH, Kaufingerstraße 24, 80331 München, Germany

A Library of Congress record exists under LCCN: 33032212

ISBN: 978-1-041-24088-4 (hbk)
ISBN: 978-1-003-74008-7 (ebk)
ISBN: 978-1-041-24092-1 (pbk)

Book DOI 10.4324/9781003740087

The Indian Tariff Problem

In Relation to Industry and Taxation

Hirendra Lal Dey

Routledge
Taylor & Francis Group

Routledge Revivals

The Indian Tariff Problem

First published in 1933, *The Indian Tariff Problem* offers a critical analysis of the policy and administration of Protective Tariffs, introduced following India's attainment of Fiscal Autonomy in 1921. Chapter one examines the implications, reactions, and limitations of tariffs as a tool for reallocating national resources and income. The subsequent seven chapters provide a detailed and realistic study of India's tariff policy and administration, focusing on three major industries of the time: cotton, steel, and sugar. The final chapter summarizes the arguments and conclusions, advocating for a more rational approach to tariff policy and improved administration techniques, supported by better and more comprehensive data. This work remains a significant historical reference for scholars and researchers of India's economic history.

THE INDIAN TARIFF PROBLEM

IN RELATION TO

INDUSTRY AND TAXATION

by

HIRENDRA LAL DEY

D.Sc.(Econ.) (London), M.A.

Lecturer in Economics, University of Lucknow

LONDON

GEORGE ALLEN & UNWIN LTD

MUSEUM STREET

FIRST PUBLISHED IN 1933

PRINTED IN GREAT BRITAIN BY
UNWIN BROTHERS LTD., WOKING

PREFACE

THE object of the present volume is a critical review of the policy and administration of Protective Tariffs, on which India embarked on the attainment of Fiscal Autonomy in 1921. The existing literature on the subject of Indian tariffs deals either with the evolution of the customs tariff through successive stages, with special reference to the fiscal autonomy controversy of the last quarter of the nineteenth century, or with general arguments along well-known, orthodox, lines on the merits and demerits of a policy of protection for India. So long as India had no right to regulate her tariff policy in accord with the wishes and opinions of her people, there was a pronounced, natural, tendency not only to emphasise her right to the exercise of fiscal autonomy, but also to assume that a policy of protection was the only, or at any rate the best, cure for many of her industrial weaknesses. Now that she has attained the long desired fiscal autonomy and freely exercised that right for a decade, the time has come when we should begin to ask how far the assumptions of the protective policy have been justified by the facts of experience. It is with the finding of an answer to that question that this book is largely concerned.

Perhaps a few words may be added on the scope and plan of the work. Since a protective tariff is, first and foremost, a machinery for taxation and redistribution of the National Dividend, the implications, reactions, and limitations, of the Indian tariff as an engine for a reallocation of the national resources and income, both with reference to the general interest on the one hand and important sections of specific interests on the other, are examined and set out in Chapter I. The succeeding seven chapters are devoted to a detailed, realistic, study of India's tariff policy and administration with specific reference to three of the typical major industries of the country—the cotton, the steel, and the sugar industries. The conclusions regarding the necessity, efficacy, and relevancy, of the protective tariff as a remedy for the present competitive weakness of these industries are stated in each case separately. The last chapter contains a résumé of the arguments and conclusions, and ends with a plea for formulating the tariff policy on more rational lines, and improving the technique of tariff administration with the aid of fuller and better data than have been used in the past.

I am deeply indebted to Professor A. J. Sargent for being good enough to read patiently through the whole book in MS., and for advice and criticisms which have been of the utmost value to me in improving the argument at many points.

I wish to express my thankfulness to my teacher and friend Sir Jehangir Coyajee, Member of the Indian Fiscal Commission and the Royal Commission on Indian Currency and Finance, Sir Padamji Ginwala, lately President of the Indian Tariff Board, Dr. Vera Anstey, Professor J. Coatman, and Professor Harold J. Laski for encouragement and helpful suggestions at different stages of the work.

I am under obligations to the Librarians of the British Museum, the India House, the India Office, and, in a special sense, to Mr. B. M. Headicar of the School of Economics and Political Science, for their unfailing courtesy and assistance.

My grateful acknowledgements are also due to my friends Dr. P. Datta and Mr. M. L. Bhatia for the drawings of the graphs.

H. L. D.

London School of Economics
October, 1931

CONTENTS

LIST OF GRAPHS

INDIAN COINAGE, WEIGHTS AND MEASURES

The unit of the Indian currency is the silver rupee. At the present rate of exchange, the rupee is equal to 1s. 6d. sterling. The rupee is divided into 16 annas, and the anna into 12 pies.

The method of numerical notation in India differs from that prevalent in Europe. Large numbers are not punctuated in hundreds of thousands and millions, but in lakhs and crores. A lakh is one hundred thousand and written out as 1,00,000. A crore is one hundred lakhs and written out as 1,00,00,000.

The standard unit of weights in India is the maund. The maund is divided into 40 seers, and the seer into 16 chhattacks. The maund is equal to 82·28 lb. Av.

THE INDIAN TARIFF PROBLEM
IN RELATION TO INDUSTRY AND TAXATION

CHAPTER I

INTRODUCTION: TAXATION AND TARIFFS IN INDIA

1. THE PRINCIPLE OF PROGRESSIVE TAXATION

The structure and the content of the tax system of a country are determined partly by the fiscal traditions of the past, partly by the economic and social organisation of the people, and partly also by the general lay-out and functions of the different parts of the governmental machinery. Since there have been in the past and there are likely to persist in the future the most marked differences among different states in fiscal traditions as well as in the organic structures and functional relations of the governmental machinery, we would naturally find the greatest divergencies and disparities in the fiscal practices of modern states. Nevertheless, as the result of a long process of abstract analysis and comparative studies in public finance, there have already emerged certain broad principles or standards which are now being increasingly accepted as the tests of the soundness of the fiscal system of a country. Among these various principles of taxation, there is perhaps none which has found a wider measure of acceptance in theory and practice than the principle of taxation according to ability. Now, as there are great inequalities among different social groups and classes in wealth, income and taxable capacity, the canon of taxation according to ability has come to be commonly interpreted as progressive taxation.[1] We can, therefore, observe in practically every modern country a marked tendency to so devise and interrelate the different taxes within the fiscal system as a whole that the distribution of the burden of taxation among

[1] Cf. Seligman, *Essays in Taxation*, pp. 21 et seq.

the members of the several income groups may conform at least approximately to the principle of progression.

In practice it is found that while direct taxes on income and property may be made to satisfy largely the ideal of progression, most of the indirect taxes on consumption often result in the inequity of sharp regression. Although the correct proportions to be observed between progressive direct taxes on income and property on the one hand and largely regressive indirect taxes on consumption upon the other must, in the last analysis, depend upon the size and shape, and the nature and standard of consumption, of the different income groups within the society, nevertheless, in the absence of adequate statistical data for the exact measurement of the distribution of taxable capacities and tax burdens of the different classes, it may be assumed that the larger the proportion of the total revenues raised by direct taxes on property and income, the greater is the degree of approximation to the principle of progression, and the larger the proportion of the revenues contributed by indirect taxes on consumption, the greater is the likelihood of the inequity of regression.[1] It, therefore, follows that if the distribution of the burden of a tax system as a whole is to be based on the principle of progression, the taxes on consumption must play a comparatively subordinate rôle, while the taxes on income and property must exercise a dominating influence. It is on account of the observance of such a due balance and harmony between the direct and the indirect taxes that, as brought out by the recent investigation of the Committee on National Debt and Taxation, the distribution of the burden of national taxation among the different income groups in Great Britain shows an admirable approximation to the ideal of progression.[2] The glaring contrasts between the British and

[1] Cf. Stamp, *Current Problems in Finance and Government*, Chapter X, "The Relation between Direct and Indirect Taxation."

[2] Cmd. 2800, p. 95. From the table on that page, it will be seen that the sharply regressive effect of the indirect taxes is largely counterbalanced by the much steeper upward graduation of the direct taxes, the net result being a slight regression for the incomes up to £500, and marked progression for the higher grades.

the Indian tax systems in respect of the percentage contribution of direct and indirect taxes to the total tax revenue which are presented in the following table would, on the contrary, tend to show that the Indian tax system suffers from the grave defect of regression and thus falls far short of the ideal of distributive justice in the matter of the imposition of tax burden on the different economic classes in the country.

TABLE I

PERCENTAGE CONTRIBUTION OF DIRECT AND INDIRECT TAXES IN INDIA AND THE UNITED KINGDOM

1926–29

	(1) INDIA* (Central and Provincial)		(2) UNITED KINGDOM† (Great Britain and Northern Ireland)	
	Amount in Crores of Rupees	Percentage of the Total	Amount in £ Million	Percentage of the Total
1. Income Tax and Super Tax.. ..	16·16	11·47	305·85	44·92
2. Stamps (Taxes on transactions and fees)	14·95	10·61	27·28	4·00
3. Estate and Death Duties	—	—	75·07	11·03
4. Land Revenue ..	34·57	24·54	—	—
5. Land Tax and Land Values Duties ..	—	—	0·83	0·12
6. Customs and Excise	75·14	53·38	271·85‡	39·93
Total	140·82	100·00	680·88	100·00

* *Statistical Abstract for British India.*
† *Statistical Abstract for the United Kingdom.*
‡ Including Motor Vehicles Duties.

2. EXTREME REGRESSIVENESS OF THE TAX SYSTEM OF INDIA

The above table, showing as it does the significant contrast between the tax systems of the United Kingdom and India, does not, however, fully bring out the sharply regressive character of the Indian tax system as a whole. For purposes of strict comparison between the Indian taxes and those of other countries, land revenues should be omitted from the list of Indian taxes, because, for the greater part of India, land revenue partakes of the nature of a share of the rent claimed by the state as part owner of land. Its administration and incidence are altogether different from those of taxes on income in at least four essential points: (1) There is no exemption from land revenue even for the tiniest holdings amounting to less than an acre and with an annual income of Rs. 20 or Rs. 30. (2) Except in the permanently settled districts where the land revenue demand has been fixed in perpetuity since 1793, the revenue demand of the Government is a fixed proportion of the economic rent, generally between 20 and 50 per cent of the latter. (3) The amount of land revenue is either fixed for ever as in the permanently settled areas, or for 20, 30 or 40 years as in the other provinces, and does not vary from year to year in response to the needs of the state. (4) Most important of all, the state, throughout the whole of India, provides irrigation facilities, agricultural loans, and improved seeds, and thus supplies the element of active partnership with the actual cultivators, which in other countries is done by the landlords. Hence, whatever the legal aspect of Indian land revenue might be, from the economic point of view it would seem that it is only a share of the rent of land claimed by the state by right of landlordship, partial or complete.[1] If, for these reasons, we

[1] Cf. *The Report of the Indian Taxation Enquiry Committee* (1926), pp. 66–67. The Committee was unable to reach any clear and definite conclusion on the point whether the land revenue is a tax or rent, but would seem rather inclined to the view that it is a tax. Due to the existence of powerful vested interests in the matter of land revenue, there is observable a marked reluctance in all quarters to give a plain, direct and decisive answer to the question whether the land revenue is a tax or rent. If it is a tax, the present assessment being between 20 and 50 per cent on all agricultural profits, there can be hardly any room for further taxation of agricultural income. On the other hand, if it is only a share of the rent, then agricultural incomes are at present altogether exempt from any income tax, and may, like all other kinds of income, be subject to the same.

In view of the well-known inequity of the incidence of the land revenue in India, under which we have at one end of the scale large and substantial

omit land revenue from among the Indian taxes, the percentage contribution of direct and indirect taxes in India compared with the corresponding position in Great Britain would be as follows:

TABLE II

PERCENTAGE CONTRIBUTION OF DIRECT AND INDIRECT TAXES IN INDIA AND THE UNITED KINGDOM (EXCLUDING LAND REVENUE IN THE CASE OF INDIA), 1926–29

	India Percentage of the Total Tax Revenues	Great Britain and Northern Ireland Percentage of the Total Tax Revenues
1. Income Tax and Super Tax ..	15·21	44·92
2. Stamps (Taxes on transactions and fees)	14·07*	4·00
3. Estate and Death Duties ..	—	11·03
4. Land Tax, Land Values Duties	—	0·12
5. Customs and Excise	70·72	39·93
Total	100·00	100·00

* A small part of the stamp receipts in India is derived from probate duties and is thus of the nature of the death duties in the United Kingdom.

The marked contrasts revealed in this table between the United Kingdom and India in respect of the relative weights of the direct and indirect taxes on the tax system as a whole would tend to show that, whereas the preponderating influence exercised by direct taxes on the fiscal system of the United Kingdom makes the distribution of the burden of taxation in that country conform to the equitable principle of progression, the overwhelming pressure of indirect taxes on the fiscal system of India, on the contrary, makes for a distribution of

land-holders, many of whom are creations of the British Government, contributing only a portion of their big unearned incomes to the state, while at the other end there are the small cultivators of the uneconomic holdings paying a substantial share of their precarious and inadequate incomes towards the revenues of the state, the principle of equity, no less than the growing financial needs of the self-governing India of the near future, is certain to compel the responsible authorities in India to courageously answer the question whether the incomes from the ownership and use of land cannot, like the incomes from all other investments and occupations, be subject to the income tax.

the burden of taxation in the latter country, which can be reasonably assumed to be heavily regressive, and, therefore, unjust and inequitable in character.

3. CONSUMPTION TAXES AND THEIR EFFECTS

A further contrast between the tax system of the United Kingdom and that of India is that, whereas in the former country by far the largest proportion of the consumption taxes is derived from taxes on luxuries, in the latter country a considerable part of the corresponding revenues is raised from the taxation of necessaries of life and means of production. This marked divergence between the consumption taxes of the two countries is brought out in the following tables:

A

INDIA

(1926–29)*

(*a*) Customs and excise duties on the necessaries of life and means of production.

	Crores of Rupees
CUSTOMS:	
1. Sugar	7·09
2. Mineral oils	1·67
3. Cotton manufactures	6·58
4. Non-protective duty on iron and steel and railway plant and rolling stock	0·90
5. Raw materials and articles mainly unmanufactured, other than metallic ores	0·75
6. Cutlery, hardware, implements and instruments	1·38
7. Metals other than iron and steel	0·87
8. Protective import duty on iron and steel ..	2·99
9. Protective duty on paper and stationery ..	0·27
EXCISE:	
10. Motor spirits	1·24
11. Kerosene	0·98
CUSTOMS AND EXCISE:	
12. Salt	6·98
Total	31·70

* *Statistical Abstract for British India.*

	Per Cent
(*b*) Taxes on the necessaries of life and means of production as percentage of the total customs and excise revenue (Rs. 75·14 crores)	42·19
(*c*) Taxes on the necessaries of life and means of production as percentage of the total tax revenue, excluding land revenue (Rs. 106·25 crores)	29·84

B

UNITED KINGDOM

(1926–29)*

(*a*) Customs and excise duties on the necessaries of life and means of production.

	£ Million
1. Tea	5·82
2. Sugar	17·60
3. Hydrocarbon oils	12·98
4. Railway passengers' duty	0·38
5. Key industries and safeguarding of industries duties (excluding duties on lace and embroidery, gloves and pottery)	1·27
Total	38·05

	Per Cent
(*b*) Taxes on the necessaries of life and means of production as percentage of the total tax revenues (£m. 271·85)	14·36
(*c*) Taxes on the necessaries of life and means of production as percentage of the total tax revenues (£m. 680·88)	5·59

* *Statistical Abstract for the United Kingdom* and *Report of the Commissioners of His Majesty's Customs and Excise.*

C

(1926–29)

	India Per Cent	United Kingdom Per Cent
(*a*) Taxes on the necessaries of life and means of production as percentage of the total customs and excise ..	42·19	14·36
(*b*) Taxes on the necessaries of life and means of production as percentage of the total tax revenues	29·84	5·59

Table C would show that the proportion borne by the taxes on the necessaries of life and means of production to the total customs and excise revenues of India is nearly thrice as great, and to the total tax revenues considerably more than five times as great, as the corresponding proportion in the United Kingdom.

The objection in principle to the raising of large revenues through the taxation of the necessaries of life and means of production is that, whereas consumption taxes on luxuries, like the income tax, fall on taxable margins of income, taxes on the necessaries of life and means of production fall upon the 'beginnings of income.' Taxes on the means of production, moreover, encroach upon business capital instead of business profits.[1] Thus, on the one hand the taxes on the necessaries of life press with undue severity upon a large number of persons in India who live on the margin of subsistence, and on the other hand the taxes on the means of production handicap the unsheltered, the unprotected, and the exporting industries in their competition with foreign products.

To sum up: the principal effects of the consumption taxes in India, from the point of view of the distribution of the burden of taxation, may be stated as follows: (*a*) Since they contribute a comparatively large proportion of the total tax revenues of the country, they exercise a predominantly regressive influence on the tax system as a whole and thus lead to a violation of the principle of equity which is sought to be increasingly realized in modern times through a large resort to direct taxes on income and property on a markedly progressive basis. (*b*) Further, since a considerable proportion of these consumption taxes is raised by the taxation of necessaries of life, they tend to encroach to a large extent upon the 'subsistence units' of the income and thus press with undue severity upon a large number of persons in India who, according to all authentic accounts, live on a bare and precarious margin of subsistence. And (*c*) lastly, since a fairly large percentage of these indirect taxes is contributed by the taxation of means of

[1] Cf. Alfred Marshall, *Memorandum on the Fiscal Policy of International Trade*, Sec. 71; also *The Australian Tariff: An Economic Enquiry*, App. M, pp. 185–89.

production (the proportion being 14·70 per cent in 1926–29), they impinge upon costs of production and thus tend to undermine the competitive strength of the unsheltered and the unprotected industries in the home market and of the exporting industries in the foreign market. In this last connection it is also important to observe that, agriculture being the basic foundation on which the elaborate structure of India's economic life rests, and the prosperity of that agriculture being largely dependent upon the maintenance of a considerable export trade in the face of exceedingly severe competition from the scientifically developed and thoroughly organised agricultural industries of the New World, the increasing taxation of the means of production and transport in India in recent years has tended considerably to retard the progress and prosperity of agriculture and thus by way of reaction also to slacken the growth of secondary industries.[1]

4. PROTECTIVE DUTIES AND THE DISTRIBUTION OF THE NATIONAL DIVIDEND

Consumption taxes on the necessaries of life and means of production, besides exercising a predominantly regressive influence on the tax system as a whole, sometimes also directly bring about a redistribution of the National Dividend in the direction of greater inequalities of income among the different economic and social groups in the country, and in this way often tend to aggravate the inequity of the regressiveness of those taxes to a considerable extent. This result is generally produced by nearly all protective import duties on the necessaries of life and means of production.

The usual effect of the operation of protective import duties on the distribution of the National Dividend may be explained as follows: Before the imposition of the duties, the prices of the

[1] Cf. *The Australian Tariff: An Economic Enquiry*, pp. 85–86, where it is pointed out that the major part of the burden of protection in Australia has been borne by a few of the primary industries, and that the limit of capacity for bearing such a burden has already been reached.

imported and of the competing indigenous articles are approximately the same. On the imposition of the duties, as a rule the prices of the imported articles tend to rise to the full, or nearly to the full, extent of the duties, and this leads to a corresponding rise in the prices of the competing indigenous articles as well. Due to the import duty, therefore, the consumer has to pay a higher price whether he purchases the imported article or the competing indigenous product. Now, while the margin of difference between the old and the new prices paid for the import is only a contribution by way of taxation to the general revenues of the state, the corresponding margin paid on the indigenous article remains with the native producers as a subsidy from the consumers of the country, and it is this subsidy that gives the element of differential advantage to the native as against the foreign producers under a system of protective duties. Thus, while all indirect taxes on the necessaries of life and means of production negatively make for an aggravation of the inequalities of income by their regressive effect, the protective duties among them have the further demerit of positively increasing these inequalities by transferring incomes largely from the general mass of consumers, who consist in every country, and specially in India, largely of the poorer members of the society, to the favoured groups of entrepreneurs, investors, and wage-earners who are connected with the protected industries. Since protective duties on the necessaries of life and means of production are thus both negatively as well as positively responsible for widening the inequalities among the different income groups in the society, they must be regarded as at least twice as objectionable as non-protective indirect taxes from the point of view of fiscal justice.

5. ARGUMENTS FOR PROTECTIVE DUTIES

Now, although protective import duties, regarded as a mechanism of taxation, are thus exceedingly inequitable in their negative as well as positive effect on the redistribution of the National Dividend and tend as such to reduce considerably the aggregate economic welfare,[1] their claim to a conspicuous place in the general fiscal system of a protectionist country is said to rest largely upon other and more important considerations than those that arise directly out of their operation as a machinery of taxation and redistribution of the National Dividend. In so far as the adoption of a system of protective duties in India is concerned, these 'other and more important' considerations have been elaborately restated by the Indian Fiscal Commission, and their central thesis may be briefly stated as follows:

(*a*) That a more rapid and extensive development of industries in India is desirable, since it would (i) reduce the excessive dependence of the country on agriculture, which makes the economic life extraordinarily unstable; (ii) increase the demand for labour and tend to raise urban wages and by way of reaction also rural wages, and thus augment the staying power of the agricultural population against the hardships of scarcity and famines; (iii) develop the capital resources of the country by facilitating the accumulation of capital in a form in which it is readily available for investment; and (iv) last, though not least, by creating newer outlets and opportunities for the exercise of diverse faculties, lead to the growth of a vigorous national character.

That, further, there are certain special industries, the existence of which within the country itself it is highly important to ensure, either because they are essential for military purposes or because they are key industries.

(*b*) That the necessary degree of industrial development in India along general as well as specific lines is being effectively impeded by conditions of unequal competition between India and foreign producers, both because most of her industries

[1] Cf. Dalton, *The Inequality of Incomes*, pp. 9–10. The argument is that so long as the primary and urgent wants of life remain unsatisfied among the lower income groups, any reduction of inequality by a redistribution of the National Dividend would tend to increase economic welfare, and conversely, any increase of inequality through the same means would tend to diminish the aggregate of economic welfare.

are infant industries and because her general economic environment is in an undeveloped state.

(*c*) And that, therefore, the development of industries in India should be artificially stimulated through state assistance, largely in the shape of protective import duties.[1]

It is necessary to enquire whether, in this presentation of the case for industrial protection by the Indian Fiscal Commission, we are not once again confronted with the old, crude, and dangerous economic fallacies that can be traced as far back as the era of mercantilism (A.D. 1500–1750) and that have been trotted out again and again for over a century now by pseudo-economic thinkers, nationalist-cum-militarist politicians and journalists, and last, though not least, by the numerous agents and supporters of industrial plutocrats who in many countries wield almost unlimited power to buy opinions as well as votes. Careful students of tariff literature must have observed, in the case of practically every country where protectionism has been adopted as a definite state policy, how intense emotions and sentiments of a nationalistic type are generated by wars and rumours of wars, how these outbursts of mass emotions and sentiments are exploited by the organised forces of powerful vested interests for the popularisation of state economic policies that are calculated first and foremost to increase their own gains at the expense of the nation at large, and how, last of all, these very policies receive the blessings of plausible but ill-founded economic theories. Since it would take us beyond the limits of our present study to investigate the psychological and political background of the protectionist policy in India, we would confine ourselves to an examination of the protectionist thesis as set out by the Indian Fiscal Commission, with special reference to the economic conditions of India.

[1] *Report of the Indian Fiscal Commission*, pp. 23–41.

6. INDUSTRIALISATION AS A REMEDY FOR FAMINES

Although it is undoubtedly true that the recurring phenomena of droughts and floods seriously affect the basic agricultural industry of India and thus cause widespread misery through scarcity and famines among the agricultural classes, it is not incontestably true that the hastening of industrial development through protection is the most economical or the most effective remedy against the hardships. For, in the first place, since, due to the development of efficient means of internal as well as external transport in recent decades, the scarcity of supply in the affected areas can be quickly and effectively met by importation either from the unaffected surplus-grain areas within the country or from external sources, famines in modern times resolve themselves largely into a question of the supply of purchasing power. It follows that the most direct remedy against the hardships of natural calamities like famines and floods is to increase the productivity and profits of the agriculturist in normal times through the spread of irrigation facilities, extension of transport, improvement of marketing, promotion of credit facilities so as to reduce the exorbitant rate of interest on his unproductive and productive loans, and thus to augment the savings of the good years that would give him a stronger staying power during the bad years. On the other hand, a policy of protective tariff will, at any rate for a considerable period, have the effect of seriously aggravating his present relative position by, as already explained, increasing the relative burden of his taxation and causing a loss of his purchasing power for the benefit of some of the better-off economic classes within the country, and also by reducing the demand for his exportable surplus in foreign countries owing to the reduction of Indian demand for foreign imports.

Even if a sufficiently long-range view be taken so as to allow for considerable industrial development in the country, the amount of new industrial employment created thereby is likely to be relatively too small and too diffused to appreciably affect the level of agricultural wages and thus compensate for the losses suffered by the agriculturist in the earlier years in consequence of the policy of protection. This view is based upon a consideration of the following facts: At the Census of 1921, over 73 per cent of the population of India was returned under 'exploitation of animals and vegetation'; of the remaining 27 per cent, again, the major portions are connected with agriculture and rural life generally, e.g. rural transport, rice pounders and flour grinders, village teachers and officials, etc. Although the Indian Census statistics do not permit of an exact division of non-agricultural occupations as between urban and rural, we may perhaps put the percentage of population dependent on rural occupations at between 85 and 90. Again, while the number of actual workers engaged in the exploitation of animals and vegetation in 1921 was 105·69 millions, the average daily number of persons employed in large-scale industries in the whole of India in 1928 was as small as 1·68 millions. Even on the most optimistic and extravagant supposition that there could be a doubling of industrial production in the next ten years, the additional industrial employment created thereby would absorb only 1·6 per cent of the agricultural workers. It is, therefore, clear that it would be vain to hope that a policy of industrial protection would effect any appreciable improvement in the conditions of the agricultural workers within a reasonable period of time. And lastly, the preliminary figures for the Census of 1931 show that during the last intercensal decade the population of India has increased by no less than 32·51 millions, i.e. an average annual increase of 3·25 millions. This huge annual increase in the population is almost exactly double the number employed in all the large-scale industries of India. These figures would make it clear that, even with the most rapid and extensive industrial development, not more than a mere fraction of this great annual addition to the number could be absorbed in new industrial employment, while all the vast balance must needs throw itself upon the staple agricultural industry of the country. It is also worth while remembering in this connection that, due to the swift and multiform progress of modern mechanisation, industrial expansion is not always or necessarily accompanied by a proportional expansion of employment. As a matter of fact, the industrial reorganisation of the post-war years has been accompanied by such far-reaching mechanisation that it has actually led to an appreciable reduction in employment in all the highly industrialised countries of the world.

In this connection, it may further be observed that since the agricultural workers form by far the largest single, and at the same time the least educated, the least resourceful, and the least organised economic group in the country, who often fall easy and helpless victims not only to the natural calamities like floods, famines, and epidemics, but also to the exploitative activities of the more intelligent, shrewd and powerful social classes within the country, the well-known socio-economic maxim of the greatest good of the greatest number would seem clearly to demand, not that this worst-off group should be made to suffer a loss of wealth and welfare for the benefit of the better-off classes, as is sought to be done under a policy of protective tariffs, but that the latter should be required to contribute towards ameliorating the far too unsatisfactory economic conditions of the former.[1]

And lastly, it is also exceedingly important to point out that in the years immediately ahead the Indian agriculturist will be, as well as the Indian manufacturer, called upon to face the competition of foreign rivals who are now being increasingly strengthened with all the resources of science and organisation. Since agriculture is and must remain for long the foundation

[1] Cf. *India in 1929–30*, p. 116, where occurs the following statement: "In any case, it is clearly a fact that a large proportion of the inhabitants of India are still beset with poverty of a kind which finds no parallel in Western lands, and are living on the very margin of subsistence. This is indeed the normal state of the millions of agricultural labourers who do not hold land themselves, and whose income consists mostly of customary wages paid in kind."

of the general economic life of India as a whole, it follows that the degree of security and stability of India's economic structure will be determined by the measure of success that can be achieved by the agriculturist in his competition with the farmers of foreign countries. The degree of success that can be achieved by him in this matter will, in its turn, be conditioned by the extent of his equipment in education, organisation, agricultural science and finance. From this point of view, again, it is clear that there is still vast room for safeguarding the stability of the economic life of the country in general and improving the economic conditions of the agriculturist in particular in more direct and effective ways than through a policy of artificially stimulated industrial development under a regime of protectionism which, as already explained, is accompanied by an inequitable distribution of the burden of taxation, an increase in the inequality of wealth, a diminution of the aggregate national welfare, and last, but by no means least, a lowering of the economic position of the agriculturist both relatively as well as absolutely.

7. INDUSTRIALISATION AND GROWTH OF CAPITAL RESOURCES

The proposition that the rapid promotion of industries in India will develop the capital resources of the country by facilitating the accumulation of capital in a form in which it is readily available for investment contains not only a serious fallacy, but also a damaging admission. The underlying implications of this proposition may be expounded as follows: "At present a large part of the savings of the population is not available for industrial investment, partly because of the habit of hoarding, partly because of large and widespread investment in ornaments, and partly also because of the absence of traditions of industrial investment among the rural population. Since these uses, or rather abuses, of national savings are wasteful and unproductive, it is clearly desirable in the economic interests of the nation to adopt a policy that would divert them into channels of productive investments. The only, or at any rate the best, method of effecting this change in the direction of the flow of savings would be to accelerate the rate of industrial development under a policy of protection, because, firstly, it would automatically transfer a part of these savings from the rural classes to the industrial investment classes in the shape of higher prices resulting in higher dividends and higher reserve funds, and secondly, it would stimulate the demand for capital through new openings for investment and thus tempt out the wealth from the hoards and also educate the people to put their savings into productive investment rather than in unproductive ornaments."

The above analysis of the proposition in question would show that while a protective policy for accelerated industrial expansion would result in an automatic transfer of wealth from the rural classes to the industrial investment classes, no claim can be, or indeed has been, put forward that such a policy would increase the aggregate amount of savings in the country. On the contrary, since it would effect a transfer of wealth from the comparatively poorer and more conservative rural classes to the relatively richer industrial groups who are accustomed to an urbanised and more expensive standard of living, the net result of the policy is likely to be a diminution of the aggregate amount of potential capital (i.e. savings) in the country. The fact that a major part of this diminished aggregate amount of potential capital, now transferred to the industrial groups, would be actually converted into invested capital instead of remaining, as before, locked up idly and unproductively in the hoards, is no adequate justification for a policy that would not only transfer incomes from the weaker to the stronger economic classes, but also cause a diminution of the aggregate amount of savings in the country, because the most effective cure for the habit of hoarding is not a virtually compulsory transfer of wealth from the illiterate and ignorant rural population to the more advanced investing groups, but the spread of education and, as amply indicated by the experience of the war and the post-war period, the popularisation of the modern methods of investing small savings through post office savings banks, cash certificates, and co-operative societies; furthermore, in view of the crushing burden of agricultural indebtedness and the usurious rates of interest prevalent in the rural areas of India,[1] and also bearing in mind the unlimited scope for agricultural and rural development in the country, it would certainly be a wiser economic policy to conserve and utilise all the available savings of the rural areas to promote rural welfare than to transfer these to the ownership and control of the urban and industrial classes for the extension of industrial activities.

8. INDUSTRIALISATION AND NATIONAL CHARACTER

But perhaps the most powerful argument in favour of a rapid policy of industrialisation in India is that it will help to build up a more alert, practical, and vigorous national character. "Finally," state the Indian Fiscal Commission, "one of the most important results that can be anticipated from the development of industries in India is one that cannot be measured in terms of money. A country industrially undeveloped tends to suffer from a certain intellectual deadness. The outlets for diversity of talent are few. Those who might have shone in a wider sphere have their energies and ambitions cramped in the mould of uniformity. It is hardly too much to say that a certain measure of industrial life and opportunity is an essential condition for building up a vigorous national character. And with regard to India the effect on the national character is likely to be particularly marked and particularly beneficial. It has long been felt that education in India has not been producing a type of mind with a sufficiently practical grasp of affairs, and industrial training is calculated to provide the corrective required."[2]

[1] Cf. M. L. Darling, *The Punjab Peasant in Prosperity and Debt* (1925), Chapters I and X. The Indian Central Banking Enquiry Committee have estimated the amount of rural indebtedness in India at no less than Rs. 900 crores (£m. 675).

[2] *Report of the Indian Fiscal Commission*, p. 28. Also cf. List, *National System of Political Economy*, Chapter XVII.

Now, although it is undeniably true that the number of persons with a sufficiently practical grasp of large affairs is relatively small in India, a close study of the factors that have influenced the character of the people would show that this particular deficiency is at bottom due partly to the debilitating effect of the climate, partly to the traditions of asceticism and other-worldliness inculcated by religion, partly to the too purely literary and cultural bias imparted by an ill-balanced educational system, and partly also to the lack of opportunities for training in the more responsible duties of administration. To attribute this characteristic defect in the intellectual make-up of the average educated Indian entirely, or even largely, to the absence of extensive industrial development in the country, is only to take a purely superficial view of the matter.

It is obvious that the introduction of the necessary degree of realistic bias in the mind of the average member of the intelligentsia must necessarily wait upon the slow process of changes in modes of living so as to counteract the disabilities imposed by climate as well as in deep-rooted social and religious traditions, upon thoroughgoing alterations in the content and methods of education, and upon the right development of self-governing political institutions.

Furthermore, it should be pointed out that, since industrial activities represent only one department of national life, the claim of industrial training must be examined not by and of itself as a matter of paramount importance, but alongside the similar claims of practical training in other at least equally important departments of national life.

And lastly, we must remember that the strength and vigour of national character are ultimately dependent, not so much upon the exceptional ability and training of a few individuals in the enjoyment of specially favourable opportunities, as upon the physical and moral stamina and intellectual training of the average individual. Hence, a policy of industrial development under a regime of protectionism, in so far as it diminishes the purchasing power of the income of the average individual and thereby reduces the material means of his personal development, actually tends to weaken national character at many more points than strengthen it.

9. MILITARY AND BASIC INDUSTRIES

Besides the arguments examined above, there are certain special arguments that are urged by the Indian Fiscal Commission for the protection of specific industries. It is held that there are two classes of industries in particular that possess extraordinary claims to protection—first, industries of military importance, and second, basic industries. The iron and steel industry is cited as belonging to both these classes. Now, without going into the merits of the military and the key industries arguments as general propositions, it may be pointed out that in the special circumstances of India those arguments are really of a very limited application. Since modern warfare is based upon a very extensive foundation of armaments and munitions, and since, further, India's membership of the British Empire would not make it politically necessary, and the general poverty of her economic resources as well as the weakness of her economic structure would not make it economically feasible for her to be self-efficient in the matter of armaments and munitions,[1] the military argument must be examined in relation to, and only as a part of, a co-ordinated policy of Imperial Defence. If, in the execution of a definite and well-defined policy of Empire Defence, it is decided that India would be the best place for the development of certain industries of military importance, the further question has to be answered as to what part of the cost of such a development should be borne by India and what parts by the rest of the Empire. Again, even when the selection of industries to be so promoted has been made, the choice will lie between the

[1] The great difficulty, if not the impossibility, of a reasonable selection of industries of military importance would be realised from the fact that under the first part of the British Safe-guarding of Industries Act of 1921, which protected the so-called Key Industries that were thought to produce articles of military importance, the number of articles protected was over 6,000.

alternative policies of development through state ownership and management on the one hand and private ownership and control with state assistance on the other. Since, in the nature of the case, the losses and risks of such industrial enterprises must in large part be borne by the state, the interests of the tax-payers would seem to demand that the profits of such enterprises, if and when they accrue, should also be gained by the state through state ownership, or at any rate through state partnership.

We may now pass on to a consideration of what are called basic industries, which have been defined by the Indian Fiscal Commission as "industries of which the products are utilised as raw materials by numerous other industries in India."[1] Here, again, although the definition is simplicity itself, its application in the selection of particular industries will be found to be surrounded with extraordinary difficulties. These difficulties may be well illustrated with reference to the steel industry. While on the one hand it is true that the steel industry provides an important raw material for, say, the railway industry, the engineering industry, the ship-building industry and the mining industry, on the other hand it is equally true that these industries, in their turn, are essential to the existence and expansion of the steel industry itself, either as providing raw materials, or transport facilities, or markets. All these industries, again, are of as great, if indeed not greater, basic importance to the economic development of the country than the steel industry itself. It therefore follows that to the extent that the growth of these other basic industries is impeded by the direct and indirect burdens of the protection of the steel industry, there must inevitably be an unfavourable reaction to a corresponding extent on the growth of the steel industry itself.

[1] *Report of the Indian Fiscal Commission*, p. 60.

10. THE PLACE OF INDUSTRIALISATION IN A SCHEME OF NATIONAL DEVELOPMENT

The analysis given in the three preceding sections would show that most of the arguments, that have been set forth by the Indian Fiscal Commission in favour of a policy of rapid industrial development along general as well as specific lines with the aid of protective tariffs, are one-sided, superficial, and at best of a limited degree of application to the particular economic conditions of India. Nevertheless, conceding that a certain degree of industrial development is essential to the building up of a well-rounded economic structure in a country, and further, that the expenditure of a certain amount of national income may legitimately be incurred in the promotion of such a development, there would still remain two important preliminary questions to be solved. In the first place, in view of the undoubted claims of development in other departments of economic and social life, e.g. education,[1] sanitation, agri-

[1] At the Census of 1921, the percentage of literacy among males of 5 years and over was 12·2 and among females of 5 years and over 1·8, the percentage for both sexes together being 7·15. Among adults of 20 years and over, the percentage was 17·1 for males, 2 for females, and 9·7 for both sexes together. In spite of a marked expansion of education during the last ten years, the figures for which are not yet available in sufficient detail, perhaps the present day percentage of illiteracy among the adult population could safely be put at around 80. Since universal literacy, besides being a desirable end in itself, is also practically indispensable to the efficient working of self-governing institutions, the figures quoted above would suggest the urgency of educational expansion in India. Regarding the deplorable condition of public health in India and its reaction on the wealth and welfare of the people, we would only quote the following resolution passed by the All-India Conference of Medical Research Workers in 1926: "This Conference believes that the average number of deaths resulting every year from preventable disease is about five to six millions, that the average number of days lost to labour by each person in India from preventable disease is not less than a fortnight to three weeks in each year, that the percentage loss of efficiency of the average person in India who reaches a wage-earning age is about 50, whereas it is quite possible to raise this percentage to 80 or 90. The Conference believes that these are under-estimates rather than exaggerations, but, allowing for the greatest possible margin of error, it is absolutely certain that the wastage of life and efficiency which results from preventable disease costs India several hundreds of crores of rupees each year. Added to this is the great suffering which affects many millions of people every year."

culture, transport and banking, etc., it has to be decided as to what proportion of the national income may appropriately be devoted to the encouragement of industrial enterprises, and also how the burden of the expenditure should be equitably distributed among the different sections of the community. It is hardly necessary to point out that no country in the world has so far been able either to assemble the necessary data or to build up a sufficiently efficient administrative machinery to provide any answer to either part of this question. The result is that in the actual administration of protection, while on the one hand the due observance of the necessary balance and harmony among the divergent claims of different departments of national life is often neglected, on the other hand the burden of protection is in large part thrown on shoulders that are least able to bear it.

Different Methods of Industrial Development

A second, and no less important, question that has to be decided is to find out which among the various alternative methods of encouragement of industrial enterprise would be the most economical and the most effective in removing well-ascertained deficiencies and weaknesses so that the industries in question may ultimately be able to stand upon their own legs. Because protective duties are not the only, nor often the most economical, way for the promotion of industries, other avenues of progress, particularly those that are collectively known under the comprehensive name of 'rationalisation' touching practically every aspect of industrial organisation,[1] should be frequently explored and examined, and freely adopted. Specially is the consideration of such alternative methods of progress of great importance in India where, as the succeeding chapters of this work will abundantly show, the main obstacles to industrial expansion are defective organisation, inadequate and unsatisfactory technical equipment in personnel as well as machinery, both insufficient supply and extravagant use of capital resources,

[1] Read L. Urwick, *The Meaning of Rationalisation.*

lack of adaptation to changed conditions of markets and marketing, inefficiency of labour and in at least one important case, viz. the cotton industry, the prevalence of serious labour unrest. Both in the case of the cotton industry as well as that of the steel industry of India, there is sufficient evidence to show that protection has actually impeded the necessary process of rationalization and thus amply supported the contention of free traders that protection tends to perpetuate inefficiency and slacken the tempo of economic progress.

11. BOUNTIES *versus* IMPORT DUTIES

Again, of the two usual methods of protection, bounties and import duties, while the administrative difficulties of both are probably evenly balanced,[1] the former possess certain special merits which often make them distinctly preferable to the latter. In the first place, since both its burdens as well as its benefits are direct and definite, the administration of a bounty system is calculated to be more careful and rational on the one hand and subject to greater public scrutiny on the other, and therefore more efficient on the whole than the administration of protective import duties. In the second place, unlike protective duties, it does not involve, and indeed may altogether dispense with, the inequitable distribution of the burden of protection among the different income groups within the community. In the third place, since the cost of a bounty system is a definite and ascertained sum, it easily lends itself to being administered from the point of view of a wise distribution of the aggregate available funds among the different alternative lines of national development. And lastly, while a system of protective duties, like monetary inflation, produces a comprehensive and all-embracing series of changes in the economic relations among the several producing and consuming groups within the community, and thus introduces in course of time far-reaching

[1] With regard to the endless difficulties of tariff administration, cf. Gregory, *Tariffs, a Study in Method*; Higginson, *Tariffs at Work*; and Page, *Making the Tariff in the United States*.

alterations in the structure of the economic society, a bounty system does not give rise to such serious consequences. Therefore it is much easier and more practicable to terminate a system of bounties than one of protective duties.

In anticipation of the criticism on the administrative ground that a bounty system would call for the provision of additional funds within the budgetary system, it may be pointed out that it would merely mean an alteration in the route through which the tax-payers' money would be remitted to the industries concerned. In fact, the administration of a bounty system would involve nothing more serious or radical than the simple addition of a new spending department to the many others, e.g. departments of agriculture and public health, that are already in existence, and it can and should be financed exactly in the same way as the other departments are.[1]

12. PRINCIPLES OF DISCRIMINATING PROTECTION

It is only when the scope and limitation of a policy of industrial development through state aid has been properly defined as suggested in Section 10 and the practical limits of the bounty method of protection have been exhausted as indicated in Section 11, that the claim of a protective tariff to a place in a rationalised system of state economic policies may be conceded. The administration of a protective tariff, again, is, as is clearly brought out in the pages of a recent authoritative work on American tariff-making,[2] beset with an almost interminable series of difficulties. To secure the administration of protective tariffs in India against the well-known dangers of political corruption, encouragement and perpetuation of inefficiency, and excessive burden on any group or class in particular and the community in general, the Indian Fiscal Commission insisted on the need for discrimination and laid down certain guiding principles for the practical

[1] Cf. *The Australian Tariff: An Economic Enquiry*, pp. 109–11.

[2] Thomas Walker Page, *Making the Tariff in the United States.*

exercise of such discrimination. The main principles may be summarised as follows:

(*a*) The institution of a Tariff Board to be an integral part of the scheme of protection.

(*b*) In dealing with applications for protection, the Tariff Board should, in the first instance, examine whether the industry that claims protection is one which

(i) possesses "natural advantages such as an abundant supply of raw material, cheap power, a sufficient supply of labour, or a large home market;

(ii) "without the help of protection either is not likely to develop at all or is not likely to develop so rapidly as is desirable in the interests of the country"; and

(iii) "will eventually be able to face world competition without protection."

(*c*) Industries that are subject to the law of increasing returns as well as those which are potentially capable of supplying the entire home market should be regarded as possessing additional claims to protection.

(*d*) Even though the protection of a particular industry should involve injury to the interests of other related industries, the Tariff Board should not withhold protection from that industry, provided that such protection is calculated to result in a net economic advantage to the country.

(*e*) While protection should ordinarily be granted to what are called infant industries, it may also be extended to industries that are in a state of temporary deterioration or atrophy and even to a strong and prosperous industry which might thereby be induced to develop a new branch.

(*f*) Tariff protection should not as a rule be granted to new industries.

(*g*) The rate of protection should be neither too low nor too high, and should be determined primarily in the light of comparative costs. And

(*h*) The Tariff Board should be directed to review periodically the protection given to different industries so as to indicate the desirability of the continuance, or modification, or withdrawal, of protection.[1]

The policy of discriminating protection was adopted by the Government of India and the Assembly in 1923, and the Tariff Board was appointed in June, 1924. During the last seven years, only three of the major industries of India have

[1] *Report of the Indian Fiscal Commission* (1922), Chapter VII.

been granted the benefit of protection, viz. the Cotton, the Steel, and the Sugar Industries. Since each of these three industries, in its own way, occupies a place of great importance in the general economic life of India, the extension of a protective tariff to them involves grave issues of state economic policy. Again, partly due to the widely varying nature of the economic factors affecting their competitive efficiency and partly due to the divergent lines of development they have followed, these three industries between them give rise to many of the more important problems of tariff administration.

In the following chapters, therefore, we propose to examine in detail the conditions of these three industries in order to find an answer to the following questions: (*a*) What are the principal weaknesses of these industries from the competitive point of view? (*b*) How far are those deficiencies remediable through the application of the principles and methods of rationalisation? (*c*) Whether and to what extent is a policy of protection warranted by the facts of each case? And (*d*) to what extent has the administration of protective tariffs conformed in practice to the principles of discriminating protection as laid down by the Indian Fiscal Commission?

CHAPTER II

THE COTTON TARIFF
BRIEF HISTORY AND RECENT DEVELOPMENTS

1. 1859–78: REVENUE DUTIES ON COTTON MANUFACTURES

Before the Sepoy Mutiny the import duties on cotton manufactures varied from 3½ to 5 per cent, but until 1848, these duties were doubled in the case of goods imported in foreign ships. In 1848, the discrimination against foreign shipping was discontinued, but the duty on foreign goods continued to be double that of goods imported from the United Kingdom.

The Mutiny was responsible for an enormous increase in the expenditure of the Government of India, and among other financial measures the customs duties on various classes of goods were also raised. Under the Tariff Act of 1859, the duty on cotton piece-goods was raised from 5 to 10 per cent, and that on twist and yarn from 3½ to 5 per cent. In the following year the latter duty was also raised to the general level of 10 per cent, the Finance Member holding that there was hardly any reason for making a distinction between twist and yarn on the one hand and cotton manufactures on the other. In 1861, Mr. Laing, who was then Finance Member, began to be haunted by free-trade scruples and wanted to reduce the duty on all cotton manufactures from 10 to 5 per cent, but due to the estimated deficit in the budget, satisfied his conscience by effecting the reduction only in the case of yarn, while the duty on piece-goods had to be left intact as it yielded a considerable amount of revenue. In regard to the reduction of the duty on yarn in particular, the Finance Member pointed out that the case was an important one, because the high duty of the previous year had already begun to produce its protective effect in that spinning machinery was being imported and spinning mills set up.[1] In 1862, a fair amount of budgetary surplus was estimated, and the duties on piece-goods and yarn were brought down to 5 per cent and 3½ per cent respectively. The reasons assigned by the Finance Member for these reductions in the import tariff were: Firstly, since the major part of the import trade consisted of British goods, the duty adversely affected Britain and Britain alone, and so it looked like striking a deliberate blow by one part of the Empire at another, which could not be defended either on moral, or political, or commercial principles. Secondly, as the duty on the imported cloths was a tax on a necessity, there was no equity in taxing the consumers of one class of cloth, while exempting from taxation the users of indigenous products. And thirdly, as India had natural advantages in respect of abundant raw material, and patient, ingenious and cheap labour, endowed with fine skill and delicate touch, there was every probability of India being able to produce certain lines of cotton manufactures both for her own requirements as well as for exports, and for these, evidently, no protection was required.[2]

These duties, that is, 5 per cent on piece-goods and 3½ per cent on twist and yarn, imposed solely for the purpose of revenue, and without the slightest intention of a protectionist nature behind them, were left unaltered for the long period of sixteen years, 1862–78.

2. 1878–82: THE COTTON DUTIES CONTROVERSY

In 1874, the Manchester Chamber of Commerce submitted a memorial to the Secretary of State for India for the removal of the cotton duties on the ground that these duties were proving prohibitory in the case of low-priced and coarser varieties of yarn and piece-goods, and that they were adversely affecting the consumption of cloths by the poorer classes. They also pointed out that the number of cotton mills set up in India was on the increase. When this memorial was forwarded

[1] *Financial Statement*, 1861–62.

[2] Ibid., 1862–63.

to India, the Government of India appointed a Tariff Committee to examine the whole question of import and export duties. The Committee pointed out that the spheres of production of cloths in Manchester and Bombay were quite different, because the finer kinds of yarn and cloth could not be produced in India on a remunerative basis. By a careful analysis, they further showed that while the total import duty on piece-goods yielded a revenue of over Rs. 80 lakhs, the duty on coarser varieties of goods in which alone there was competition produced only a sum of Rs. 4 lakhs, so that the abolition of the duty on the non-competing finer fabrics would involve the sacrifice of revenue to the extent of 76 lakhs, which the Government of India could ill afford to do at the time.[1] Accordingly, no change was made in the cotton tariff under the Tariff Act of 1875. In the same year, however, a duty of 5 per cent was imposed on imported raw cotton not produced in Continental Asia or Ceylon, with the object of discouraging the Indian mills from the use of American or Egyptian cotton.[2]

The Secretary of State for India, however, strongly objected to the import duties on cotton manufactures, not, it should be noted, on account of their protective effect because they had none, but by reason of their being a tax on a first necessity of life of the people of India, and also their being opposed to the general trade policy of the Empire. Accordingly, he urged the repeal of the cotton duties as soon as the finances of the Government of India would permit.[3] No action for the repeal of the duties could, however, be taken till 1878. In 1878, the coarser varieties of imported cotton goods, with which Indian manufactures had begun to compete, were exempt from duty. These were (1) unbleached T cloths under 18 reed, jeans, domestics, sheetings and drills, but containing finer yarn than 30's, and (2) yarn of the qualities known as 20's water and 32's mule, and lower numbers. At the same time, the duty on

[1] P.P. 56, H.C. 1876.
[2] C. N. Vakil, *Financial Development in Modern India*, p. 411.
[3] P.P. 56, H.C. 1876.

imported raw cotton was also abolished.[1] It is interesting to note that in proposing the above changes in the import tariff, the Finance Member, Sir John Strachey, laid down the following principles which were to govern the future customs tariff of India:

(*a*) "That no duty should exist which affords protection to native industry, and as a corollary, that no duty should be applied to any article which can be produced at home, without an equivalent duty of excise on the home production; and also that no duty should be levied except for purely fiscal purposes.

(*b*) "That as far as possible the raw materials of industry and articles contributing to production should be exempt from customs taxation.

(*c*) "That the duties should be applied only to articles which yield a revenue of sufficient importance to justify the interference with trade involved by that machinery of collection.

(*d*) "As regards exports—the duties should be levied on those commodities only in which the exporting country has practically a monopoly of production."[2]

After this enunciation of principles by the Government of India, it was only a question of time before the remaining duties on cotton manufactures were taken off. Meanwhile, the Manchester Chamber of Commerce continued their vigorous agitation for the extension of the principle of exemption to other varieties of cotton yarns and piece-goods in which an element of direct and indirect protection might be found. The Tariff Commission appointed by the Government of India examined the question and concluded that the exemption limit of 30's for all grey cotton goods would completely eliminate all vestiges of protection, while the then existing limits of 20's water and 32's mule for yarns excluded all possibility of direct protection for the Indian yarns. Accordingly, the Government of India extended the 30's limit to all grey cotton goods,[3] and left the yarn duties intact.

The exemptions granted under the measures of 1878 and

[1] *Financial Statement*, 1878–79. [2] Ibid.

[3] The tariff of 1878 had exempted only a few specific kinds of grey cotton goods from duty.

1879, led to a large-scale substitution of the duty-free coarser fabrics for the dutiable finer ones in the export trade from Lancashire to India, with the result that there was a heavy decline in the yield of the cotton duties. Finding that these had now become comparatively unimportant as revenue producers, the Government of India prudently decided to put an end to the controversy by abolishing them altogether as soon as possible. The opportunity came in 1882, when the budget estimate showed a revenue surplus of over £m. 3. In that year, therefore, they repealed all the remaining cotton duties. At the same time, nearly all other import duties, which had been only minor sources of revenue, were also abolished. The only duties that were allowed to remain in the tariff schedule were the special duties on wines, spirits, arms, ammunition, salt and opium.[1]

3. 1882–1918: PRINCIPLES OF FREE TRADE: THE COTTON EXCISE DUTY

The measure of 1882, which gave full effect to the doctrine of free trade for the comparatively long period of twelve years, freed the Government of India from the embarrassing position in which they had been placed by the bitter tariff controversy of the previous eight years. And the Finance Member was able to congratulate himself on being able to apply in full to India the lessons of free trade derived from English experience and English economic history.

But this policy of excluding customs duties from among the sources of the public revenues of India could not be adhered to for a long time. The happy state of a budgetary equilibrium reached in 1882 soon passed away. Due to the growth of military expenditure brought about by the frontier troubles, the military expedition to Burma, the construction of large public works, the progressive reduction of opium revenue, and lastly, the steady decline in the rupee-sterling exchange on account of

[1] *Financial Statement*, 1882–83.

the falling price of silver, the Government of India were again faced with growing financial difficulties. In 1886 the Income Tax was reimposed. In 1888 the duty on salt was increased, and an import duty was laid on petroleum. Expenditure on productive public works was curtailed, the Famine Grant was stopped, and revenue assignments to the Provincial Governments were considerably reduced.[1]

In spite of all these measures for the restoration of the financial equilibrium by increased taxation and reduction of expenditure, the position continued to be unsatisfactory, and in 1894, the Government being faced with a deficit of Rs. 3½ crores, the financial situation became quite acute. The Herschell Committee on Indian Currency, which had sat in 1892 to examine the causes and suggest remedies for the depreciation of the rupee-sterling exchange, had reported that of all alternative measures for fresh taxation, customs duties would be the one least likely to excite opposition in India. The Government of India welcomed this suggestion and enacted a Bill levying a general 5 per cent duty on all imports except cotton goods and doubling the duty on petroleum. The omission of the cotton goods from the new tariff was due to the refusal of sanction by His Majesty's Government, and excited much strong criticism in India.[2] The new duties, however, proved insufficient to fill up the huge gap between the revenue and the expenditure of the Government of India. The Secretary of State for India, therefore, intimated his readiness to waive his objection to the imposition of cotton import duties, provided that there was either an exemption for those imports which competed with Indian manufactures or, in the alternative, there was a countervailing excise duty levied on the latter. In accordance with these directions the Government of India, in December, 1894, enacted two measures under which the following tariff changes were introduced: (*a*) a 5 per cent import duty on all cotton piece-goods, and on all yarns above

[1] *Financial Statement*, 1884–85 to 1893–94.

[2] *Proceedings of the Governor-General's Legislative Council*, March, 1894.

20's; and (*b*) a corresponding excise duty of 5 per cent on all yarns of count 20's and above produced in the Indian mills.[1]

The cotton import and excise duties of 1894 satisfied neither the cotton mill-owners of Lancashire nor those of India. The mill-owners of India complained that, as they were producing non-competing goods, the imposition of a countervailing excise duty on the Indian yarn was unjust and unfair. The Lancashire manufacturers, on the other hand, contended that the exemption of Indian yarns below 20's from the excise duty introduced certain elements of protection which favoured Indian yarns and woven goods at the expense of the Lancashire products. In other words, the anomalies and difficulties introduced by the drawing of an artificial line to distinguish competing from non-competing cotton manufactures, which had been experienced after the passing of the measures of 1878 and 1879, appeared once again.

The Secretary of State for India, to whom strong representations on the subject had been made by the cotton manufacturers of Lancashire, directed the Government of India to recast the duties in a suitable form so as to remove from them all grounds for constant complaint on the score of inequality of treatment.[2] Accordingly in 1896 the Government of India enacted two measures, the chief features of which were as follows: (*a*) both the import as well as the excise duty on yarns was abolished; and (*b*) the import duty on cotton manufactures was reduced from 5 per cent to 3½ per cent, and a corresponding excise duty of 3½ per cent was levied on all piece-goods produced in the Indian mills.[3]

[1] *Proceedings of the Governor-General's Legislative Council*, December, 1894.

[2] Cmd. 8078 of 1896.

[3] Acts II and III of 1896. It should be noted that the products of the hand-looms, which are estimated to contribute between one-third and one-fourth of the total consumption of piece-goods in India, were exempted from the excise duty.

4. 1918–1922: LARGE INCREASES OF THE CUSTOMS DUTIES DUE TO THE EXIGENCIES OF THE WAR AND POST-WAR FINANCE

These scales of duties remained in force till the year 1917–18. As the war dragged on through 1914–15 and 1915–16, it became increasingly evident that the financial position of the Government had to be considerably strengthened by expanding the old as well as by tapping new sources of taxation. In 1916–17, the general import duty was raised from 5 per cent to 7½ per cent, while increases were made in the rates on iron and steel, sugar, arms, liquors, tobacco and silver manufactures. Jute and tea, two of the principal items of Indian exports, became subject to export duties. The duty on cotton manufactures, however, which had been under a 3½ per cent import duty since 1896, remained at the old level. The non-official members of the Governor-General's Council strongly criticised the omission to enhance the cotton duties. The Finance Member, however, informed the Council that the Government of India had themselves proposed to raise the cotton duties to an appreciable extent, but had been dissuaded by the Home Government from taking the step on the ground that it would revive the old and bitter controversies regarding the cotton duties.[1]

In the next year, however, the omission was supplied. Although there was a small surplus in the Budget, increased resources were called for in order that India might make a fairly substantial monetary contribution to the expenses of the war. The Government, therefore, had no alternative but to act upon the oft-repeated suggestion of the non-official members of the Council to raise additional revenue by enhancing the duties on the importation of cotton manufactures. The import duties on cotton manufactures were raised to the general rate of 7½ per cent, while the cotton excise duties remained at the old level of 3½ per cent. This measure was received with a universal chorus of approval by the non-official members of the Legislature, and the main reason for this jubilation was that it

[1] *Financial Statement*, 1916–17.

had not only introduced an element of protection to the Indian cotton industry, but what was more important, it was also the first step in the direction of an ever-increasing degree of manipulation of the customs tariff for the benefit of all kinds of indigenous industries.[1]

No further changes in the cotton tariff were made till 1921–22. In that year the Government of India were faced with an estimated budget deficit of over Rs. 18 crores, and had to impose fresh taxation. The largest part of this deficit was proposed to be covered by changes to the import tariff, which were estimated to bring in a revenue of Rs. 8 crores. Among other large and important changes in the rates of import duty, the general rate of duty, which had been placed at 7½ per cent in 1916–17, was enhanced to 11 per cent. While the enhanced general rate of 1916–17 had left out the cotton manufactures from its scope, the general increase in the rate effected in 1921–22 included the cotton manufactures as well. And since the excise duty on the Indian mill-made piece-goods was retained at the old rate of 3½ per cent, the tariff change of this year contained an appreciable element of protection to the Indian Cotton-mill Industry in that the net effect of the new import duty was to lay a differential burden of 7½ per cent on all imported cotton manufactures as against those of Indian mills. In consideration of this substantial benefit conferred on the Cotton-mill Industry, however, the concession granted in the then existing tariff of allowing the exemption of all spinning and weaving machinery as well as mill stores from the import duty was withdrawn. Now, though this substantial increase in the cotton duties was calculated to be undoubtedly protective in its effect, the Finance Member took care to make it plain that his intention in proposing this measure was the production of badly needed revenues on a larger scale, and not protection of any kind. At the same time, he could not help admitting that the effect of many of the revenue duties in their then existing high level was bound to be somewhat protective in character. He there-

[1] *Financial Statement*, 1917–18.

fore suggested that before proceeding any further in the direction of high revenue duties or, which is the same thing in effect, protective duties, the whole subject of Indian fiscal policy in all its different aspects should be examined by the Fiscal Commission, which was going to be immediately appointed.[1]

In the next financial year the position became more serious still, and the stupendous problem of rescuing the finances of the Government from the dangerous state of insecurity and uncertainty into which they had been thrown during the war, and more especially during the post-war period of rising prices and excessive expenditure, presented itself in a challenging form and demanded serious attention and sustained efforts. A few figures will make the position clear: In 1918–19, the Government of India had a budgetary deficit of Rs. 6 crores; in 1919–20, mainly due to the Afghan War, the deficit swelled to the disturbing figure of Rs. 24 crores; in 1920–21, it increased to Rs. 26 crores; and again, in the year 1921–22, there was a big jump to Rs. 34 crores. During the four years, 1918–19 to 1921–22, therefore, the total excess of expenditure over revenue amounted to the huge sum of Rs. 90 crores. This was about 43 per cent more than the proceeds of the principal heads, and only 17 per cent less than the entire revenue and commercial income of the Government of India in 1921–22.[2]

But this was not the whole of the story. On the basis of the then existing taxation, the Finance Member estimated another deficit of about Rs. 32 crores for the year 1922–23. In the face of such large figures of recurring deficits in five successive

[1] Vide the Budget of the Government of India for 1921–22. It may be noted that in view of the fiscal autonomy convention established under the Montagu–Chelmsford Reform of 1919–20, His Majesty's Government thought it necessary to abstain from all interference with the tariff proposals of the Government of India, even though there was a terrible depression in the cotton industry of England and strong representations had been made by the mill-owners of Lancashire.

[2] According to the revised estimate of 1921–22, the yield of the principal revenue heads was Rs. 63·70 crores, while the total income from all sources was Rs. 108·97 crores.

years, therefore, it was only a question of financial prudence and honesty to impose fresh taxation. For it was clear that if India was to escape from the financial insolvency and currency disorganisation witnessed in many of the Central and Eastern European states in the years succeeding the war, the dangerous state of disequilibrium between the revenue and the expenditure, revealed in five successive years, had to be immediately ended. And since, on account of large recent increases in civil and military expenditure brought about partly by high prices and partly by the war, much relief could not be expected from retrenchment, the Government and the Legislature could not avoid facing up to the unpleasant and unpopular task of imposing fresh taxation on a large scale.

The Finance Member proposed various measures calculated to bring in an additional revenue of over Rs. 29 crores. Of this, however, about 14·90 crores, or slightly more than half, was to be raised from the customs duties, and only Rs. 2¼ crores from income tax and super tax. Considerable enhancement was made in the rates on all the important articles of import. The most important change in the customs tariff proposed by the Finance Member was, however, the increase of the general revenue duty of 11 per cent to 15 per cent, including the duty on cotton piece-goods. But as the increase in the import duty alone would impose a larger burden on the consumers of imported piece-goods, he proposed to equalise the extra taxation on all consumers of cloths by raising the cotton excise duty from 3½ to 7½ per cent. On the refusal of the Legislative Assembly to sanction the increase in the cotton excise duty, however, the import duty on piece-goods was retained at the old level of 11 per cent. Another measure relating to the cotton tariff that was passed in this particular year was the imposition of a duty of 5 per cent on imported twist and yarn, which had been on the free list since 1896.[1]

[1] Vide the Budget of the Government of India for 1922–23.

5. RECENT DEVELOPMENTS. THE ABOLITION OF THE COTTON EXCISE DUTY. THE BEGINNINGS OF PROTECTIONISM

The fact that the cotton excise duty of 1896 had been imposed, not for the purpose of revenue on the initiative of the Government of India, but primarily as a countervailing duty at the instance of the Home Government under pressure from the cotton manufacturers of Lancashire, had inevitably invested that ill-fated duty with a considerable amount of political bias and prejudice, and therefore it never received from the Indian public any dispassionate consideration on its own merits as a purely taxational measure. As a natural consequence, the Indian public, throughout the whole of its existence covering a period of thirty years, 1896–1925, demanded its abolition more on constitutional than on economic grounds. It is also worthy of note that both official and non-official opinions in India repeatedly expressed their disapproval of the cotton excise duty largely on account of its historical origin. Accordingly, in 1916, the Government of India publicly announced their view that the excise duty should be abolished as soon as financial circumstances permitted. Meanwhile, however, the permission given by the Home Government to the Government of India to raise the cotton import duty from 3½ per cent to 7½ per cent in 1917–18, and again to 11 per cent in 1921–22, had the undoubted effect of shedding the countervailing characteristic from the cotton excise, and with the great expansion of the Indian cotton industry in many new directions as well as along the old lines under the stimulus of the war and the duties of 1917–18 and 1921–22, of converting the cotton excise duty into a purely taxational measure of large and increasing importance. This new aspect of the cotton excise duty was realized by the Government of India in a short time. We therefore find that, although up to the year 1916–17 they had been definitely opposed to the continuance of the excise duty, partly on account of its small yield and partly by reason of its pressure on a largely non-competing industry in the early stages of its growth, in the years of post-war financial stringency they began rightly to look upon it more and more rather as an important and growing source of revenue than as an unfair burden on a weak and infant industry.[1]

On the other hand, however, although the differential fiscal measures of 1917–18 and 1921–22 had undoubtedly eliminated the ground for the political bias against the cotton excise duty, the bias itself continued. This is evident from the opinions of representative witnesses who appeared before the Indian Fiscal Commission of 1921–22. Thus, three of the most prominent among the industrialists of Bombay, for example, made it clear that their objection to the cotton excise duty was not one of economic principle, but one largely directed against the manner and circumstances of its origin. Similarly, another representative of the Cotton-mill Industry of Bombay, Sir Purushattamdas Thakurdas, who occupies an outstanding position in the commercial as well as political life of the country, said that he would ask for the abolition of the cotton excise duty first and foremost as a concession to the political sentiment of the people, and that, once it was abolished and India given the right to 'write on a clean slate,' he would be prepared to reconsider it afresh on its own merits.[2]

The Indian Fiscal Commission, which examined this question in all its different aspects, while condemning the cotton excise duty on account of the circumstances of its origin, pointed out that the enhancement of the import tariff in 1917–18 and 1921–22 had the effect of raising the prices of all piece-goods in India, imported as well as indigenous, and that, therefore, the excise duty was a proper form of taxation in as much as it enabled the Government to receive a part of the sacrifices made by the consumers of Indian cloths in the shape of high prices consequent on the levy of import duty, thus satisfying the canon of economy laid down by Adam Smith, which says that "every tax ought to be so contrived as both to take out and

[1] *Assembly Debates*, September, 1925.

[2] *Report of the Indian Fiscal Commission*, p. 97.

keep out of the pockets of the people as little as possible, over and above what it brings into the public treasury of the state." They therefore held that the purely taxational aspect of the cotton excise duty should be placed by the Government of India before the Legislature, and expressed the hope that the latter would decide the question on its own merits. From this dispassionate judgment on the question delivered by the majority of the Commission, the minority of five, four of whom, it is interesting to note, were directly connected with the cotton industry of India, dissented strongly and emphatically. They only expressed their own opinion that the continuance of the cotton excise duty would be contrary to the "unanimous sentiment of the people of India," and recommended its immediate abolition irrespective of fiscal considerations.

The Government of India accepted the proposal of the minority, and while prevented by a series of unbalanced budgets from giving immediate effect to the decision, gave the pledge for its abolition as soon as their finances would permit it.

In 1923, the Cotton Industry of Bombay, and to a lesser extent that of Ahmedabad, began to feel the effects of the general trade depression which had set in in Europe two or three years earlier. Falling prices, reduced sales, intensified competition over a narrowing field, and accumulating stocks showed their effects in the diminishing rates of profits in most, and the appearance of loss in some, of the cotton-mill companies, especially in Bombay. The Bombay Mill-owners' Association, therefore, early in 1924 began a vigorous and widespread propaganda for the abolition of the cotton excise duty, and besides initiating a systematic Press campaign, sent some representations to the Government of India and invoked the support of the Government of Bombay. In September of the same year, the Legislative Assembly, on the initiative of the Ahmedabad Mill-owners' Representative, passed a resolution recommending to the Government of India to take early steps for the repeal of the cotton excise duty. In the course of the debate, however, Sir Charles Innes, Member for Commerce in the Government of India, indicated sufficiently strong reasons for the decision of the Government that the excise duty could not be immediately abolished, and pointed out, among other things, that the Cotton-mill Industry of Bombay had, during the eight boom years, 1915 to 1922, been in so prosperous a condition that they had been able to pay away a sum of over Rs. 50 crores on dividends, which worked out on an average to 53 per cent per annum on the paid-up capital.[1]

In spite of this declaration of the Government of India, the Bombay Mill-owners' Association continued their efforts towards the abolition of the duty. By July, 1925, the crisis in the mill industry of Bombay had become somewhat acute, and the Mill-owners' Association, so far baffled in their endeavour to seek relief from the abolition of the excise duty, now fell back upon the one thing to which the manufacturers almost always and inevitably turn their attention in bad times, viz. the reduction of wages. They notified a general reduction of 11½ per cent in the wages of all labourers, and when negotiations for a compromise failed, there was a widespread strike about the middle of September, 1925. The City of Bombay had already in the previous year suffered grievously from the dislocation of its economic life through a wholesale strike in the Textile Industry extending over nearly ten weeks. The Government as well as the public of Bombay, therefore, could hardly contemplate with indifference the prospect of another big strike in the year 1925. His Excellency the Governor of Bombay, therefore, lent the weight of his official support to the representations made by the mill-owners to the Government of India for the repeal of the excise duty.[2] In September, once again, the Assembly, on the initiative of the Cotton-mill Industry of Bombay, passed a resolution recommending that, in view of the critical state of the Cotton Industry, the collection of the cotton excise duty should be suspended forthwith.[3] No longer

[1] *Assembly Debates*, September, 1924.

[2] *Report of the Bombay Mill-owners' Association* for the year 1925.

[3] *Assembly Debates*, September, 1925.

able to resist the pressure of the great and growing volume of opinion in favour of the repeal, and prompted by the desire to bring about industrial peace in Bombay,[1] the Government of India suspended the cotton excise duty as from the 1st of December, 1925, by an ordinance, and finally repealed it in the beginning of the financial year, 1926–27, when the estimates showed a budgetary surplus of over Rs. 3 crores.[2]

6. TOWARDS A PROTECTIVE TARIFF. THE TARIFF BOARD ON THE COTTON INDUSTRY

Those who had closely watched the trend of the agitation organised and carried on by the Mill-owners' Association of Bombay in 1924 and 1925 for the repeal of the cotton excise duty did not have much difficulty in foreseeing that the repeal of the excise duty was sure to be followed by the protectionist demand for a considerable enhancement of the import duty on yarn as well as cotton piece-goods. As a matter of fact, the Assembly Resolution of September, 1924, moved by Mr. Kasturbhai Lalbhai (representative of the Ahmedabad Mill-owners' Association), as originally proposed, intended to kill two birds with one stone, and recommended the abolition of the cotton excise duty as well as the appointment of a Tariff Board to examine the question of protection to the Cotton-mill Industry. The Bombay Mill-owners' Association, however, were more shrewd and businesslike, and they were doubtful whether a sufficiently strong case could be made out to secure the benefit of two first-class measures at one and the same time. Accordingly, they advised that the question of protection should be dropped for the time being. As we have seen, the Mill-owners' Association continued their representations to the Government of India throughout the greater part of the year 1925. In the course of the discussions that took place, the Viceroy and his

[1] The Government of India made it clear that the immediate object of the relief was to enable the mill-owners to continue to pay the old rate of wages.

[2] The yield of the cotton excise duty in 1924–25 was Rs. 218 lakhs, and for the first eight months of 1925–26, Rs. 147 lakhs.

Government intimated that they were proposing, on their own initiative, to ask the Tariff Board to examine the conditions of the cotton industry "for the purpose of determining whether it is in need of protection, and if so, what modifications are required in our tariff duties, whether on imports generally or on imports from particular countries."[1] When, therefore, in March, 1926, they had achieved their first object of having the excise duty finally repealed, the Mill-owners' Association almost immediately proceeded to take the necessary steps for the fulfilment of their second object, that is, the enhancement of the import duty with the intention of obtaining further relief. Their representation to the Government of India was sent on the 19th of May, and the Tariff Board was appointed on the 10th of June, 1926. The terms of reference were as follows:

(1) to investigate the condition of the cotton textile industry in India, with special reference to the industry in Bombay and Ahmedabad;

(2) to examine the causes of the depression in the industry and to report whether they are of a temporary or permanent character;

(3) in particular, to consider whether, and if so to what extent, the depression is due to the competition of other countries in the home and export trade.

(4) to report whether, having regard (i) to the fact that the industry has long been firmly established in India, and (ii) to the interests of the consumer and to all other interests affected—

(*a*) the industry is in need of protection;
(*b*) if so, in what form and for what period protection should be given; and
(*c*) to make any other recommendations that are germane to the subject.

The Board signed the report on January 21, 1927. All three Members of the Board agreed in the view that one of the main external causes of the depression in the Indian Cotton Industry was the severe competition of Japan in the yarn trade as well as in certain lines of coarse and medium grey goods, and that in this there was an element of unfairness owing to the adoption by Japan of a double shift system rendered possible

[1] Vide His Excellency the Viceroy's Reply to the Mill-owners' Deputation, August 24, 1925.

by the nonfulfilment by that country of the Washington Labour Convention both in regard to the limitation of hours as well as the employment of children and women at night. The 'unfair advantage' arising out of this was calculated to be 4 per cent. In so far as the competition with the other important country, the United Kingdom, in the import trade was concerned, they also agreed that, as the imports of piece-goods from that country were of such varieties as were not produced in India, there was no direct competition between the two.

While agreeing in this analysis of the causes of the depression, however, they differed fundamentally in the suggestion of remedies. The two Indian members of the Board held that although the obvious remedy was to adopt discriminating duties against Japan, they were precluded from recommending this course mainly on political grounds.[1] They therefore recommended that the necessary protection to the Indian piece-goods should be given by means of an additional duty of 4 per cent on all imports, irrespective of the country of origin. On the question of yarn, however, in which also there was an element of unfair competition from Japan, they realised that any enhancement of the duty would be a severe handicap to the important but struggling hand-loom industry which contributes more than a quarter of the total consumption of piece-goods in the country. Instead of an increase in the rate of import duty, therefore, they recommended the grant of a bounty of one anna per lb., or its equivalent, on yarn of 32's and higher counts. The President of the Board, however dissented from the members on both these points. He held that the demand for protection came only from Bombay and Ahmedabad, and not from the other centres of the Textile Industry in India, that the depression in Bombay was as much due to internal as to external competition, and that therefore the only legitimate claim for protection that could be substantiated

[1] Another reason was that the yield of a higher duty against Japan alone would not produce sufficient money for the bounty which they proposed to be given on the production of yarn.

was the one based on the "unfair competition" of Japan. On this view of the case, therefore, he maintained that the needs of the case would be adequately met by an enhancement of the duty by 4 per cent against Japanese yarn as well as piece-goods only. This, he pointed out, would be "a measure of protection which will assist the Bombay industry, will impose the minimum burden on the consumer, and will not, at the same time, give the industry in other centres assistance of which it does not really stand in need." His objections to the grant of a bonus on the production of yarn of counts 32 and over were equally strong. These were: (1) There was no case for granting an artificial stimulus to the development of the spinning of higher counts at the cost of the tax-payer; (2) its administration would necessitate the carrying out of inquisitorial inspections of the spinning mills; (3) it would not eliminate the internal competition from which Bombay was suffering; and (4) it would accentuate the tendency of the Indian mills, which had been admitted by many witnesses in the course of the enquiry, to spin higher counts of yarn out of inferior Indian cotton, resulting in inferior product, lower output and discontented labour.[1]

7. THE VACILLATING POLICY OF THE GOVERNMENT OF INDIA; THE COTTON MILL-OWNERS' PROPAGANDA; PROTECTION FOR COTTON YARN

The Government of India took more than four months in formulating their conclusions on the Report of the Board, and even then, as we shall presently see, these conclusions were destined to pass through successive modifications as they felt more and more the impact of political opinion in the country. In their Resolution No. 341 T (27), dated the 7th of June, 1927, they communicated their decision to the public as follows:

(1) They agreed to abolish the import duty on textile machinery and mill stores.

(2) They accepted the finding of the Tariff Board that in the

[1] *Report of the Tariff Board* (*Cotton Textile Industry*), pp. 216 et seq.

manufacture of yarn Japan enjoyed an 'unfair' advantage due to the non-compliance with the Washington Labour Convention, which made it possible for her to adopt a double-shift system in spinning by the employment of women at night. The difference in the cost of production of yarn in Japan and India, attributable to this factor, they agreed with the Tariff Board, would be, if allowance were made for a reasonable return on capital over and above the bare cost of production, 10 per cent. It was therefore conceded that the Tariff Board were right in their finding that the manufacturer of yarn in India could justly ask for protection against unfair competition. Now, as a bounty was already ruled out, the only other alternative method of granting protection would be an increase in the existing duty from 5 per cent to 10 per cent. But this they were not prepared to do, because an increase in the duty on yarn would prejudicially affect the hand-loom industry of the country.

(3) With regard to the increase of the duty on piece-goods, although it was true that the advantage to Japan due to 'unfair competition' could be approximately taken at 10 per cent, this difference, they held, was more than covered by the then existing revenue tariff of 11 per cent, and hence called for no further increase in import duties.

It will therefore be evident that in their first decision on the recommendations of the Tariff Board, the Government of India had clearly taken the position that there was no case for the grant of assistance to the cotton Textile Industry, either by means of a bounty or by an enhancement of the tariff. The Bombay Mill-owners' Association, however, after their successful experience in the matter of abolition of the cotton excise duty, had well learnt the value of propaganda, and could therefore be hardly expected to rest satisfied with the decision of the Government of India. On the 20th of June, 1927, they convened a Conference of the owners of cotton weaving and spinning mills from all over India and, of course, had the Conference to pass resolutions urging upon the Government to reconsider their decision and to grant adequate protection to the Textile Industry of India. Three weeks later, on the 12th of July, 1927, a deputation waited on His Excellency the Viceroy, as a result of which the leader of the deputation was able to inform the public on the 18th of July that the Government could not now "possibly disregard the strength of our case, and of public opinion throughout the country, and persist in an attitude which is calculated to inflict grave injury to the best interests of India."[1]

Exactly four weeks later, on the 16th of August, we find the Government of India issuing a *communiqué*, in which they rediscuss the relevant recommendations of the Tariff Board, refer to the representations of the Mill-owners' Association, and agree to grant protection to the Indian yarn of 40 counts and below so as to neutralise the unfair advantage enjoyed by Japan. With regard to the effect of the duty on the Hand-loom Industry, anxiety for which had decided them against raising the duty on yarn only three months earlier, they were now satisfied that the consequences of the enhancement of the duty would not be serious!

This reversal of the decision of the Government of India with regard to the enhancement of the duty on yarn, clearly brought about by the pressure of the cotton mill-owners of Bombay, was in utter disregard of the evidence tendered to the Tariff Board by the Directors of Industries of Madras, Assam, Central Provinces, Burma, and Behar and Orissa, to the effect that the important Hand-loom Industry of these provinces would be adversely affected thereby. This was also contrary to the view of the Indian Fiscal Commission and the Textile Tariff Board that no enhancement of the duty on yarn should be made, because it would seriously increase the handicap of a large number of poor artisans,[2] who had had a hard struggle to

[1] Mr. H. P. Mody's Statement issued to the Press on July 18, 1927.

[2] According to the Census Report of 1921, the number of hand-looms in existence at the date of the census was 2 millions. As this number was exclusive of the figures for several native states and British provinces, the total number may safely be taken at 2½ millions. The Textile Expert to the Government of Behar and Orissa in the Note submitted to the Textile Tariff Board estimated that the industry supports 5 million persons and turns out an output valued roughly at about Rs. 50 crores. The importance of this industry will be further realised when we are informed that in Madras alone there are as many as 174,000 hand-looms, which produce a large quantity of special varieties of coloured piece-goods for export, and that in Behar and Orissa, one of the poorest of provinces in India, the hand-looms supply no less than 40 per cent of the consumption of piece-goods in the province. (Vide the speech of Mr. R. D. Bell, late Director of Industries, Bombay, *Assembly Debates*, March 20, 1924.)

keep themselves alive in competition with the well-organised and powerful Mill Industry, and whose position was exceedingly weak, insecure and unstable due to the lack of finance and commercial ability. It was, therefore, but natural that the measure should have met with a considerable volume of opposition in the Assembly from the representatives of Bengal, Behar and Orissa, and Madras, the three provinces where the Hand-loom Industry plays a very important part in the economic life of the people.[1]

8. EXAMINATION OF THE INDIAN TARIFF (COTTON YARN AMENDMENT) ACT, 1927: THE BURDEN ON THE HAND-LOOM INDUSTRY

The Bill was passed and became law on the 22nd of September, 1927. The net effect of the measure may be explained as follows: Under the then existing tariff, the duty on imported twist and yarn was 5 per cent. The new measure provided that the duty should be 5 per cent *ad valorem* or 1½ annas per pound, whichever was higher. The result was that all twist and yarn, of which the price was less than Re. 1 and 14 annas a pound, became subject to a much heavier rate of duty than the higher-grade varieties. Taking the average declared value of different grades of yarn in 1927–28 as the basis of calculation, we find that on yarn of counts 1–20 the duty worked out to about 11 per cent, on counts 21–30 to 7 per cent, on counts 31–40 to 10 per cent, on counts 41–50 to 7½ per cent, and on higher counts, where the price was more than Re. 1 and 14 annas a pound, it was less than 5 per cent, and therefore ineffective.

Further light on the effect of the duty on the price and production of different varieties of yarn would be thrown by a consideration of the relation between internal production and imports. In the year 1927–28 the position was as follows:

[1] Vide the speeches of Messrs. K. C. Neogi, M. S. Shesha Ayyangar, B. Das, and Nilkanta Das, *Assembly Debates*, August 22, and September 6, 1927.

THE QUANTITATIVE RELATION BETWEEN IMPORTS AND INDIAN MILL OUTPUT IN THE YARN TRADE OF INDIA* (1927–28)

Grades		Imports (Million lb.)	Indian Mill Output (Million lb.)	Total (2 + 3) (Million lb.)	Imports as Percentage of the Total
1–20	..	2·5	494·8	497·3	0·5
21–30	..	0·9	263·0	263·9	0·3
31–40	..	27·3	33·8	61·1	44·7
Above 40	..	8·0	11·1	19·1	42·0
Total	..	38·7	802·7	841·4	4·6

* *Review of the Trade of India*, 1927–28. The table excludes from the import column "two-folds," because there is no production of these in India; on the other hand, from the column of Indian output, it excludes "wastes," etc., which do not occur in the imports statistics.

It will be observed from the above Table that in yarn of lower counts, that is, 1's to 30's, the Indian mills have a practical monopoly of the market, while in yarn of medium counts, 31's to 40's, as well as in that of higher counts, above 40's, they have a position that is somewhat stronger than that of the importers.

Sir George Rainy, while introducing the Indian Tariff (cotton yarn amendment) Bill, made an attempt to show that the burden of the increased duty on the Hand-loom Industry would not be a serious one by assuming that the price of Nos. 1 to 30 would remain unaffected, that the price of yarn above No 40 would be slightly affected, and that it was only in the case of Nos. 31 to 40 that the price would rise considerably. Accordingly, so he held, the effect of the duty would be least felt by the consumers of the coarser varieties of cloths, only slightly felt by the consumers of finer grades of piece-goods, while its full force would be felt by users and consumers of counts Nos. 31 to 40. And as Nos. 31–40 represented the range in which alone the Japanese competition was severely felt, the change in the tariff would have the effect of giving the due degree of protection only at the point where it was needed, while, as analysed above, it would not injure the consumers of cotton goods which were either below or above that particular range.[1]

Now, although Sir George permitted himself these very convenient and apparently reasonable assumptions with regard to the non-effectiveness of the duty in raising the price of yarn of count 30's and below due to the practical monopoly of the market held by the Indian mill-owners, the assumptions were based on too charitable a view of human nature to be always borne out by the facts of experience. Even if it be granted that in these lower ranges of counts of yarn, the price of yarn in the Indian market is determined by the selling price of the Indian manufacturers and not by the import price plus duty, as was contended by Sir George, the probability that in a period of falling prices and declining profits the Indian mill-owners would exploit the fullest possibilities of the tariff in maintaining prices at a sufficiently high level is a much stronger one than that they would, as assumed by the Member for Commerce to the Government of India, allow their prices to remain unaffected by the duty. In any case, from the consumer's and tax-payer's point of view, it is more safe to assume that the prices would be so affected by the full amount of the duty.

In this view of the case, therefore, it would appear that the net effect of the enhancement of the yarn duty was that it enabled the mill-owners to exact a tribute equal to the full amount of the duty from all users of cotton yarn. As a result, in addition to giving them a great stimulus in the production of count 31's and above, in which there was serious competition with imports to be overcome, it also enabled them to increase their profits, or at any rate to reduce their losses, by raising the prices of yarn of count 30's and below, in which they have had a practical monopoly of the home market, and to which, therefore, there could obviously have been no case for the extension of protection or artificial stimulus of any kind. In so far, therefore, as this analysis of the probable effect of the Act

[1] *Assembly Debates*, August 22, 1927.

XXIII of 1927 is concerned, one may reasonably raise the question whether the Government of India as the tariff-making authority had been at all well advised in enacting a measure which extended protection much beyond the needs of the case, and which, therefore, had the effect of putting about 5 millions of hand-loom weavers and mills with weaving sheds only in a position of competitive weakness, and that, at a time when they were, equally with the yarn manufacturers, experiencing extreme financial distress in a period of falling prices, narrowing markets and vanishing profits. And this question assumes a still greater pointedness when we are reminded that the financial sacrifices that these several classes of yarn consumers were made to undergo were intended to contribute directly to the avoidance of loss and increase of profit on the part of those who are also, in most cases, in serious competition with them in the home market for piece-goods.

9. FROM SAFE-GUARDING TO PROTECTION

The President and the Members of the Tariff Board were, as we have seen, in complete agreement in the view that the only important ground on which the Cotton Industry of India could claim the assistance of the state was the 'unfair' advantage enjoyed by Japan in respect of the employment of women and children. But while the President suggested that the proper remedy against the evil was the safeguarding of the Indian Industry by means of additional differential duties against the cotton manufactures of Japan, the two members appear to have gone much beyond the necessary degree of safeguarding when they recommended that a bounty of one anna per pound should be given on the production of yarn of 32's and higher counts so as to stimulate the production of superior counts of yarn, in which, however, the cotton mills of India had shown little aptitude so far. There seems, therefore, to have been a fundamental difference of opinion between the President and the Members as to whether the assistance of the state could be legitimately granted only for safeguarding the industry as it is against the 'unfair' conditions of competition, or whether it could also be extended so as to bring into existence some new branch of an old industry as well. If we accept the former view of the case, then state assistance can be given by way of safeguarding only to the extent and for the period of the 'unfair' competition. On the other hand, if the latter view prevails, then we are faced with what is called the "infant industry" argument, and the state must be prepared to guarantee the continuance of the assistance of the tariff or the bounty, as the case may be, as long as this new branch of the industry is not able to stand on its own legs. In other words, while the acceptance of the 'safeguarding' point of view would narrow the scope and duration of state assistance, the admittance of the protectionist point of view would widen the scope and prolong the period much further.

In the original Bill as introduced by the Government, the preamble contained the words "in order to safeguard the manufacture of cotton yarn in British India," and showed clearly the view of the Government that the purpose of the Bill was the 'safeguarding' of the industry as it is, and not the granting of protection so as to stimulate further development in new directions. But the Select Committee, to which the Bill was referred, widened the purpose of the Bill and committed the country to an indefinite period of protection for the Cotton Industry by deliberately substituting the word 'protection' for 'safeguarding.'[1] Accordingly, in the Bill as finally passed, the preamble contained the words "in order to protect the Cotton Textile Industry in British India against competition in cotton yarn produced under industrial conditions which enable such yarn to be produced at a cost below that at which it can be produced in British India."[2] A careful analysis of the wording of the preamble would show that, although the words "against competition in cotton yarn produced under industrial conditions" would seem to convey a weak suggestion of

[1] *Assembly Debates*, September 6, 1927.

[2] The Indian Tariff (Cotton Yarn Amendment) Act.

The Problem of Discriminating Protection

It will be remembered that in 1927, when the Indian Tariff (Cotton Yarn Amendment) Bill was passed, the Government of India had taken the view that the duty on coarser and medium counts of yarn was to be increased as a measure of safeguarding against what might be regarded as 'unfair' advantage enjoyed by Japan in the matter of hours of labour and employment of women and children at night. In July, 1929, however, the new Factory Law of Japan, under which hours of labour for women had been at least equalised with those in force in India, had become operative. Accordingly, the question of granting assistance to the Indian Cotton Mill Industry could no longer now be regarded from the point of view of safeguarding, but became one of protection, pure and simple, and the intention of the measure as incorporated in the preamble is stated to be "to protect the Cotton Textile Industry in respect of the manufacture of cotton piece-goods."[1] The Government of India, however, tried to soften the real nature of the measure as a purely protective one by declaring that it had been designed as a temporary emergency measure to save the Textile Industry of Bombay from a grave crisis, and that the question of protection on its own merits would be considered afresh by the Tariff Board after the lapse of three years.[2] It would, therefore, appear that, although the Government had no better ground for giving protection to the Cotton Industry in 1930 than they had had in 1927, they nevertheless felt themselves persuaded at the later date to impose an extra taxation on the consumers of India in order to reduce the losses of some and increase the profits of other cotton mills in India under the popular and attractive guise of protection.

In their desire to grant an additional measure of assistance to the Cotton Mill Industry by an enhancement of the import

[1] The Cotton Textile Industry (Protection) Act, 1930.

[2] The Budget Speech of Sir George Schuster, *Assembly Debates*, February 28, 1930.

duty, the Government of India were, however, also influenced by another and a far more powerful consideration. The Budget Estimates for 1930–31 had disclosed an anticipated deficit of Rs. 4, 10 Lakhs on the basis of the then existing taxation, and, therefore, the Government had already decided on raising the import duty on piece-goods from 11 to 15 per cent for the sake of additional revenue, quite independently of protective considerations.[1]

It will be recalled that the Tariff Board in 1927 held that the necessary degree of assistance would be derived by the Cotton Industry if the import duty on piece-goods were raised from 11 to 15 per cent. By 1930, however, the condition of the Textile Industry in Bombay and to a lesser extent in other parts of India had become worse, and the Government of India, therefore, having first decided that relief ought to be given to the mill-owners in their financial difficulties, came to the conclusion that the new rate of 15 per cent would not be sufficient to meet the needs of the case, but would have to be supplemented by other measures of a suitable nature. The problem, as it was analysed and defined in Mr. Hardy's Report, was to devise a tariff measure under which the greatest amount of protection would be secured to the Indian mills in respect of plain grey goods of medium qualities, a lesser amount in bordered grey and coloured goods, and a still lesser amount in bleached goods. Under this scheme of differentiation, by far the largest proportions of Japanese goods would automatically be subject to the higher rate of duty, while, on the contrary, by far the larger proportions of British goods would fall under the lower rate. From the point of view of discriminating protection, therefore, two alternatives were open to the Government of India, either to levy a surcharge on Japanese goods alone, and treat all the other countries on an equal footing, or to give a preferential lower rate on British goods, in which the competition with Indian mill products was admittedly not

[1] The Budget Speech of Sir George Schuster, *Assembly Debates*, February 28, 1930.

serious, and put the imports from all the other countries under the higher rate of duty. The principal objection against the first alternative was that it would involve the abrogation of the Anglo-Japanese Convention, under which Japan could claim the right to the most-favoured-nation treatment from India, and which required a notice of six months for its annulment. Moreover, as Japan was by far the largest importer of Indian cotton and pig iron, that course of action was also fraught with the grave and incalculable dangers of retaliation. Against the second alternative, however, the objection was not economic but political, and was based on the ground that it would introduce a principle of Imperial Preference in Indian tariff and would thus be liable to arouse the suspicion of infringing the fiscal autonomy convention. The Government of India, however, in complete agreement with the Bombay Mill-owners' Association, chose the second alternative, as the one more suited to meet the needs of the case from the economic point of view, and, at the same time, gave all assurance to the Legislature that the measure did not involve the acceptance of Imperial Preference as a matter of principle. Accordingly, although the Bill undoubtedly encountered a large measure of opposition from those who stressed the purely constitutional aspect of the case, it received a sufficient measure of acceptance from the majority of members who looked at it merely as a complicated economic question, and was ultimately passed as the Cotton Textile Industry (Protection) Act of 1930.

The Provisions of the Act

It would be recalled that it was in plain grey goods that the severe pressure of competition was felt by the Indian mills, and that, therefore, it was that class of indigenous piece-goods that required to be guaranteed a price, as far as such a guarantee could be given by means of an import duty, below which the imported piece-goods could not be sold. Accordingly, the Act provided for a minimum specific duty of 3½ annas per pound on all plain grey goods, whether of British or of non-British origin. The only preference that was provided was to be found in the alternative *ad valorem* rate, 15 per cent for grey goods of British manufacture, and 20 per cent for those of non-British manufacture. The result of this combination of differential *ad valorem* rates with the non-differential minimum specific duty may be explained as follows: So long as plain grey goods of British origin have a c.i.f. price equal to or less than 23½ annas per pound, they would be subject to the minimum specific duty of 3½ annas per pound exactly in the same way as plain grey goods of non-British origin. That is to say, Britain will have no preference whatsoever in plain grey goods of coarser and medium qualities, in which there is a three-cornered competition among Britain, Japan and India. On the other hand, as soon as the c.i.f. price of British plain grey goods rises above 23½ annas per pound, the 15 per cent rate becomes effective. But, as the classes of cloth with a price of 23½ annas per pound and upwards are of superior qualities which are neither imported from Japan nor made in India, the only consequence of the effectiveness of the lower preferential rate of duty in this range of cloths would be that, while it would not in the least interfere with the degree of protection claimed by and necessary to the Indian products, it, at the same time, would allow the consumers of these costlier types of cloths to satisfy their requirements after the payment of a tax of 15 per cent, and not 20 per cent. On the other hand, the application of the higher rate of duty, that is, 20 per cent to this class of cloth, would have been that, while the consumers would have been greatly penalised, the Indian producers would have derived small benefit from it.

In respect of the other varieties of piece-goods, that is, bleached (white) goods and coloured (dyed, printed or woven) goods, there is no provision for a minimum specific duty as in the case of plain grey goods. Here the Act provides for a simple differential *ad valorem* rate, 15 per cent against piece-goods of British origin, and 20 per cent against those of non-British origin. In these classes also, however, the effective degree of preference is really less than what would appear to be the case at first sight. In bleached goods, which are practically all luxury goods, the Indian output is less than 1 per cent, there being no large-scale up-to-date bleaching factory in India, while the imports from Britain amount to 95 per cent. In this also, therefore, the real effect of the application of the 20 per cent rate would have been to place an unduly large burden on the consumers for the sake of a very small benefit to the producers. The benefit that may, at the most, be derived by British manufacturers in this particular case is that as the foreign manufacturers would be handicapped in the Indian market by the 5 per cent additional duty, the former may take advantage of the difference in capturing the remaining 5 per cent of the market from the latter.[1]

In coloured goods (printed, woven or dyed), on the other hand, however, while in respect of finer classes, which are imported largely from Britain, the question of special advantage does not arise at all; in respect of medium and coarser qualities, she will derive an advantage as against the other external competitors, that is, Japan, Holland and Italy.

The Indian Tariff (Cotton Yarn) Amendment Act of 1927, which had been enacted for a period of two and a half years, had been intended to protect the Indian manufacturer against the 'unfair' advantage enjoyed by Japan. This so-called 'unfair' advantage had been, however, meanwhile eliminated by the operation of a stricter factory law in that country from July, 1929. The Act should, therefore, have been allowed to lapse at the end of March, 1930, as was the original intention and purpose of the Government. But, instead of that, they discovered a fresh ground for its continuation for another three years in the inferior labour conditions of China, from which country, for the first time, cotton yarns amounting to 10½ million pounds on the average of the two years 1928–29 and 1929–30, had been exported to India. A new law had indeed

[1] During 1927–28 to 1931–32, the share of the United Kingdom declined from 95 to 74 per cent, while that of Japan increased from 1 to 22 per cent.

been passed in that country, which was stricter in all respects than that in India or Japan, but there was no certainty as to when that law would be actually enforced. The information at the disposal of the Government of India was to the effect that the conditions of employment of women and children were far worse and the rates of wages much lower in China than those in India. Accordingly, the protective measure of 1927 was incorporated with the Cotton Textile Industry (Protection) Act of 1930.[1]

II. AN ESTIMATE OF THE BURDEN OF HIGHER PRICES LAID ON THE CONSUMERS IN CONSEQUENCE OF PROTECTIVE DUTIES ON COTTON MANUFACTURES

The Cotton Textile Industry (Protection) Act of 1930 is too recent a measure to enable us to make an estimate of the amount of burden placed on the consumers for the benefit of the producers. The figures of imports, internal output, and of prices for the recent months have been greatly vitiated by an intense political agitation, effective boycott of foreign cloths, and also by a terrible depression in the trade in agricultural produce, which has very considerably diminished the purchasing power of the hundreds of millions who are dependent on agriculture alone. Nevertheless, some idea of the burden of import duties on cotton piece-goods may be formed by an examination of the effects of the 11 per cent duty which had been put into operation in 1922. We, therefore, proceed to estimate the burden of cotton import duties laid on the consumers in the period 1922–23 to 1928–29. This has been done in the four tables that follow.

The sources and nature of the statistical data and the assumptions involved in interpreting them may be briefly summarised as follows:

(*a*) The figures for the duties realised from the imports are given

[1] Speech of Sir George Rainy, *Assembly Debates*, March 13, 1930.

in the Government statistical publications on finance and commerce. We assume that the whole of this duty is paid by the consumers.[1]

(*b*) The quantities of cotton piece-goods produced by the cotton mills in British India and Native States are given in the Monthly Statistics of Cotton Spinning and Weaving, published by the Government of India. The problem is to find out the value of these piece-goods corresponding to the c.i.f. landed price of imported piece-goods. The difficulties of an exact valuation are almost insurmountable, because, apart from the fact that in the Indian piece-goods market at least a hundred different classes are recognised, the price of each class is dependent on a great number of independent factors such as quality of yarn, weave, reed and pick, dimensions, borders and headings, filling and finishing, printing, dyeing, assortment, fold and packing, and, last of all, trade-marks.[2]

We have three alternative methods of valuation open to us:

(i) to assume the average price of exported Indian piece-goods to be equal to the average price of those consumed within the country;

or (ii) to assume that the average price of imports and exports is equal to the average price of the indigenous piece-goods consumed within the country;

or (iii) to accept the valuation of Indian mill-made piece-goods as given by the Government Customs Department for the purpose of the excise duty under the Act of 1896.

We have accepted the third alternative as the one nearer to the facts than the other two, and that for two important reasons:

(i) We found, by actual calculation, that the valuation under the first two alternative methods would be at least 25 per cent to 30 per cent above the valuation given by the Government.

(ii) As the Government valuation was made under the law[3] by the Customs Department for the purpose of the excise duty, we may safely assume that this valuation would be approximately accurate.

[1] Without going into a theoretical discussion of the incidence of import duties under varying conditions, we need only point out that the weight of evidence tendered by economists before the Colwyn Committee was overwhelmingly in favour of the assumption. The assumption was also made by Sir Herbert Samuel in his examination of the taxation of the various classes of people in the United Kingdom (vide *Journal of the Royal Statistical Society*, March, 1919).

[2] *Hardy Report*, op. cit., Chapter II.

[3] Although the Act was applicable only to British India, in practice the statistics were also collected for native states as well.

(*c*) The excise duty being abolished in December, 1925, the statistics of value were discontinued from the year 1926–27. The statistics of quantities of output under fifteen different headings are, however, still continued. On examination, it has been found that the average price per yard of Indian piece-goods under the scheme of tariff value was 25 per cent lower than the average c.i.f. landed price per yard of imports and exports as given in the *Review of Trade*. The value of Indian mill-made piece-goods for the years 1926–27 to 1928–29 has, therefore, been arrived at by multiplying the quantity produced[1] by an average price per yard, which is less than the corresponding average price for imports and exports by 25 per cent.[2]

(*d*) A large amount of cloths is also produced by the hand-loom weavers of India as well. We have to find out both the quantity and the value of their output. From the figures of imports, Indian mill output, and exports, we know the total quantities of yarn converted into cloths by the Indian mills and hand-looms together. Mr. A. C. Coubrough in 1921 estimated that the cotton mills on an average produced 4·76 yards, and the hand-looms 4 yards of cloth out of 1 pound of yarn.[3] By deducting from the total amount of yarn consumed in India the amount required by the mills to produce known quantities of piece-goods in yards, we estimate the quantity of yarn consumed by the hand-looms, and convert this into cloths at the average rate of 4 yards to a pound.

The hand-looms produce cloths of two extreme qualities, very coarse qualities, corresponding to the greater part of the

[1] It should be noted that the statistics of output for 1926–27 and subsequent years relate to the total output, while those for the earlier years referred to the goods that were actually issued out of the mills. We have neglected the difference in the calculation of the burden of taxation.

[2] Mr. A. C. Coubrough in 1921 assumed the average price of Indian piece-goods $= \frac{W + T}{2}$, where W = average price of imports, and T = average price of mill-produced goods as estimated by the Customs Department for the purpose of excise duties. We have been unable to find the grounds for this assumption, and, therefore, we have rejected the formula given by him.

[3] *Notes on Indian Piece-goods Trade*, by A. C. Coubrough, 1921.

output of Indian mills, and very fine qualities, much superior in quality and price to the average of mill-made cloths.[1] As both the coarser and the finer varieties of hand-loom products satisfy a very special demand, incapable of being satisfied either by imports or by the Indian mills, we are inclined to think that the average value of hand-loom products is appreciably higher than that of Indian mill-made cloths. There is no way of finding out even approximately the extent to which this would be so. Accordingly, to be on the safe side, we have followed Mr. A. C. Coubrough in assuming equality of value for the hand-loom and mill products.

(*e*) From the total value of mill-made and hand-loom made cloths, we deduct the value of exports, and thus obtain the value of indigenous piece-goods consumed in India. After arriving at the value of the piece-goods made by the Indian mills and hand-looms and consumed in India, we find out the total burden of taxation laid on the consumers by the import duty, calculating at a flat 11 per cent rate on such value.

To find the net benefit of the Indian producers from the import duties on cotton piece-goods, however, we have to deduct for excise duties on piece-goods and the import duty on yarn, which may be taken to be the repayment to the public of a portion of the tribute that the producers are enabled to levy from the consumers by reason of the existence of the import duty.[2]

[1] Cf. *Hand-loom Weaving in Madras Presidency*, by D. M. Amalsad, Textile Expert to the Government of Madras; *A Note on Hand-loom Weaving in India*, by K. S. Rao, Textile Expert to the Government of Bihar and Orissa, 1924, and *Report on the Survey of Cottage Industries in Bengal*, 1929.

[2] The duty on yarn being a charge on a semi-manufactured good cannot be passed on to the consumers of piece-goods under competitive conditions. It is, therefore, borne by the hand-loom weavers and those mills which have only weaving-sheds. The benefit of the higher price due to the duty is divided as follows: in so far as the imports are concerned, it produces revenue for the public exchequer; on the other hand, in so far as the surplus yarn of Indian mills is concerned, the effect is to enable the spinning mills to levy a tribute from hand-loom weavers and those mills which have weaving-sheds only

TABLE I

QUANTITY OF INDIGENOUS PIECE-GOODS CONSUMED IN INDIA

(Millions of Linear Yards)

1 Year	2 Mill Output	3 Hand-loom Output	4 Export	5 Internal Consumption (2 + 3 − 4)
1922–23 ..	1,725	1,341	186	2,880
1923–24 ..	1,702	1,005	201	2,506
1924–25 ..	1,970	1,256	230	2,996
1925–26 ..	1,954	1,160	164	2,950
1926–27 ..	2,295	1,731	197	3,829
1927–28 ..	2,410	1,312	168	3,554
1928–29 ..	1,937	1,077	149	2,865
Annual Average	1,999	1,269	185	3,083

TABLE II

GROSS BURDEN OF THE CUSTOMS DUTY ON THE CONSUMERS OF INDIGENOUS PIECE-GOODS

1 Year	2 Quantity Consumed (Millions of Yards)	3 Value per Yard* R.	 A.	 P.	4 Total Value (Lakhs of Rupees)	5 Total Amount of the Burden at 11 Per Cent. on the Total Value (Lakhs of Rupees)
1922–23	2,880	0	5	6	99,00	1,089·00
1923–24	2,506	0	5	0	78,30	861·30
1924–25	2,996	0	4	10	90,50	995·50
1925–26	2,950	0	3	10	70,70	777·70
1926–27	3,829	0	4	0	95,70	1,052·70
1927–28	3,554	0	3	10	85,10	936·10
1928–29	2,865	0	3	9	67,10	738·10

* The average value per yard for 1922–23 to 1925–26 is that given by the Customs Department for the purpose of excise duties; that for 1926–27 to 1928–29 is equal to the average of import and export prices less 25 per cent. (See explanation *c*, supra.)

TABLE III

NET BENEFIT DERIVED FROM THE CUSTOMS DUTY BY THE PRODUCERS OF INDIGENOUS PIECE-GOODS

(In Lakhs of Rupees)

1 Year	2 Gross Benefit (see Column 5, Table II)	3 Import Duty on Yarn	4 Excise Duty	5 Net Benefit 2−(3 + 4)
1922–23	1,089·00	48·86	187·34	852·80
1923–24	861·30	42·74	156·52	662·04
1924–25	995·50	51·41	217·67	726·42
1925–26	777·70	43·38	146·60	587·72
1926–27	1,052·70	36·45	—	1,016·25
1927–28	936·10	43·45	—	892·65
1928–29	738·10	45·80	—	692·30
Annual Average	921·49	44·58	101·16	777·75

TABLE IV

TOTAL BURDEN PLACED ON THE CONSUMERS OF INDIGENOUS AND IMPORTED PIECE-GOODS ON ACCOUNT OF THE IMPOSITION OF THE IMPORT DUTY

(In Lakhs of Rupees)

1 Year	2 Net Gain to Indian Producers (Column 5, Table III)	3 Excise Duty and Customs Revenue from Piece-goods	4 Total Burden (2 + 3)
1922–23 ..	852·80	826·37	1,679·17
1923–24 ..	662·04	772·64	1,434·68
1924–25 ..	726·42	991·43	1,717·85
1925–26 ..	587·72	753·15	1,340·87
1926–27 ..	1,016·25	621·04	1,637·29
1927–28 ..	892·65	625·17	1,517·82
1928–29 ..	692·30	604·48	1,296·78
Annual Average	775·75	742·04	1,517·78

PRINCIPAL FEATURES OF THE TABLES

Table I.—Here the outstanding fact is the important place still occupied by the hand-loom weavers in the supplying of piece-goods consumed in the country. The ratio of mill output to hand-loom output is 61·39. That is to say, the supply of piece-goods from the hand-looms is about two-thirds that from the mills. But this by itself does not give a sufficient idea of the relative importance of the Hand-loom Industry. We have, therefore, to look also at the comparative volume of employment available in the two branches of the Cotton Industry. The number of hands employed in the Cotton-mill Industry is about 370,000, whereas the number of hands employed in the Hand-loom Industry has been estimated at about 5 millions. From this point of view, the latter may be taken to be about fourteen times as important as the former in the national economy of India.

This would, therefore, suggest that in any scheme for the promotion of the Indian Cotton Industry as a whole, at least as much attention should be given to the difficulties of the hand-loom weavers as to those of the Mill Industry. The condition of hand-loom weavers has been investigated by the Industrial Commission of 1916–18 as well as by the provincial departments of industries set up under the reformed constitution of 1920. These first-hand enquiries show that what the hand-loom weaver requires for the improvement of his position are education, facilities for the purchase of raw materials and disposal of finished products, introduction of improved appliances like the fly-shuttle, and cheap finance. It is evident that these are matters that require steady help and work on the part of the departments of education, co-operation and industry in the different provinces. Any amount of increase in the import duties cannot by itself solve any of the problems with which the hand-loom weaver is faced. On the other hand, any profits that may be derived from the higher prices due to the increase of the import duty will merely go to swell the profits of the middleman-money-lender, who plays the double rôle of the financier and the entrepreneur in the case of the Hand-loom Industry. In the case of hand-loom weaving, therefore, the import duty penalises the consumer without yielding any appreciable benefit to the producer. Moreover, as the import duty reduces the consumers' capacity to pay further taxes, it may be regarded as drying up the source from which the provincial governments are to derive the revenues that are needed to give the hand-loom weavers the kinds of assistance that are really and permanently beneficial to him.

Table III.—This shows that the producers of piece-goods in India were able to levy an annual tribute from the consumers amounting to over Rs. 921 lakhs. The only redeeming feature of the situation was that the state as representing the consumers was able to take back a small portion of this money, amounting to less than 16 per cent of the whole, in the shape of import duty on yarn and excise duty on piece-goods.

Table IV.—The total burden of the duty placed upon consumers was over Rs. 15 crores per annum. This is nearly equal to the proceeds of the entire income-tax of British India, the figure for the income-tax revenue varying between Rs. 15 and 16 crores during the years 1925–26 to 1927–28.

Another important feature is that rather more than half the total sum paid by the tax-payers did not reach the coffers of the state, but went as a bonus to the producers.

If the sum shown as the net gain of Indian producers is divided in the ratio of 60 to 40 per cent as between the mill-owners and hand-loom weavers, the share of the former would be Rs. 465·45 lakhs per annum. The total paid-up capital of the Indian Cotton-mill Industry in recent years may be estimated at approximately Rs. 4,000 lakhs.[1] During the period in question, therefore, the consumers contributed in the shape of higher prices a sum of money, which works out to between 11 and 12 per cent per annum on the entire paid-up capital of the Cotton-mill Industry in India.

[1] Mr. A. S. Pearse, in his book, *The Cotton Industry of India*, puts the figure at Rs. 4,162 lakhs for August 31, 1929.

CHAPTER III

THE COTTON INDUSTRY AND THE TARIFF

1. 1851–1890

MANY economists and historians have indeed given us glowing accounts of the beautiful muslins and fine calicoes that were produced by the hand-loom weavers of India, and exported to Europe as late as the eighteenth century, but it is important to remember that the problems and requirements of the modern Cotton Industry are, in many respects, fundamentally different from those with which the hand-loom weavers of India were concerned in the days before the advent of the modern factory, the railway, and the steamship. The first modern cotton mill in India was founded by an English Company, called the Bowreah Cotton Mills Company Ltd., on the banks of the Hughly near Calcutta in 1817,[1] and its successor is still in existence. But the real foundation of the Cotton-mill Industry of India was not laid until thirty-four years later, when in 1851 the first cotton mill of Bombay was set up by the Bombay Spinning and Weaving Company under the able guidance of a Parsee gentleman named C. N. Davar. Progress of the Mill Industry in Bombay was, however, exceedingly slow at first, only two more mills having been added during the decade ending 1860. Then came the American Civil War, 1860–65, and this proved to be a great boon to the cotton merchants of Bombay. The extraordinary high prices realised for Indian raw cotton in the markets of Europe brought them large and unexpected wealth, which found a ready and ever-widening outlet for investment in the newly started Cotton-mill Industry of the city. Another factor which contributed to the expansion of the industry was the beginning of the yarn trade with China. In 1865, at the close of the American Civil War, Bombay had 10 mills with 250,000 spindles and

[1] *The Commercial Products of India*, by Sir George Watt, p. 618.

TABLE I

PROGRESS OF THE INDIAN COTTON MILLS

1890–1914*

Year Ending June 30th	Number of Mills	Number of Spindles (in Thousands)	Number of Looms (in Thousands)	Average Number of Hands Employed Daily (in Thousands)	Approximate Quantity of Cotton Consumed, Bales of 392 lb. (in Thousands)
1890	137	3,274	23	103	1,008
1895	148	3,810	35	139	1,342
1900	193	4,946	40	161	1,453
1905	197	5,163	50	195	1,879
1910	263	6,196	83	234	1,935
1914†	271	6,779	104	260	2,143

* Memorandum of the Bombay Mill-owners' Association, Tariff Board, *Minutes of Evidence*, Vol. II, pp. 71–72.

† Year ending August 31.

closing decade of the nineteenth and opening decade of the twentieth century.[1]

It will be seen from the above table that during the period of twenty-four years, 1890–1914, the number of mills increased by 98 per cent, the number of spindles 107 per cent, the number of looms 345 per cent, the average daily number of hands 153 per cent, and the approximate quantity of raw cotton consumed 113 per cent. The most striking feature of this table is that while the spinning branch of the industry at the end of the period only grew to a little more than twice its size at the beginning of the period, the corresponding growth of the weaving branch was nearly four and a half times as large. This disparity in the growth of the two branches of the industry is to be explained by the fact that the mill-owners of India, realising the insecure and uncertain nature of the yarn trade with China, turned their attention towards capturing a greater and greater share of the home market for piece-goods by weaving an increasingly larger share of the yarn into finished cloths for the home consumers than they had done before. The remarkable progress in weaving also reflects the effect of the growing national sentiment, known as 'swadeshi,' in favour of native manufactures.

It will be recalled that up to 1894 there was no cotton tariff, from 1894 to 1896 there was an import duty of 5 per cent on piece-goods and an import duty and a countervailing excise duty of 5 per cent on yarn, and, lastly, from 1896 to 1914, while there was no duty on yarn, there was an import duty and a countervailing excise duty of 3½ per cent on piece-goods. That is to say, practically throughout the whole of this period the Cotton Manufacturing Industry of India derived no advantage from the import duty. We must, therefore, attribute the remarkable progress of the Indian Cotton Industry during this period also entirely to the factors of natural advantage accessible to it.

We may further recall that it was during this period that the

[1] *Report of the Indian Industrial Commission*, p. 66.

TABLE II

THE WAR AND THE POST-WAR PERIOD PROGRESS OF THE COTTON-MILL INDUSTRY IN INDIA

1913–14 TO 1928–29*

Year Ending August 31st	Number of Mills	Number of Spindles (in Thousands)	Number of Looms (in Thousands)	Average Number of Hands Employed Daily (in Thousands)	Approximate Quantity of Cotton Consumed in Bales of 392 lb. (in Thousands)
1913–14	271	6,779	104	260	2,143
1918–19	258	8,690	118	293	2,044
1919–20	253	6,763	119	311	1,952
1920–21	257	6,870	124	332	2,120
1921–22	298	7,331	135	344	2,204
1922–23	333	7,928	145	347	2,152
1923–24	336	8,313	151	357	1,918
1924–25	337	8,511	154	368	2,226
1925–26	334	8,714	159	374	2,113
1926–27	336	8,703	162	385	2,417
1927–28	335	8,704	167	361	2,010
1928–29	344	8,807	175	347	2,161

* The Table is reproduced from Mr. A. S. Pearse's book, *The Cotton Industry of India*, 1930, p. 22.

GRAPH I

PROGRESS OF THE COTTON-MILL INDUSTRY OF INDIA

1913–14 TO 1928–29

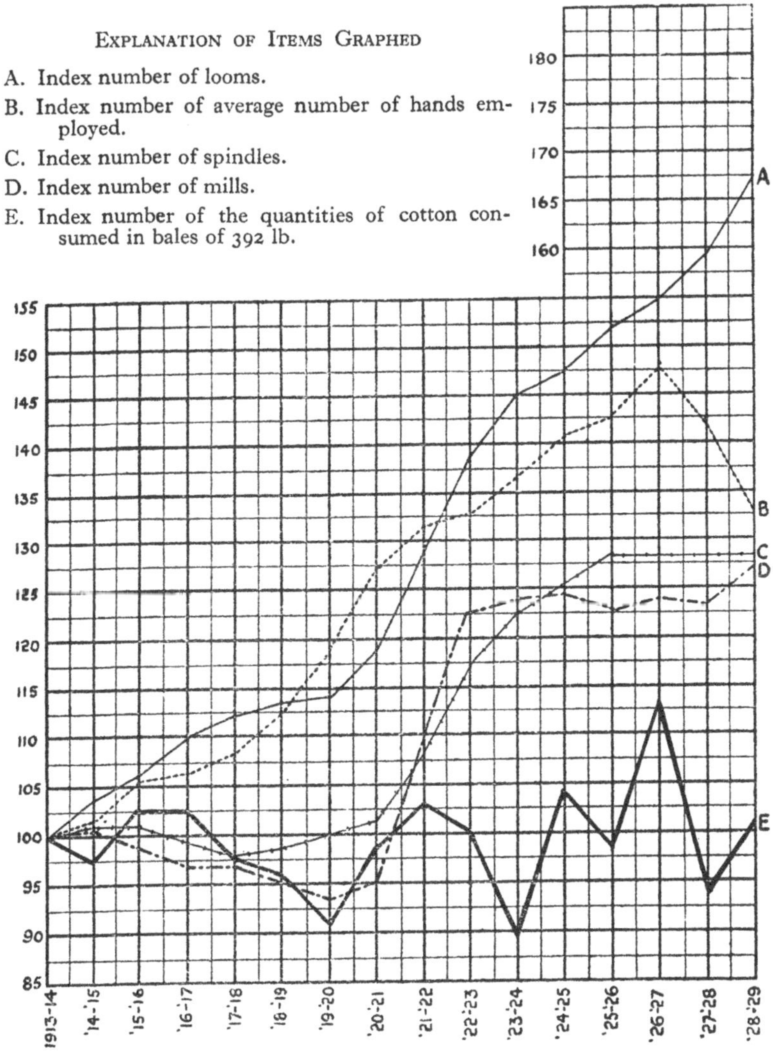

countervailing cotton excise duty was imposed. In the previous chapter we noticed that although the cotton excise duty fulfilled the 'canon of economy' in taxation, it was nevertheless condemned by public opinion in India as a great burden on a young and growing industry. In the light of the above record of expansion registered by the industry, however, the conclusion seems to be justified that the industry enjoyed sufficient natural advantages and commanded a fair degree of enterprise and vitality so as to be able to more than hold its own in the matter of free and open competition without any kind of artificial assistance whatsoever at the expense of the tax-payers. In this view of the case, therefore, it would appear that, in spite of the bitter and violent criticism directed against it, the cotton excise duty had the supreme merit of not allowing the owners of the Cotton-mill Industry to enjoy, out of the tax-payers' money, a considerable bonus, which would have accrued to them in the absence of the excise duty, but which was not at all essential to normal and natural growth of the industry in India.

3. 1913–14 to 1928–29[1]

The year 1920–21 marked the end of the period of exceptional profit, 1921–22 to 1923–24 were years of considerable extensions of the Cotton-mill Industry out of the profits made during the boom, and lastly, the period 1924–25 to 1928–29 was a period of pronounced depression. It will, therefore, be convenient for us to take these three periods separately.

1913–14 to 1920–21.—The decline in the number of mills accompanied by a small increase in the number of spindles, and an appreciable increase in the number of looms, clearly indicates that the size of the unit of production was undergoing some expansion. The number of spindles declined during each of the last three war years, but it again began to rise from 1918–19 onwards, and by 1920–21 it showed an increase of 91,945, or 1·4 per cent over that of the pre-war year. The number of looms, however, increased steadily every year, and at the end of

[1] This section is to be read with Table II on p. 96 and Graph I on p. 97.

the period it was about 19 per cent bigger than in the pre-war year. What happened was that there was a very considerable reduction of the export of yarn to China, partly due to the competition of the Japanese and the Chinese mills, and partly due to the shortage of the available freight, and that, therefore, increasing quantities of yarn were being turned into cloths to supply a larger share of the home market and also to build up a growing export trade to East Africa, Persia, Asiatic Turkey, Ceylon, Malay and Straits Settlements.[1]

While the number of spindles increased by 1·4 per cent, and the number of looms by 19 per cent, the average number of hands employed daily showed an increase of no less than 28 per cent. This would seem to indicate that the efficiency of labour, as measured by the number of looms or spindles looked after by each man, declined to a certain extent.

Figures in the last column are somewhat puzzling at first sight. The consumption of raw cotton in each of the years, 1918–19 to 1920–21, was less than that of 1913–14, and this decline in the consumption of raw cotton was accompanied by an increase in the number of spindles, e.g. in 1920–21. This anomaly is to be explained by the fact that the mills were changing over to a certain extent from the coarser to the finer counts of yarn,[2] and were, consequently, making a progressive substitution of the medium-stapled cotton imported from East Africa for the short-stapled Indian cotton.

1921–22 to 1923–24.—The years 1916–17 to 1921–22 were boom years—years of high prices and high profits. Thus, during that period the cotton mills of Bombay, with an average paid-up capital of about Rs. 13 crores, were able to earn average annual profits of no less than Rs. 5·65 crores.[3] That is to say, the profits earned by the cotton mills of Bombay during those six years amounted to more than two and a half times the entire

[1] *Review of the Trade of India*, 1913–14 to 1920–21, Statistical Tables.

[2] Thus, while in the pre-war quinquennium, 1909–10 to 1913–14, yarn of counts 1's to 20's and of 21's to 30's amounted to 74 and 23 per cent respectively of the whole output, the corresponding percentages for 1920–21 were 67·2 and 30·2.

[3] *Report of the Tariff Board*, Appendix V.

paid-up capital of the industry. Similar profits were presumably made by the owners of the cotton industry in other parts of India as well. This vast accession of wealth to the investing classes could not, however, be reinvested in the extension of the industry by laying down new machinery and plant until after the year 1920–21, due to the fact that the engineering works of Great Britain and U.S.A. had received such huge orders for machinery during the post-war boom that they could not execute these orders in any appreciable quantities before the year 1921–22.[1] We, therefore, find that although the boom period had come to an end by 1921–22, the expansion of the industry actually took place in the subsequent three years, 1921–22 to 1923–24. Thus, while in the seven years, 1914–15 to 1920–21, the average number of spindles added per annum was just over 30,636 and that of looms 6,535, the corresponding figures for the three-year period, 1921–22 to 1923–24, were 480,823 and 9,234 respectively.

1924–25 to 1928–29.—The post-war boom had completely disappeared by the end of 1922–23. Prices began to fall and profits diminished. A general depression in trade set in. As the years 1924–25 to 1926–27 succeeded each other, the pressure of the depression was more and more keenly felt, specially by the cotton mills of Bombay. As we saw in the last chapter, the grave financial position of the Cotton-mill Industry of Bombay was the principal cause of the agitation for protection which culminated in the passing of the Indian Tariff (Cotton Yarn Amendment) Act of 1927 and the Cotton Textile Industry (Protection) Act of 1930. We will analyse in a later section the special causes that brought about the financial crisis in the Bombay Cotton Industry, and discuss, in the light of that analysis, how far the protective measures of 1927 and 1930 rested on sound economic reasons. Meanwhile, taking the country as a whole, we find from the table that, in spite of the trade depression of 1922–23 and the following years, the Cotton Industry of India made continuous, if not marked,

[1] *Review of the Trade of India*, 1921–22.

progress from 1924–25 to 1928–29. Thus, during the period the number of mills, already enormously inflated during the post-war boom, instead of remaining stationary, increased somewhat from 337 to 344, while the number of spindles rose by 493,791 or by 98,758 per annum, and the number of looms by 23,507 or by 4,700 per annum. We should not fail to notice that this rate of growth compares very favourably with that in the period, 1914–15 to 1920–21, when the annual rate of addition was only 30,636 in the case of spindles, and 6,535 in the case of looms. When we remember that the period 1914–15 to 1920–21 was for the greater part an exceptionally prosperous period, and then compare the rate of growth in 1924–25 to 1928–29 with that of 1914–15 to 1920–21, it would be difficult for us to resist the conclusion that the Cotton Industry of India as a whole possesses sufficient vitality so as to be able not only to overcome the difficulties of a period of depression, but also to make steady progress in both spinning and weaving without artificial aid of any kind at the expense of the consumers.

4. THE RELATIVE POSITION OF THE IMPORTS AND THE INDIGENOUS PRODUCTS IN THE HOME MARKET

Another fruitful line of study would be to survey the development and the present condition of the Indian Cotton Industry in the light of the comparative position of the imports and the Indian mill output. We would now turn to a consideration of this aspect of the problem.

The variations in the number of spindles in the different periods which we noticed in Table II are reflected with an approximate degree of accuracy in Table III, showing the variations in the output of Indian yarn and its relative position in the total trade. Throughout the period 1913–14 to 1919–20, while the consumption of indigenous yarn remained fairly steady, the figures for net imports showed a very marked decline, with the result that the percentage share of indigenous yarn in the total consumption of yarn in the country rose from 93 in 1913–14 to 98·3 in 1919–20. Nevertheless, it will be observed

TABLE III

VARIATIONS IN THE CONSUMPTION OF IMPORTED AND INDIAN MILL YARN

1913–14 TO 1929–30*

1 Years	2 Net Imports (Million lb.)	3 Indian Mill Output (Million lb.)	4 Export of Indian Yarn (Million lb.)	5 Net Consumption of Indian Yarn (3 − 4) (Million lb.)	6 Total Consumption of Yarn in India (2 + 5) (Million lb.)	7 Percentage Share of Indian Mill Yarn in the Total Consumption of Yarn
1913–14	35·9	683	207	476	512	93·0
1918–19	32·0	615	73	542	574	94·4
1919–20	7·9	636	161	475	483	98·3
1920–21	43·7	660	89	571	615	92·8
1921–22	53·5	694	88	606	660	91·8
1922–23	53·0	706	64	642	695	92·4
1923–24	39·5	617	46	571	611	93·5
1924–25	50·5	719	46	673	724	92·9
1925–26	50·6	686	32	654	705	92·8
1926–27	48·5	807	42	765	814	94·0
1927–28	50·9	809	25	784	835	93·9
1928–29	42·5	648	24	624	667	93·7
1929–30	43·4	834	25	809	852	95·0

* Vide *The Annual Statements of the Sea-borne Trade of British India*, and *The Monthly Statistics of Cotton Spinning and Weaving in Indian mills.*

GRAPH II

VARIATIONS IN THE CONSUMPTION OF IMPORTED AND INDIAN MILL YARN

1913–14 TO 1929–30

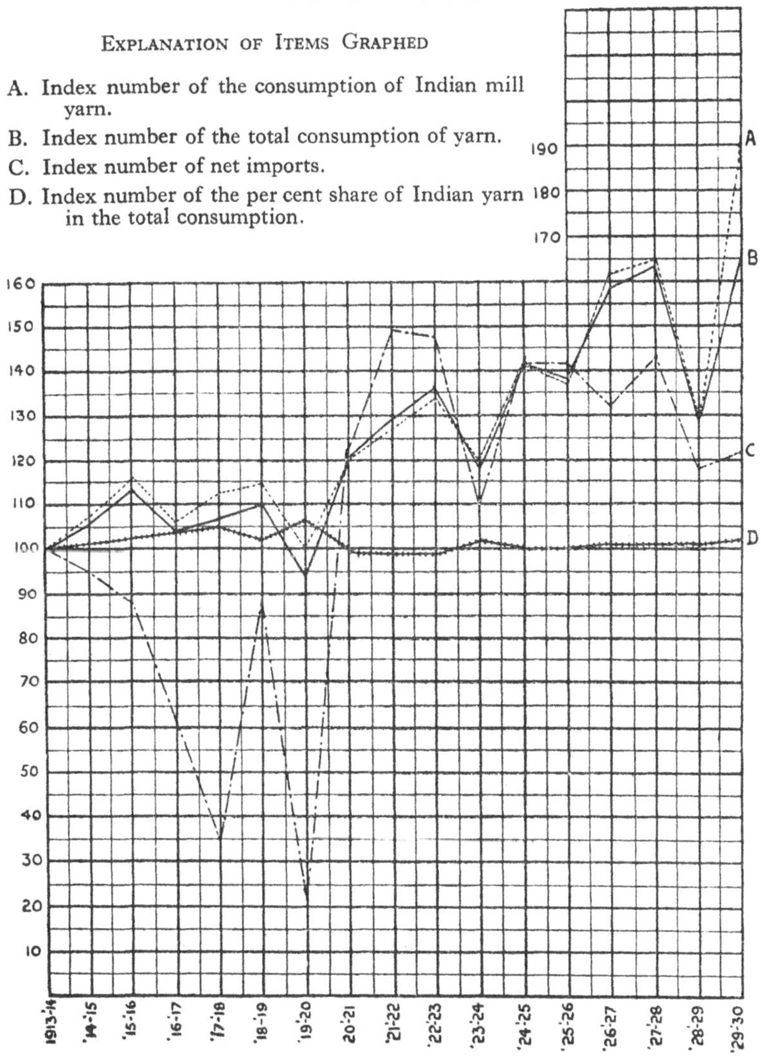

TABLE IV

VARIATIONS IN THE CONSUMPTION OF IMPORTED AND INDIAN (MILL-MADE) PIECE-GOODS

1913–14 TO 1929–30*

1 Year	2 Net Imports (Million Yards)	3 Indian Mill Output (Million Yards)	4 Exports of Indian Mill-made Piece-goods (Million Yards)	5 Balance of Indian Cloths Available for Consumption in Indian (3 − 4) (Million Yards)	6 Total Consumption of Imported and Indian (Mill-made) Piece-goods in India (2+5) (Million Yards)	7 Percentage Share of Indigenous (Mill-made) Piece-Goods (5) in the Total Consumption (6)
1913–14	3,042	1,164	104	1,160	4,202	27·6
1918–19	955	1,451	158	1,293	2,248	57·5
1919–20	836	1,640	207	1,433	2,269	63·2
1920–21	1,405	1,581	140	1,441	2,846	50·6
1921–22	980	1,732	154	1,578	2,558	61·3
1922–23	1,467	1,725	152	1,573	3,040	51·7
1923–24	1,374	1,702	164	1,538	2,914	52·8
1924–25	1,710	1,970	193	1,777	3,487	51·0
1925–26	1,529	1,954	122	1,832	3,361	54·5
1926–27	1,759	2,259	151	2,108	3,867	54·5
1927–28	1,939	2,357	127	2,230	4,169	53·5
1928–29	1,912	1,893	108	1,785	3,697	48·3
1929–30	1,897	2,419	100†	2,319	4,216	55·0

* Vide *Review of the Trade of India* and *The Monthly Statistics of Cotton Spinning and Weaving in Indian mills.*

† The total exports in this year were 133 million yards; the exports of coloured goods to Ceylon and Straits Settlements, which are the two largest markets for the hand-loom goods of Madras, were 36 million yards; we have assumed that of this, 33 million yards were hand-loom products.

For Note to Table, see p. 108.

GRAPH III

VARIATIONS IN THE CONSUMPTION OF IMPORTED AND INDIAN (MILL-MADE) PIECE-GOODS

1913–14 TO 1929–30

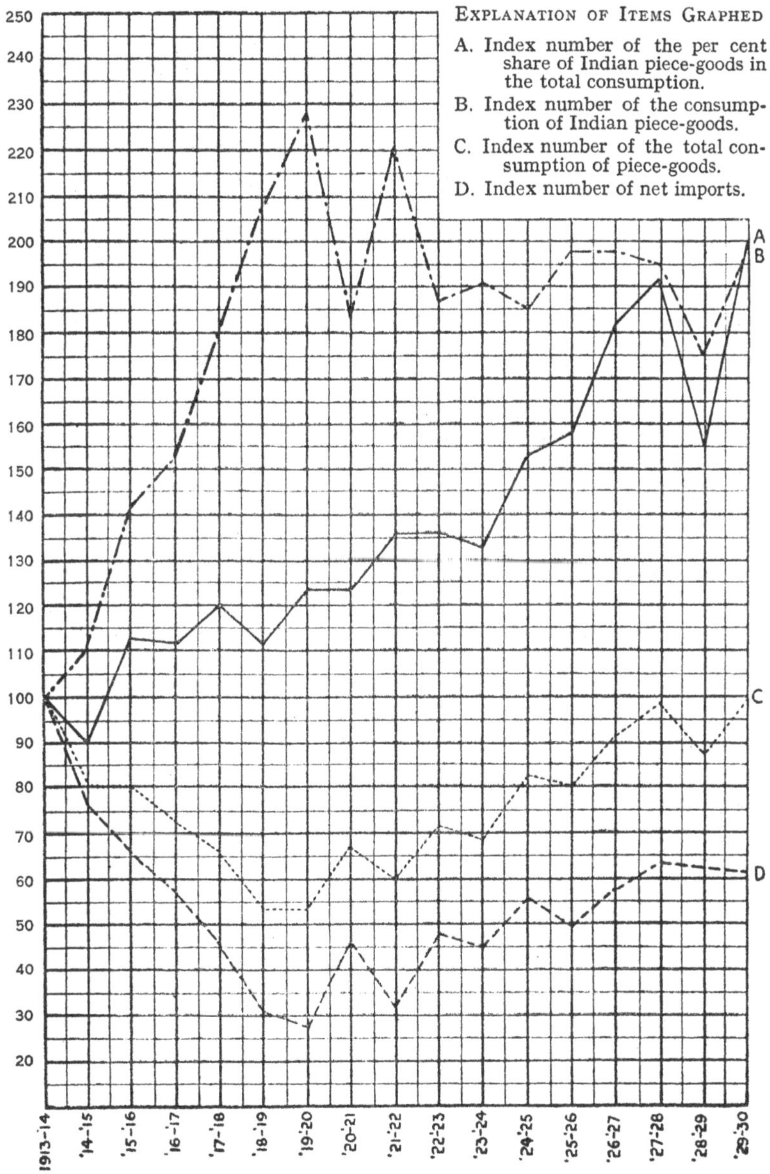

(*c*) There was a rapid decline in the consumption of cloths in India from 1913–14 to 1919–20. In terms of quantity, the decline during the seven-year period was 1,933 million yards, or 46 per cent. Since 1920–21, however, there was again a fairly continuous rise till it attained the pre-war position in 1929–30.[1]

(*d*) The percentage contribution of the Indian mills to the total consumption of piece-goods in India rose rapidly from 27·6 in 1913–14 to 63·2 in 1919–20. There was a slight decline in the percentage share in the period 1920–21 to 1924–25, after which there was again an upward tendency which continued down to 1929–30.[2] Taking the whole period together, it would appear that the strong and predominant position in the home market attained by the Indian Cotton Industry during and immediately after the war, had only been slightly weakened during 1922–23 to 1924–25, the first three years of the depression, but was again increasingly recovered in the five years, 1925–26 to 1929–30.

5. CAUSES OF THE 'ATROPHY' OF THE COTTON-MILL INDUSTRY OF INDIA IN RECENT YEARS

Our survey of the development of the Cotton Industry of India from its early beginnings down to recent years has clearly shown that that industry throughout the whole course of its history registered steady, continuous, and sometimes even marked, progress. We also saw that up to 1921–22, the import duty, being either altogether non-existent or very nominal, played little part in promoting that development. We further noticed that both the spinning and weaving branches of the

NOTE.—The exports of Indian piece-goods contain a large quantity of the products of the hand-loom industry, specially from Madras. These are coloured fabrics, and commonly known as handkerchiefs, saris and lungis, and are in large demand in Ceylon, Malaya and Straits Settlements, where there are large numbers of Indian settlers, and also in Java and Anglo-Egyptian Sudan. It is quite probable that small quantities of hand-loom products are also exported from other ports. But as the Madras exports consist mostly of hand-loom products, we have assumed that the entire exports of coloured, printed and dyed goods from Madras are hand-loom products. We have, therefore, deducted the figures for exports of coloured goods from Madras from the figures for total exports of piece-goods in order to arrive at the figures for the exports of mill-made cloths.

---

[1] During 1930–32, the total consumption fell by 661 to 3,555 million yards, or 16 per cent.

[2] The percentage rose to 74 in 1930–31, and 79 in 1931–32.

Cotton Industry were able to capture a substantial and increasing share of the home market before obtaining the small differential advantage under the tariff of 1921–22 and subsequent years. And lastly, we found that the steady expansion of output as well as the predominant position in the home market continued during the general trade depression that set in in 1922–23.

On the basis of this testimony of important and varied groups of facts that point to the attainment of independent 'adult' stage by the Cotton Industry of India even in the pre-war period, we are entitled to presume that that industry would not possibly stand in need of artificial advantage of any kind at the cost of the general body of consumers. It would also be reasonable for us to hold that an industry, which was able to overcome the varying difficulties caused by changes in currency, exchange and external competition during over sixty years of steady growth, would also possess sufficient strength and resourcefulness to tide over the financial strain and stress inevitable in a period of world-wide trade depression, without asking for a bonus from the consuming public.

Nevertheless, as we saw in the previous chapter, the mill-owners of Bombay and Ahmedabad were able to make some sort of a case for protection and succeeded in obtaining it in two stages, firstly, through the abolition of the cotton excise duty in December, 1925, and secondly, through the Indian Tariff (Cotton Yarn Amendment) Act of 1927 and the Cotton Textile Industry (Protection) Act of 1930. In order that we may be able to arrive at a balanced judgment on these protectionist measures, it is necessary for us to take up and examine some of the principal grounds on which the claim for protection was urged by the cotton mill-owners of India, accepted by the Tariff Board, and granted by the Government of India.

At the outset we have to note that the demand for protection was not presented with equal intensity by all the sections of the Indian Cotton-mill Industry. The mills in Northern India, Madras, and other up-country centres were on the whole doing satisfactorily from the financial point of view, and accordingly, their demand for protection was weak and half-hearted. On the other hand, the financial position of the cotton mills of Ahmedabad was rather unsatisfactory, while that of the cotton mills in Bombay was critical. The case for protection, therefore, was presented in elaborate detail by the Bombay Mill-owners' and to a lesser extent the Ahmedabad Mill-owners' Association.[1] The significance of these two Associations will be readily understood from the fact that in 1925, out of a total of 274 mills working in the whole of India, 135 or 49 per cent of the whole were located in these two largest and oldest centres of the Cotton-mill Industry in the country. Again, the importance of Bombay alone may be measured by the fact that in 1924–25, it produced 45 per cent of the entire yarn output and 47·1 per cent of the entire cloth output of the cotton mills in India.[2]

Because the financial crisis was most acute in Bombay, and because the Bombay mills represent the largest section of the Cotton-mill Industry of India, the issues involved in the demand for, and the grant of, protection will be made clear to us if we examine them with special reference to the position of the Cotton-mill Industry in Bombay. Sir George Rainy (Member for Commerce and Railways in the Government of India), in introducing the Cotton Textile Industry (Protection) Bill in the Legislative Assembly, stated that the scheme of protection proposed under that measure had only a limited objective, and that that limited objective was to save the Presidency of Bombay from the serious economic consequences of a collapse of the Cotton Industry of the Bombay City and Island. Another member of the Government of India, Sir George Schuster, informed the Assembly that the purpose of the measure was merely to save one important section of the Indian Cotton Industry, i.e. the Bombay section, from a state of special

[1] The representatives of the Ahmedabad Mill-owners' Association in the course of their oral evidence before the Tariff Board frankly admitted that had it not been for the vigorous lead given by the sister institution at Bombay, they would not have asked for protection. Cf. Report of the Tariff Board, *Minutes of Evidence*, Vol. II, p. 410.

[2] Ibid., Vol. I, pp. 20–28.

deterioration or 'atrophy.' It is, therefore, clear that the primary object of the Cotton Textile Industry (Protection) Bill, according to the tariff-making authority in India, was to rescue the Cotton-mill Industry of Bombay from an impending collapse due to the acute financial position of the mills.

We, therefore, now proceed to an examination of the nature and extent of this 'atrophy,' its causes and cures.

TABLE V

TABULAR STATEMENT OF THE FINANCIAL POSITION OF THE BOMBAY COTTON MILLS*

(000 *omitted*)

Year	Capital Paid Up (Rupees)	Net Profit or Loss after Depreciation (Rupees)	Dividend (Rupees)	Percentage of Dividend to Paid-up Capital
1917	7,65,67	3,02,07	1,69,62	22·2
1918	8,10,46	2,28,08	1,91,96	23·7
1919	9,40,11	6,15,67	3,77,20	40·1
1920	16,98,67	10,10,63	5,98,16	35·2
1921	17,83,11	8,46,45	5,34,79	30·0
1922	17,96,29	3,87,52	2,94,44	16·4
1923	19,18,62	33,13	93,69	4·9
1924	19,28,16	—91,70	60,85	3·2
1925	19,20,96	—1,33,65	43,11	2·2
1926	18,96,00†	—1,95,41	—	—
1927	18,08,00†	—7,36	—	—
1928	17,15,00†	—2,98,78	—	—

* The figures in the above table up to 1925 are taken from the *Report of the Tariff Board*. Complete data for the subsequent years are not available. The figures for losses in 1926, 1927 and 1928 are taken from the brief and very incomplete statement on the audited accounts that the Bombay Millowners' Association have been pleased to vouchsafe to the public in their Annual Reports in recent years.

† These are from an article entitled "The Cotton-mill Industry in India," by G. Findlay Shirras, published in *Capital*, "Industries, Trade and Transport Supplement," December, 1930.

It will be noticed that the years 1917 to 1922 were years of extraordinary prosperity and high profits, and that the position became increasingly unsatisfactory from 1923 onwards. We may regard the losses incurred in 1924 and the subsequent years as the apparent symptoms of the 'atrophy' to which the

Finance Member of the Government of India referred in his statement to the Assembly. From the table it would be clear that, if the profits of the six boom years, 1917–22, had been wisely used in building up an appreciable reserve fund, it would not at all have been beyond the capacity of the Bombay Cotton-mill Industry to tide over the difficulties of the depression that inevitably followed on the boom. Let us rearrange the figures in the table on a somewhat different line and see what follows. It is now generally held in India that 8 per cent per annum is a reasonable return on capital.[1] On the basis of a uniform 8 per cent dividend on the paid-up capital, the above table may be reconstructed as follows:

TABLE VI

(000 *omitted*)

Year		Capital Paid Up (Rupees)	Net Profit or Loss (Rupees)	Dividend at 8 Per Cent on Paid-up Capital (Rupees)	Reserves and Carry Forward (Rupees)
1917	..	7,65,67	3,02,07	61,25	2,40,81
1918	..	8,10,46	2,28,08	64,84	1,63,24
1919	..	9,40,11	6,15,67	75,21	5,40,46
1920	..	16,98,67	10,10,63	1,35,89	8,74,74
1921	..	17,83,11	8,46,45	1,42,65	7,03,80
1922	..	17,96,29	3,87,52	1,43,70	2,43,81
			Total, 1917–22	..	27,66,86
1923	..	19,18,62	33,13	1,53,49	− 1,20,36
1924	..	19,28,16	− 91,70	1,54,25	− 2,45,95
1925	..	19,20,96	− 1,33,65	1,53,68	− 2,87,32
1926	..	18,96,00	− 1,95,41	1,51,68	− 3,47,09
1927	..	18,08,00	− 7,36	1,44,64	− 1,52,04
1928	..	17,15,00	− 2,98,78	1,37,22	− 4,36,00
			Total, 1923–28	..	− 15,88,76
			Total, 1917–28	..	11,78,10

This table would make it clear beyond a shadow of doubt that, if the Mill-owners of Bombay had followed a cautious policy of

[1] *Report of the Tariff Board*, Vol. I, p. 62.

dividend distribution and built up a suitable reserve fund, they could have continued to give a reasonable dividend to the shareholders and at the same time succeeded in maintaining a strong financial position. Instead, they allowed themselves and their shareholders to indulge in a policy of extravagant dividends, with the result that when the losses of the period of depression appeared, they had insufficient reserves to meet them. It is, therefore, clear that if the Bombay Cotton-mill Industry found itself in a state of 'atrophy' in the last few years, that atrophy was due partly to the lack of foresight on the part of the management and partly to the wild desire of the shareholders for abnormal rates of dividends.[1]

[1] The extravagant financial management of the Bombay mills will be apparent from the following instances: In 1920, 2 mills paid dividends of over 200 per cent, 14 mills 100 per cent and more, 20 mills 40 per cent and more. In 1921, 11 mills paid dividends of 100 per cent and over. In 1922, 4 paid dividends of 100 per cent and over. In 1923, the first year of the depression, 7 mills paid dividends of 40 per cent and over (vide *Report of the Tariff Board*, Vol. I, p. 83).

Mr. A. S. Pearse instances an extreme case where the shareholders were not satisfied with a 400 per cent dividend, but expected a 500 per cent one (vide *The Cotton Industry of India*, p. 65).

Note on the financial condition of the cotton mills in India in recent years:

From the data collected from the *Investors' India Year-Book*, we get the following results:

Out of 65 cotton mills for which the returns are available, 41 are located in Bombay, and 24 in the up-country centres.

Out of the 41 mills in Bombay, one mill was established in 1920 and paid dividends only in 1922. This may be left out as an exceptional case of boom product. Of the remaining 40, 20 were able to pay dividends ranging from 3 to 32 per cent, and 20 were unable to pay any dividends at all, during the years 1926–28. The first 20 had paid dividends ranging from 3 to 175 per cent in the boom period, 1917–22, while the last 20 had paid dividends amounting to between 6 and 120 per cent in the same period. From this it would appear that, though the payment of high dividends in the boom period was undoubtedly one of the principal causes of the aggravation of the financial position of some of the mills in the period of depression, there were certainly other elements of weakness which also contributed to the same result.

Out of the 24 mills in the up-country centres, 18 continued to pay dividends ranging from 6 to 70 per cent, and only 6 were unable to do so, in the years 1926–28. This shows that the up-country mills were on the whole much less affected than the Bombay mills during the period of depression. In the boom period, 1917–22, the first group of 18 mills had paid dividends ranging from 5 to 240 per cent, while in the case of the second group of 6 mills, the dividends ranged between 6 to 425 per cent. Out of these 6 mills, again,

The Tariff Board did indeed realise that the distribution of high dividends in the boom period was among the most important factors that had weakened the financial position of the Bombay mills. Nevertheless, they went out of their way to justify the action of the mill-owners by pointing out that the dividends paid by the mills in Bombay were, on the average, not higher than those paid by the Japanese mills in the same period.[1] This was, no doubt, offered as an explanation by the Tariff Board on behalf of the mill-owners of Bombay, but to us it seems that the explanation was altogether uncalled for, irrelevant, and misleading. For, the real point at issue was not whether the dividends paid by the mill-owners of Bombay were higher or lower than those paid by the cotton manufacturers of Japan, but whether the reckless disregard of the future shown by the mill-owners in the distribution of extravagant dividends in the boom period entitled them to any sympathy or assistance from the general public. To that question there could be but one answer, and that answer undoubtedly a negative one.

2 mills stand out pre-eminent in the matter of extravagant dividend payments; one of them had paid an annual average dividend of 241 per cent, and the other 199 per cent during the period, 1919–22. The dividends paid by these two mills in one single year, 1920, were 365 per cent and 425 per cent respectively. In the case of the up-country mills, therefore, it appears that some at least of the mills must have brought about their own financial crisis by inordinate scales of dividend payments in the boom period.

In this connection, the findings of the Tariff Board on the real causes of the liquidation of mills in Bombay and Ahmedabad will be found both interesting and instructive. They examined every single case of mills that had gone into liquidation since the commencement of the depression, and their clear and definite conclusions on the subject may best be given in their own words: "We are satisfied that no mill in India which could be regarded as run with fair efficiency and economy had up to the present been forced into liquidation as the result of the depression. None of the mills which has so far gone into liquidation had the smallest chances of surviving except in boom conditions. A study of the evidence we received at Ahmedabad will be found instructive on this point. A long list of mills which had gone into liquidation in that and adjacent centres was placed before us, but in almost every case there was very definite evidence that the liquidation was the result of incompetence and inefficiency and, in some instances, of dishonesty" (*Report*, Vol. I, pp. 18–19).

[1] Ibid., Vol. I, p. 84.

6. OVER-CAPITALISATION AND WEAK SELLING. THE NEED FOR REORGANISATION

The above analysis of the dividend payments made by the mill-owners of Bombay, though throwing a flood of light on the causes of the financial weakness of the Cotton-mill Industry in that centre, does not, however, by itself reveal the full extent to which the managing agents of the cotton mills allowed themselves to lapse from strict principles of financial management. For, following the practice common in Europe and America, they fully exploited the sharpened greed of the investors during the period of high profits, and inflated the capital value of the stocks by selling old shares and issuing new ones at many times their normal capitalised value.[1] The result was what is called over-capitalisation or stock-watering, as will be evident from the table on page 116.[2]

The figures for comparative increases in capital, spindles and looms would leave little room for doubt that, even allowing for the general rise in the cost of plant and machinery in 1919 and the following years, the enormous expansion of paid-up capital must have been due to a large extent to the speculative issue of shares to the public at exaggerated values. The payment of high dividends on these inflated capital values of shares in the years 1920, 1921 and 1922 naturally prevented the accumulation of reserves at all commensurate with the prosperity of the period. Next to the policy of high dividends,

[1] The Balfour Committee on Industry and Trade give an instructive memorandum on the meaning and effects of over-capitalisation in their volume entitled *Further Factors in Industrial and Commercial Efficiency*, pp. 170–81. The memorandum traces several different sets of circumstances under which over-capitalisation arises. Among those, the following one is applicable to the cases of over-capitalisation in the Cotton-mill Industry of India: "A Company by a revaluation of its assets at boom prices creates an apparent reserve which is made the basis of an issue of bonus shares. Boom values subsequently fall and the capital remains at an inflated figure."

[2] The figures for paid-up capital are from the *Report of the Tariff Board*, Vol. I, p. 20, and those for spindles and looms are from the Memorandum submitted by the Bombay Mill-owners' Association to the Tariff Board, Minutes of Evidence, Vol. II, pp. 69–70.

accepted, and we should add, in many cases encouraged and welcome, as a necessary process of readjustment.[1]

Experience of Western countries in recent years, therefore, suggests that combinations or amalgamations will also help the Bombay Cotton-mill Industry in not only successfully overcoming some of the difficulties of wasteful competition in the years of depression, but also in reorganising itself as a whole on a stable basis by the elimination of the weaker units of production and the concentration of production in the most efficient ones.

And this has, in fact, been long realised by the mill-owners of Bombay. Accordingly, when they found that they could not expect any relief in their difficulties at the expense of the taxpayers, they set up negotiations for the amalgamation of as many as 35 mills in 1929 and 1930, and actually invited an expert from Lancashire for the revaluation of the plant and machinery in the different mills involved in the scheme of amalgamation. If no protection to the Mill Industry had been granted in 1930, it is quite probable that the scheme of amalgamation would have been carried through, and the majority of the cotton mills would have been thereby restored to a healthy and sound position, by the end of 1930. But now it appears that, since the mill-owners of Bombay have been successful in persuading the tariff-making authority to grant them considerable financial assistance at the cost of the tax-payers, their efforts in the direction of amalgamation and rationalisation on a large scale have altogether slackened.[2]

[1] Cf. Walter Meakin, *The New Industrial Revolution*; L. Urwick, *The Meaning of Rationalisation*; *First Report of the Balfour Committee on Industry and Trade* (Cmd. 3282), p. 188; and also Sir Josiah Stamp's address on "The Present Position of Rationalisation," published in the volume *Criticism and Other Addresses*, 1931.

[2] The following note published by *Capital* in its issue of January 29, 1931, on the subject of the "Bombay Merger Scheme" is interesting, and also instructive in that it fully confirms the contention of free traders that protection tends to shelter inefficiency and to delay, if not altogether prevent, improvements: "Mr. Entwistle, the Lancashire expert, is still busily engaged on his valuation of the mills in Bombay, but nothing has been heard lately regarding the progress of the spade-work which must precede Sir N. Wadia's big merger scheme. As a matter of fact, it is not thought the project

7. INCREASING SEVERITY OF UP-COUNTRY COMPETITION

In our survey of the development of the Indian Cotton Industry in the earlier sections of this chapter, we found that when regarded as a whole, the industry showed steady and continuous progress throughout the entire period of its growth (1860–1930). We further noticed that the increase of output as well as the relative contribution of the home product to the home market showed that neither the position nor the progress of the Indian Cotton Industry as a whole was menaced by any unduly severe competition from the imports. And lastly, in our examination of the recent financial condition of the cotton mills in the different parts of India, we found that, considering the abnormal times, while the financial position of the mills in Bombay was undoubtedly unsatisfactory and perhaps even critical, that of many of the up-country mills was fairly satisfactory. These two sets of considerations tend to indicate that, while the Indian Cotton Industry as a whole cannot be said to be exposed to the dangers of an unduly severe foreign competition, the important Bombay section of it must be losing ground in the home market as compared to the other centres of the Cotton Industry in the country itself. In other words, from the statistical and the financial data so far considered, it would appear that it is the severity of the competition with the other home producers rather than with the importers that has been one of the contributory causes of the recent 'atrophy' or the general financial weakness of the Cotton Industry of Bombay.

That the position of the Cotton Industry of the Bombay City relatively to that of other parts of India has been steadily deteriorating in recent years is brought out by the following table:

has gone very far, and whereas formerly when the Mill Industry was in desperate straits people talked of the merger with enthusiasm, now that things are looking somewhat brighter there may not be the same willingness to make sacrifices which will be inevitable in such a scheme. The old rivalries between groups of mills are not easily overcome, and though 35 mills was the number originally mentioned, people 'in the know' do not think anything like this number will come into the scheme."

The merger scheme was altogether abandoned at a later date.

TABLE VIII*

RELATIVE POSITION OF THE COTTON INDUSTRY OF BOMBAY IN DIFFERENT PERIODS

1 Year	2 Number of Mills	3 Number of Spindles (in Thousands)	4 Number of Looms (in Thousands)	5 Number of Spindles to Looms	6 Mill Production of Yarn (in Millions of lbs.)	7 Mill Production of Cloths (in Millions of Yards)
1898–99 (year ending June 30th)					1899–1900 (year ending March 31st)	
Bombay	74	2,339	22	105	514	102
Rest of India	93	2,211	16	139		
Total	167	4,550	38	119	..	..
Percentage of Bombay	44·3	51·4	58·2	..	..	..
1903–04 (year ending June 30th)					1904–5 (year ending March 31st)	
Bombay	76	2,472	24	102	333	93
Rest of India	107	2,532	21	121	245	66
Total	183	5,004	45	111	578	159
Percentage of Bombay	41·5	49·4	53·6	..	57·6	58·5
1907–08 (year ending June 30th)					1908–9 (year ending March 31st)	
Bombay	79	2,654	35	77	358	107
Rest of India	139	3,008	31	95	300	85
Total	218	5,662	66	85	658	192
Percentage of Bombay	36·2	46·8	52·1	..	54·4	55·8

2–13 (year ending June 30th)					1913–14 (year ending March 31st)	
Bombay	77	2,807	45	63	355	138
Rest of India	159	3,513	47	74	328	136
Total	236	6,320	92	68	683	274
Percentage of Bombay	32·6	44·6	48·4	..	52·0	50·3
1920–21 (year ending August 31st)					1921–22 (year ending March 31st)	
Bombay	83	3,025	63	48	349	207
Rest of India	162	3,820	61	62	344	196
Total	245	6,845	124	55	693	403
Percentage of Bombay	33·8	44·1	50·7	..	50·3	51·3
1924–25 (year ending August 31st)					1925–26 (year ending March 31st)	
Bombay	79	3,378	71	48	262	200
Rest of India	196	4,715	78	61	424	265
Total	275	8,093	149	55	684	465
Percentage of Bombay	28·8	41·7	48	..	38·2	43

* NOTE.—The data for this table are from the *Report of the Tariff Board*, Vol. I, pp. 5–14. The figures in columns 2 to 5 are those covered by the year according to the Bombay Mill-owners' Association, which ended June 30th up to 1912–13, and August 31st since. The figures in columns 6 and 7 refer to the output in the next following official year, which ends March 31st.

It will be noticed that although the number of mills in the whole of India increased during the period by 65 per cent, that in Bombay remained practically stationary, with the result that the percentage of Bombay fell from 44·3 to 28·8. The variation in the number of mills, however, is no true index to the variations in the relative importance of the industry in Bombay and other places, for it is clear from the table that the expansion of the industry in Bombay proceeded by way of addition of spindles and looms to the existing mills rather than through the setting up of new mills. We must, therefore, look to other data for forming a true estimate of the relative position. In the number of spindles the percentage of Bombay fell from 51·4 to 41·7 and in the number of looms from 58·2 to 48. It will also be observed that this relative decline of Bombay in both spinning and weaving had set in since 1898–99, and though held in check for a while by the favourable conditions of the boom period, the tendency came once more into evidence in the last few years. Again, the comparison of the figures in columns 3 and 4 with those in columns 6 and 7 would show that, as judged by the output of yarn per spindle and of cloths per loom, the relative efficiency of the mills in Bombay had been distinctly higher up to the year 1921–22, but became appreciably lower since that year. Thus, while in 1921–22, Bombay with 44·1 per cent of the spindles and 50·7 per cent of the looms produced 50·3 per cent of the yarn and 51·3 per cent of the cloths respectively, in 1925–26 with 41·7 per cent of the spindles and 48 per cent of the looms, the percentage share of the output held by Bombay fell to 38·2 per cent in the case of yarn and 43 per cent in the case of cloth. That is to say, the relative importance of Bombay as a centre of the Cotton Industry of India decreased, firstly, on account of a lower rate of growth in the number of spindles and looms, and secondly, as a result of diminishing efficiency as measured by the average output per loom and per spindle.

The comparative disadvantages of Bombay as a centre of the Cotton-mill Industry in India

The decline in the relative importance of Bombay as a centre of the Cotton Industry in India, and also the greater inability of the mill-owners of Bombay to meet the losses of the period of depression, which we have traced in the preceding pages, would undoubtedly indicate that Bombay suffers from certain disadvantages as compared to the up-country centres. We, therefore, now proceed to examine some of the principal factors that have contributed to the deterioration of the Bombay Cotton Industry in recent years. These may be conveniently grouped under two broad headings: (A) Labour Unrest and (B) Higher Costs of Production.

8. LABOUR UNREST IN BOMBAY

One of the greatest disadvantages from which the Cotton Industry of Bombay has suffered in recent years as compared to the up-country centres appears to have been the prevalence of grave and recurring labour troubles in that centre. While in other parts of India the mill-owners have been able to effect considerable readjustments between costs of production and falling prices by the reduction of labour costs, the efforts of the mill-owners in Bombay in that direction have been rendered altogether unsuccessful on account of the strong resistance offered by the comparatively better organised trade unions of that City. Without going into the question as to how far the mill-owners on their part were justified in seeking to reduce wages and how far the trade unions in their turn were well advised to resist those reductions by means of strikes, we may simply point out that the prolonged and continuous labour unrest and the consequent stoppage of the mills at frequent intervals must have contributed in a great measure to seriously weaken the position of the Cotton-mill Industry of Bombay both financially and otherwise. The importance of this factor as a special handicap of Bombay in recent years of grave depression will be realised from the following:

STRIKES AND LOCK-OUTS DURING THE PERIOD APRIL 1, 1921, TO JUNE 30, 1929*

Centre		Total Number of Disputes	Total Number of Work-people Affected (in Thousands)	Total Number of Working Days Lost (in Thousands)
Bombay..	..	401	1,078	49,298
Ahmedabad	..	221	135	2,605
Sholapur	..	10	39	1,214
Total	..	632	1,252	53,117

* Memorandum submitted by the Government of Bombay to the Royal Commission on Labour in India, *Minutes of Evidence*, Vol. I, Part I, p. 127.

Now, although this table includes the disputes in all the industries in these three centres, the majority of the disputes occurred in the Cotton Textile Industry, which is far and away the most important single industry in each of these centres. Thus, out of the 401 disputes in Bombay, 317 or 79 per cent took place in the Cotton Textile Industry alone. It will be observed that, whether we judge from the number and frequency of strikes, or from the number of work-people affected, or from the total number of working days lost, the difficulties caused by labour unrest were far more serious in Bombay than in Ahmedabad, its greatest single rival in the Cotton Industry, while Sholapur, the third important centre of the Cotton Industry in the Bombay Presidency, was almost free from labour trouble.

Let us look at another set of data. In the same period, i.e. the 1st of April, 1921, to June 30, 1929, in the whole of the Bombay Presidency there were 22 strikes affecting more than one industrial concern. Of these, 17 were in the Cotton Textile Industry, out of which Ahmedabad accounted for 5, Sholapur 2, Kurla 1, Surat 1, and Bombay 8. Out of the 8 strikes in the Bombay Cotton Industry, no less than 3 affected all the mills, while a fourth one affected as many as 64 out of the 76 mills and lasted nearly six months.[1]

[1] Memorandum, *ut supra*, pp. 117–18.

The view, that the City of Bombay has within recent years suffered more seriously from labour unrest than any other centre of the Cotton Industry in India, is also confirmed by the fact that in no other place have the Government found it necessary to conduct official enquiries into industrial disputes to such an extent as in the case of the Textile Industry of that City.[1]

Some of the principal causes of the strikes in the textile mills of Bombay City in the last few years are stated below:

A. Grievances of the workers:—

(1) Direct cut in wages.

(2) Reduction in monthly earnings owing to the following indirect causes:—

(*a*) Introduction of new varieties of cloths at rates which did not bring the level of wages to those earned on the production of the old sorts.

(*b*) Reduction of piece-rates to meet unanticipated high production by individual operatives.

(*c*) Adjustments in rates to bring them in line with rates prevailing in other mills.

(*d*) No adjustments made to increase the rates in cases where mills were on fine counts.

(*e*) Introduction of artificial silk as raw material.

(*f*) Gradual withdrawal of bonuses such as good attendance and efficiency bonus, and free railway passes to workers.

(*g*) Introduction of a method of paying wages on the weight of the cloth after it had undergone a subsequent process, instead of paying on the actual weight produced on the looms.

(3) The introduction of new methods of work, involving a reduction in the number of operatives employed.

(4) The increase in the hours of work of mechanics in some mills from 8½ hours to 10 hours per day, and the declaration of a general intention to level up the hours of work for all mill operatives in all mills to 10 hours per day.

[1] See the *Report of the Bombay Strike Enquiry Committee*, 1928–29, and also the *Report of the Pearson Court of Enquiry*, 1929. These two authoritative and exhaustive enquiries clearly show that the adjustment of labour costs to prices in the Cotton Industry of Bombay has been attended with difficulties of such a grave nature as have not been experienced in any other part of India.

B. Growth of militant trade unionism, especially since 1928.

C. Lack of co-operation between the employees and the employers in respect of the necessary changes in the conditions of employment involved in a scheme of rationalisation.

D. Absence of any permanent machinery for bringing the parties together to discuss and settle points of difference.[1]

As a direct result of the state of unrest and uncertainty created by frequent strikes, quite a considerable number out of these being 'lightning' strikes, there has been a natural reluctance on the part of mill-owners to invest money either in the modernisation or in the expansion of the mills. In consequence, the Cotton Industry has tended increasingly to shift itself in recent years from Bombay to the up-country centres of British India as well as the Native States.

It is, therefore, clear that, until the relations between the employers and the employees have been established on a more satisfactory basis than has been the case hitherto, there is a great likelihood of the City of Bombay declining further and further in importance as a centre of the Cotton Industry in India. It is also equally clear that, in so far as the absence of stability and progress in the industry is due to the unsatisfactory nature of the relations between the two parties, the proper remedy is to establish some machinery of mediation for the purpose of conciliation or arbitration. In this connection it may be pointed out that the comparatively greater prevalence of a peaceful atmosphere found in the Cotton-mill Industry of Ahmedabad has been promoted in a large measure by the introduction of the method of compulsory arbitration in that centre, where in cases in which the disputes between masters and men cannot be settled by mutual negotiations, they are referred to a board of two arbitrators, one nominated by the Mill-owners' Association, and the second, generally Mr. Gandhi, nominated by the trade union. If the arbitrators fail to come to an agreement, they refer the disputes to an umpire, whose decision is binding. Thus in 1929, when there was a

[1] See the *Report of the Bombay Strike Enquiry Committee*, 1928–29, and also the *Report of the Pearson Court of Enquiry*, 1929, p. 118, et seq.

dispute between the Mill-owners' Association and the Textile Labour Union of Ahmedabad regarding the increase of wages, the mill-owners' representative and Mr. Gandhi were unable to arrive at an agreement and referred the matter to an Umpire. The Umpire's award that the wages of the weavers should be increased by 5 per cent and those of the spinners by 8 per cent were accepted by the mill-owners.[1]

In the Bombay City, on the other hand, it appears that the trade union movement as a whole has lost much of its power and prestige with the workers, mill-owners as well as the general public, on account of the disastrous and ill-advised strikes of 1928 and 1929, and that, therefore, there is not much prospect in the near future of the settlement of industrial disputes by means of mutual negotiations.[2] Hence, although a legal machinery has now been instituted for enquiring into and settling disputes under the Trade Disputes Act of 1929, it is very doubtful whether in the absence of a sound development of the Trade Union movement and some standing machinery for mutual negotiations between the employers and the employees, the Cotton Industry of Bombay can look forward to having a spell of peaceful atmosphere so as to enable it to put into effect the rationalisation scheme which was recommended by the Tariff Board in 1927.[3]

9. HIGHER COSTS OF PRODUCTION IN BOMBAY

The remaining important disadvantages of the Cotton-mill Industry in Bombay as compared to the mills in the up-country centres can best be exhibited in the form of costs sheets. It will be readily understood that any accurate ascertainment of comparative costs in an industry, of which the units vary widely in points of size and efficiency, is an exceed-

[1] *Report on an Enquiry into Wages and Hours of Labour in the Cotton-mill Industry in 1926*, Labour Office, Government of Bombay, 1929, Appendix B.

[2] Vide White Paper on the Labour Situation issued by the Government of Bombay, 1930.

[3] *Report of the Tariff Board*, 1927, and the *Report of the Strike Enquiry Committee*, 1928–29.

ingly difficult matter. Moreover, it is rarely possible to obtain the desired data owing to the fact that the firms concerned are quite unwilling to supply the data of costs of production as it is apprehended that their publication would lead to the disclosure of important trade secrets to their rivals. The Tariff Board in India were, however, able to collect fairly adequate costs sheets from 8 mills in Bombay, 6 mills in Ahmedabad, and 7 mills in the up-country centres, which throw much valuable light on the question of comparative advantages. It should, however, be noticed that while all the mills in Bombay and Ahmedabad were representative mills, those in the other up-country centres were somewhat above the average.[1]

In the two tables that follow (pp. 129–30), the data of costs of production are given in detail for Bombay and the up-country centres, while those for Ahmedabad are available only as a total. The figures relate to 1926–27.

Analysis of the comparative advantages of Bombay city

It will be observed that the figures of costs of production per spindle per day and per loom per day as given in the above tables do not by themselves offer any complete guidance as to the different items of comparative advantage. For the purpose of any satisfactory comparison we should also have the figures of outturn per spindle and per loom per day. These latter data, however, are not available to us, and so we have to be satisfied with an examination of the different items in the costs per spindle and per loom per day in the different centres.

Spinning

It would appear from the first table that, although Bombay is at a slight disadvantage in respect of manufacturing charges, and specially wages, its overhead charges are somewhat lower than those in the up-country centres, with the result that the total costs of production in Bombay are a little less

[1] *Report of the Tariff Board,* Vol. I, pp. 117–21.

than those in the up-country centres. On the other hand, the figures of total costs in Bombay are appreciably higher than those in Ahmedabad, the difference being 2·29 pies or nearly

TABLE IX

AVERAGE MANUFACTURING AND OVERHEAD CHARGES PER SPINDLE PER DAY

	Bombay Pies	Up-country Centres Pies
A. MANUFACTURING CHARGES:		
1. Fuel and power	1·87	2·25
2. Stores	1·16	1·29
3. Repairs and upkeep of machinery	0·39	0·37
4. Wages	5·04	3·86
Total	8·46	7·77
B. OVERHEAD CHARGES:		
1. Municipal taxes, Government assessment, licences, fees, etc.	0·17	0·07
2. Insurance..	0·26	0·46
3. Repairs to buildings	0·14	0·19
4. Salaries of supervising and technical staff	0·42	0·66
5. Office expenses at mill and registered office of Company	0·25	0·54
6. Miscellaneous charges	0·27	0·32
Total	1·51	2·24
TOTAL MANUFACTURING AND OVERHEAD CHARGES	9·97	10·01

AVERAGE WAGES:	Rs. a. p.	Rs. a. p.
Male	1 2 5	0 13 3
Female	0 13 2	0 6 4

The total figure for Ahmedabad is 7·68 pies per spindle per day.

30 per cent above the costs figures of the latter. The details of the costs in Ahmedabad, however, not being available to us, we cannot ascertain what are the items in respect of which Bombay compares unfavourably with Ahmedabad. As between Bombay and the up-country centres for which the details are available,

it appears that the one important single item in respect of which Bombay is at a marked disadvantage is wages. As the wages item in Table X brings out this comparative disadvantage of Bombay in a more prominent way, it would be best to

TABLE X

AVERAGE MANUFACTURING AND OVERHEAD CHARGES PER LOOM PER DAY

	Bombay Pies	Up-country Centres Pies
A. Manufacturing Charges:		
1. Fuel and power	66·06	56·71
2. Water	2·86	2·76
3. Stores	55·58	76·69
4. Repairs and upkeep of machinery	11·63	8·63
5. Wages	317·64	255·50
Total	453·77	400·29
B. Overhead Charges:		
1. Municipal taxes, Government assessment, licences, fees, etc.	6·06	1·85
2. Insurance..	8·26	10·63
3. Repairs to buildings	3·62	3·89
4. Salaries of supervising and technical staff	24·31	28·12
5. Office expenses at mill and registered office of Company..	8·62	19·43
6. Miscellaneous charges	9·49	6·96
Total	60·36	70·88
Total Manufacturing and Overhead Charges	514·13	471·17
Average Wages:	Rs. a. p.	Rs. a. p.
Male	1 13 5	1 1 10
Female	0 12 4	0 7 0

The total figure for Ahmedabad is 450·29 pies.

consider the wages item in connection with the costs per loom per day.

Weaving.

When we turn to the next table, the comparative advantages and disadvantages of Bombay become fairly clear to us. The total costs per loom per day in Bombay are higher than those of the up-country centres by about 43 pies or 9 per cent; when compared to the costs in Ahmedabad, the difference becomes as high as 63 pies or 14 per cent. The items which make up this difference between Bombay and other centres, arranged in order of importance, are: (*a*) wages, (*b*) fuel and power, (*c*) repairs and upkeep of machinery, (*d*) municipal taxes, etc. We would dispose of the last three items first and turn to the first one last.

Fuel and Power

The higher costs in fuel and power in Bombay are due to the fact that the charges for hydro-electric power which most of the mills in Bombay use under a long-period contract with the two power companies in the city have been higher in recent years than the costs of oil fuel or coal which is used by the mills up-country. As the contract between the cotton mills of Bombay and the hydro-electric power companies only expired in 1932,[1] it is evidently not possible for Bombay immediately to eliminate the comparative disadvantage under this item.[2]

Repairs and Upkeep of Machinery

It is difficult to perceive why Bombay should have any disadvantage under this item at all. As Bombay is one of the most important centres of the Engineering Industry in India, and as it saves the railway freight charges on imported machinery and parts of machinery, which the up-country centres must

[1] *Report of the Tariff Board*, Vol. I, p. 132.

[2] It is, however, important to point out that if we take the relative costs of fuel and power in spinning and weaving together, Bombay would have a net advantage as follows:

Bombay's costs per loom and 48 spindles	603·89 pies
Up-country centres' costs per loom and 61 spindles ..	608·42 ,,
Bombay's net gain	4·53 ,,

(See Tables VIII, IX, X.)

pay, it is reasonable to assume that considerable economies under this item are practicable.

Municipal Taxes

The details of comparative municipal taxes are not available to us. We can, however, state in a general way that Bombay being a far bigger city than any other centre of the Cotton Industry in India, the problems of sanitation, water-supply, roads and traffic, police and prevention of crimes, have of necessity become more serious and acute there. Accordingly, it may be stated with almost complete certainty that in the matter of municipal taxation, the comparative disadvantage of Bombay is a permanent handicap.

Wages

From the table of comparative costs of production per loom per day, it will be noticed that by far the greater disadvantage of Bombay is in respect of wages, the difference being no less than 62·14 pies. The labour costs in Bombay are as much as 24 per cent higher than those in the up-country centres. It will further be observed that the sum of 62·14 pies, which measures the disadvantage of Bombay in respect of labour costs, is even greater than the entire overhead charges in Bombay, and is only slightly less than the overhead charges in the up-country centres. Again, if the labour costs in Bombay could have been equalised to those in the up-country centres, not only would the difference in comparative costs amounting to 42·96 pies have completely disappeared, but Bombay would also come to have an advantage in comparative costs to the extent of about 20 pies.

Inelasticity of Wage-rates in Bombay

Apart from the fact that the rates of wages in Bombay have always been higher than those in up-country centres due to its higher cost of living,[1] in the post-war years of readjustment

[1] *Reports on an Enquiry into Wages and Hours of Labour in the Cotton-mill Industry*, 1921, 1923 and 1926, Labour Office, Bombay.

Bombay has experienced a much greater difficulty in reducing wages than the other competing centres in India. This will be evident from a survey of the course of wages in Bombay and also from a comparison of the prevailing rates of wages in recent years in Bombay as well as the other centres.

The basic rates of wages in Bombay were raised above the pre-war rates in 1917, and also a war bonus of 10 per cent in addition was granted in that year. In 1918 the bonus was raised to 15 per cent. In 1919 it was again increased to 35 per cent and was termed a high-prices allowance. In 1920, mainly as a result of a strike, the special allowance was raised to 70 per cent in the case of workers on fixed wages and winders, and 80 per cent in the case of all piece-workers other than winders. Due to the collapse of the boom in 1922 and also the continuous fall of prices and the cost of living from 1921 onwards, the Bombay Mill-owners' Association tried to reduce the wages by 11½ per cent in 1925. The workers replied by a strike of two and a half months' duration, and as we saw in the previous chapter, the strike was only ended by the Government of India abolishing the cotton excise duty and the Bombay mill-owners agreeing to retain the wages at the old level. In this connection it may be pointed out that the Ahmedabad mill-owners were able in 1923 to reduce labour costs by a cut of 15½ per cent in wages in spite of a strike of some ten weeks' duration. In 1929, again, in connection with the reorganisation scheme, the Bombay mill-owners proposed a cut of 7½ per cent in the wages of the weavers, and the result was another big strike. The Strike Enquiry Committee, appointed by the Government of Bombay to investigate the matter in dispute between the employers and the workers, specifically examined the subject of the proposed wage-cut in the light of the conditions of external and internal competition and also of the general financial state of the industry as a whole, and came to the conclusion that the proposed wage-cut was justified, although at the same time they observed that the mill-owners would be well advised to drop the proposal of wage reduction, if thereby they could ensure the whole-hearted co-operation of the workers in the introduction of the standardisation and efficiency schemes.[1] This, therefore, shows that the payment of comparatively high wages must be the price at which the Bombay mill-owners must buy industrial peace, which is so essential in a period of far-reaching reorganisation.

That the rates of wages in Bombay are somewhat higher than those in Ahmedabad and much higher than those in the up-country centres will be seen from the following 'standard muster' for the 1st of April, 1926. It may be explained that the 'standard muster' is the muster roll kept by each mill, indicating the number of operatives in each department and also showing the monthly rate for workers on fixed wages and the remuneration per unit for piece-workers. The average wages shown in the table against piece-workers, that is, frame-tenters, winders and weavers, are those earned during the month on the basis of the piece-rate given in the standard muster.

It will be noticed that out of the seven classes of cotton operatives, four on time-wages and three on piece-wages, represented in the table, all the four time-workers and one piece-worker, viz. frame tenters, are given rates of wages in Bombay, which are appreciably higher than the corresponding rates at Ahmedabad and much higher than those in the other up-country centres. In the case of weavers, the Bombay figures are a little lower than the Ahmedabad figures, but considerably higher than those for all the other centres. And lastly, in respect of winders, the Bombay figures are somewhat lower than those of any other centre except Nagpur. In these two last cases, however, we should not make the mistake of inferring from the higher figures for some of the up-country centres that in these the Bombay scales of wages are lower. On the contrary, as all the rates for time-workers are higher in Bombay, we may legitimately presume that the scale of remuneration for winders and weavers, too, must be higher there, and that the lower

[1] *Report of the Bombay Strike Enquiry Committee*, 1928–29, Vol. I, pp. 101–27.

TABLE XI

RATES OF WAGES IN BOMBAY AND UP-COUNTRY CENTRES*

Standard Muster April 1, 1926	Bombay			Ahmedabad			Cawnpore			Delhi			Nagpur		
	Rs.	a.	p.	Rs.	a.	p.	Rs.	a.	p.	Rs.	a.	p.	Rs.	a.	p.
Blowroom tenters (Time)	27	0	0	23	10	0	16	14	6	19	0	0	24	0	0
Cardroom tenters (Time)	27	4	0	24	7	6	23	12	0	14	0	0	24	0	0
Frame tenters (Piece)	37	12	0	29	6	0	27	3	0	25	0	0	30	12	0
Ring Frame sideboys (Time)	29	12	0	26	7	6	15	10	0	20	0	0	24	0	0
Winders (Piece)	21	4	0	23	1	0	27	13	0	25	0	0	18	8	0
Weavers (Piece)	47	12	0	47	15	9	32	7	0	35	0	0	41	0	0
Folders (Time)	29	0	0	25	11	3	14	6	0	20	0	0	24	0	0

* *Report of the Tariff Board,* Vol. I, p. 113, The figures are for a representative mill in each case.

figures shown against Bombay than against some of the up-country centres are really due to the lower efficiency of piece-workers in the former.

10. INTRODUCTION OF EFFICIENCY MEASURES

The prevalence of considerably higher wage-rates in Bombay and the inelasticity of these rates in the face of falling prices and under vastly altered conditions of competition make it clear beyond doubt that, if the mill-owners of Bombay are to hold their own against the severe and growing internal as well as external competition, they must increase the total effectiveness of labour by the introduction of efficiency measures. In so far as they are specially handicapped in the matter of labour costs, their one principal way of escape from the difficulty lies in so altering the machinery and equipment that each worker may look after more machinery than at present. There is ample evidence to show that the effectiveness of labour in the majority of the cotton mills in Bombay is not only lower than that in some of the up-country mills, but falls appreciably below what can be found in a few of the most efficient and up-to-date mills in Bombay itself. We shall take only a few specific cases for comparison. In Bombay one operative generally looks after 180 spindles. In Madras, on the other hand, the number of spindles per operative is 240, which, by the way, is also the figure for Japan. In view of the fact that Bombay has a distinct advantage in respect of spinning on account of its humid climate, there is no reason why the number of spindles per operative in Bombay also should not be raised from 180 to 240. The mill-owners of Madras made the change acceptable to the operatives by providing that the wages of the fourth operative who was retrenched as a result of the change would be divided between the mill-owners and the remaining three operatives in the proportion of one-fifth to four-fifths.[1] A similar stipulation with regard to the distribution of the savings effected as a result of the reduction in the number of operatives would also undoubt-

[1] Report of the Tariff Board, *Minutes of Evidence*, Vol. IV, pp. 518–19.

edly facilitate the introduction of a change in Bombay as well. Then, again, take the case of looms. The average number of looms looked after by each operative in Bombay is two. But there are instances in Bombay itself where an operative looks after three and sometimes even four looms. Thus, an enquiry into the wages and hours of labour in the Cotton-mill Industry in May, 1926, showed that in the City of Bombay, out of 11,758 weavers returned, 11,358 or 36·59 per cent were two-loom weavers, 327 or 2·79 per cent one-loom weavers, 6 three-loom weavers, and 67 four-loom weavers. Similarly in Ahmedabad out of 4,394 weavers returned, 4,229 or 96 per cent were two-loom weavers, 74 three-loom weavers, and 101 four-loom weavers.[1] These instances show that considerable economies may be effected by the cotton mills in Bombay by the introduction of the three-loom and the four-loom system in place of the present two-loom one. Here, again, the co-operation of the operatives may be secured by an agreed scheme under which, as in Madras, the savings effected by the reduction in the number of operatives would be divided between the management and the operatives in some suitable proportions.[2]

Scope for the introduction of similar efficiency or labour-saving measures undoubtedly exists also in the other departments of the Cotton-mill Industry of Bombay. Thus, during the three years, 1926–29, 13 of the stronger mills in Bombay were able to effect considerable economies in labour in all the preparatory, spinning and weaving departments. In this way, one single group of 9 mills were able to retrench a total muster roll of 27,000 to the extent of no less than 5,100 or about 19 per cent.[3] The least, therefore, that the cotton-mill owners of Bombay can and should do in order to improve their competitive power is to introduce the efficiency measures that have been successfully adopted by the more enterprising among their number.

[1] *Report on an Enquiry into Wages and Hours of Labour in the Cotton-mill Industry*, 1926, Labour Office, Bombay.

[2] Cf. *Report of the Bombay Strike Enquiry Committee*, 1928–29, pp. 162–65.

[3] Ibid., pp. 154–65, 243–49.

Co-operation of Labour essential: the way to get it

It is needless to point out that the hearty co-operation of labour is absolutely essential to the introduction of the above efficiency measures. That co-operation can certainly be secured, firstly, by providing for some scheme of unemployment relief for those operatives who will be retrenched as a result of the new system, and secondly, by ensuring that a reasonable proportion of the savings due to the reduction in the number of labourers is available towards the improvement of the remuneration of those who will be retained and who will unquestionably have to stand a greater strain in their work than before.

With regard to the first point, the Strike Enquiry Committee suggested that, in the absence of a state system of unemployment insurance in India, the employers and the employees should institute an "out of work Donation Fund," which would go some way towards mitigating the hardships of unemployment inseparable from a scheme of rationalisation. Under the Committee's plan, the mill-owners are to contribute one anna per operative per month and each worker is also to contribute either one anna or half-anna per month. The annual income of the Fund would be Rs. 1,68,750, if the operative contributed half-anna, and Rs. 2,25,000 if he contributed one anna.[1] In 1929, the number of operatives in the cotton mills of Bombay was approximately 150,000. Taking the maximum retrenchment possible at 20 per cent of the present number, the number of operatives thrown out of work under the reorganisation scheme would be 30,000. If the reorganisation were spread over a period of, say, three years, the average number to be relieved per annum would be 10,000 and the amount of unemployment relief available for each operative would be between Rs. 16·88 to Rs. 22·5. On the basis of the average monthly earnings of adult workers in Bombay in 1926,[2] the

[1] Cf. *Report of the Bombay Strike Enquiry Committee*, 1928–29, p. 160.

[2] The average monthly earnings in 1926 were Rs. 32 14 as. 1 pie. (Vide *Report on an Enquiry into Wages and Hours of Labour in the Cotton-mill Industry of Bombay*, 1926, p. 43.)

amount of relief available for each would be equal to the earnings of two to three weeks. This will no doubt to a certain extent mitigate the hardships consequent on the loss of work in the mills. And moreover, we have to remember in this connection that the mill operatives in India are in the majority of cases also agricultural workers, and that they can and frequently do turn to agricultural work as a source of employment.

With regard to the second point, viz. increased remuneration to the workers on account of the greater strain involved in the system of more machinery per operative, we have only to mention that some of the Bombay mills referred to above, where the efficiency measures have already been introduced, have devised a new scheme of remuneration which has proved satisfactory to both the employers and the employees alike. Under this scheme, a two-loom weaver taking a third loom would receive 46 per cent of the earnings of the third loom as his additional remuneration, and if he takes two more looms, he would receive 50 per cent of the earnings of the third and fourth looms as his additional wages. Similar provisions regarding the payment of increased remuneration in proportion to increased work have been made in respect of the Drawing Frame, Blow Room, Card Room, and Ring Frame Departments.[1] If some of the mills in Bombay have thus been able to give the necessary lead in the introduction of the more efficient and economical system of working with the co-operation of the operatives, it certainly cannot be difficult for the other mills in that city as well as up-country centres to effect considerable economies in the labour costs by following that lead.[2]

II. OTHER LINES OF IMPROVEMENT: RAW MATERIALS AND MARKETS

Apart from the disadvantages in the costs of manufacture which we have discussed above, there are two other important

[1] *Report of the Bombay Strike Enquiry Committee*, 1928–29, pp. 154–65.

[2] It may, however, be mentioned that the adoption of similar measures in the up-country centres will tend to re-establish the relative inferiority of Bombay in respect of labour cost.

matters in respect to which the cotton mills of Bombay seem to be considerably handicapped in competition with the up-country mills. The situation of the cotton mills in Madras, Nagpur, Cawnpore and Ahmedabad almost in the heart of the important cotton-growing tracts of India places them in a position of appreciable advantage in regard to the cost of the raw material. Moreover, the mills in some of these up-country centres, viz., those of Cawnpore, Nagpur, and Madras, being located in the midst of the great consuming areas of India, they are able to make considerable economies in the matter of transport charges as well. Furthermore, there is evidence to show that, as the majority of the up-country mills carry on production on a comparatively small scale, they are able to adapt their production and marketing to suit the tastes and requirements of the consuming public in a much larger degree than has been the case with the Bombay mills. Thus, while the up-country mills, through their own selling agents, have been able to keep in touch with the changing and varying requirements of the different sections of the consumers and also to push the sales of their own cloths, the Bombay mills have in the past shown comparative indifference to these important matters by having no selling agents of their own. Naturally, the result has been that the products of the Bombay mills have been ousted from many of the important consuming centres by those of the Japanese as well as the up-country mills.[1]

Now, in so far as raw cotton is concerned, the disadvantage of Bombay arising out of the greater distance from the cotton-growing tracts in India is to a certain extent counterbalanced, firstly, by the fact that while the up-country mills must buy up their entire stock in the harvesting season and thus carry a large stock for the rest of the year, the Bombay mills can buy their raw cotton throughout the year through the Cotton Exchange in the city; and secondly, by their ability to import the superior raw cotton from Uganda cheaper than the up-

[1] Report of the Tariff Board, *Minutes of Evidence*, Vol. II, pp. 242–45, 318–20.

country mills. It may be noted that in recent years there has come into evidence a tendency on the part of Bombay mill-owners to supply their requirements of raw cotton in an increasing degree through importation.[1] This advantage of Bombay in respect of imported cotton for the production of finer yarn could be considerably strengthened, if the mill-owners would follow the example of the Japanese cotton importers in combining into an association for the purchase of raw cotton, as this will secure them better terms not only in respect of the price of raw cotton but also in the matter of freight rates.

The disadvantages of the Bombay mills in respect of the internal market may be greatly reduced, if not altogether eliminated, by the establishment of their own selling agencies in the great distributive centres, and also by the maintenance of intimate and frequent contact between the mill authorities and the markets, so that, instead of having to rely entirely upon the information supplied by merchants and selling agents, they may be able to study first-hand the movements of the market and adapt their production accordingly, for, as the Balfour Committee on Trade and Industry truly observe, "no arrangement with regard to agents, however satisfactory, can dispense with the necessity that the manufacturer should himself visit the markets and become personally acquainted with his representatives, as well as with market conditions."[2]

But if the Bombay mills have some disadvantage in respect of the internal market, they have a corresponding advantage over the other mills with regard to the export markets. It will be recalled that originally the Cotton-mill Industry of Bombay was started and kept up at a high level of prosperity mainly as an exporting industry, disposing of most of its output of yarn in the Chinese market. The loss of the yarn trade with China has now been compensated to an appreciable extent by a growing market for cloths in Africa, Arabia, Persia,

[1] This is Uganda cotton of the American type and means that the Bombay mills are changing over to finer yarn.

[2] Cmd. 3282, p. 165.

Ceylon, Malay, and Straits Settlements, as will be seen from the following table:

TABLE XII

EXPORTS OF INDIAN COTTON MANUFACTURERS*

(Millions of Yards)

Class	Pre-war Average (1909–10–13–14)	War Average (1914–15–18–19)	1925–26	1926–27	1927–28	1928–29	1929–30
Grey ..	47·4	74·6	37·4	19·9	18·0	16·3	15·0
Coloured	42·4	80·4	126·5	175·9	149·2	131·5	117·2
Total ..	89·8	155·0	163·9	195·8	167·2	147·8	132·2

* *Review of the Trade of India*, 1909–10 to 1929–30. The continuous decline in the last three years is largely accounted for by an increasingly heavy fall in the exports to Persia, Iraq and Egypt, where European piece-goods are displacing those from India.

It will be noticed that the post-war exports are much larger than the pre-war ones. It is also important to notice that some of these markets, e.g. the Levant, East Africa, South Africa, Persia and Iraq are still capable of appreciable development. The Indian Trade Mission, which visited the Near East and Africa in 1928, found sufficient evidence for the conclusion that there was considerable room for the expansion of the market for nearly all classes of Indian cloths, and specially for woven coloured goods, piece-dyed goods and cotton blankets in most of these areas.[1] In all these markets Bombay, due to its position as a great seaport at the head of the Arabian Sea, has an important advantage over the other producing centres of India. This advantage could be enormously increased if the mill-owners of Bombay would establish a strong selling organisation for the export markets. It may be pointed out that the Indian Trade Mission recommended that the selling organisation should be set up on the following lines:

(*a*) The formation of a single export selling organisation with the mill-owners as members;

(*b*) All selling of goods produced by the members for the export market through this one organisation;

[1] *Report of the Trade Mission to the Near East and Africa*, 1928, pp. 232–45.

(*c*) The head office to be located in Bombay, with branch offices in those oversea markets, in which the present trade or potentialities are large, and agents in those places where the markets are comparatively small;

(*d*) Commercial travellers to be attached to the branch offices; and

(*e*) Periodical visits to be paid by the mill-owners to the branch offices, agents and customers overseas so that close and effective contact might be maintained between the manufacturers and oversea merchants.[1]

And we may add that this organisation might be utilised also in purchasing raw cotton and securing freight on advantageous terms.

12. THE MANAGING AGENCY SYSTEM: ITS WEAKNESSES; SUGGESTIONS FOR REFORM

One of the great peculiarities of the industrial and commercial life of India is the existence of large agency houses or firms. These are partnerships or private limited companies formed by the association of a few individuals with great business enterprise and large financial resources. The more important among these firms conduct a great variety of business—import and export trade, promoting, financing and managing of industrial concerns, and agency work for different types of firms, such as buyers of cotton, insurance companies, and manufacturers of machinery and stocks. They manage the great majority of the cotton mills, jute mills and other mills, iron, steel and engineering works, coal-mines and tea gardens of India. It is also important to note that the better managed agency firms have a strikingly large number of successes to their credit and therefore enjoy a high prestige with the financial world and good reputation for ability and judgment with the investing public.[2] While admitting, therefore, that the agency firm has proved itself so far as a widespread and successful business institution in India, it is nevertheless necessary for us here to point out some of the more serious defects in the system

[1] *Report of the Trade Mission to the Near East and Africa*, 1928, pp. 248–49.

[2] *Report of the Indian Industrial Commission*, pp. 12–13.

of management of mills by agency firms, as are found in the case of the Cotton-mill Industry of Bombay and Ahmedabad.

(a) *Concentration of Control and Plurality of Directorships*

In Bombay there is a great concentration of mills in the hands of a few agency firms. Thus in 1927, one single firm controlled as many as 11 mills and another 12 mills, and these two firms between them controlled no less than 50 per cent of the paid-up capital, and nearly 30 per cent of the spindles and looms of the entire Cotton-mill Industry of the place.[1]

Mainly as a result of this concentration of the control of mills in the hands of a few agency firms, we also find that a few individuals, who are in the majority of cases members of the agency firms, are appointed Directors of far too many mills to make it possible for them to take any but the most passive and superficial interest in the affairs of the mills under their charge. The following table will give us an idea of the extent of plural, and therefore also largely ineffective, directorships prevalent in the Cotton-mill Industry of Bombay:

TABLE XIII*

Serial Number	Number of Directorships held by One Single Individual	Paid-up Capital of the Companies Represented (in Crores of Rupees)	Paid-up Capital of the Companies Represented as Percentage of the Paid-up Capital of the Entire Cotton Industry of Bombay
1	30	12·82	65
2	14	2·74	14
3	13	2·71	14
4	12	8·74	44
5	8	1·68	8·6
6	6	7·26	37
7	5	7·15	36
8	5	1·78	9
9	4	1·32	6·7
10	3	1·17	5·9

* The data for this table have been collected from Mr. S. M. Rutnagur's *Bombay Industries: The Cotton Mills*, pp. 249–51. They relate to 1927.

These instances show that a few individuals, due either to their

[1] *Report of the Tariff Board*, Appendix XII, p. 258.

membership of, or influence with, the managing agency firms, exercise a controlling authority over a large number of mills without, at the same time, being able to give the necessary attention to the affairs of these concerns.

(*b*) *Lack of Technical Qualifications among the Directors*

In 1927, there were in all 175 Directors of cotton mills in Bombay. Of these, 149 were merchants, 15 lawyers, and only 11 experts.[1] It is obvious, therefore, that the amount of technical knowledge at the disposal of the mill authorities in Bombay is far too small to be effective in levelling up the technical efficiency of the industry as a whole. In order that the Board of Directors of the majority of the cotton mills in Bombay may be really competent, it is necessary that there should be less of mere window-dressing, and more of careful selection, in the constitution of the Boards. In practice, this will mean that the managing agency firms, as long as they retain their predominance in the constitution of the Boards of Directors, should contain a large number of members with the necessary technical qualifications.

(*c*) *Managing Agency a Family Business*

In some instances in Bombay, but in nearly all instances at Ahmedabad, the membership or partnership of the Managing Agency is limited to the members of the family, or at best, to a narrow circle of friends and relatives, while succession to the vacant places is determined by heredity.[2] The institution has, therefore, all the defects of a hereditary system. While the pioneers and founders are usually men of great initiative, enterprise, and resourcefulness, it will be a matter of the merest chance whether the successors are going to be competent and energetic persons, or as is much more likely to be the case, only easy-going men without any stamina or training. It is clear that a very considerable modification of the clannish and

[1] *Report of the Tariff Board*, Appendix XII, p. 258.

[2] Report of the Tariff Board, *Minutes of Evidence*, Vol. II, pp. 436–42.

hereditary principle of organisation is called for if there is to be a guarantee of continued efficiency in the Cotton-mill Industry at Ahmedabad.[1]

(*d*) *Cotton Mills Treated as Private Property*

There is evidence to show that at Ahmedabad the funds and affairs of particular cotton mills are administered as if they were the private affairs of the managing agents concerned. Thus, there are instances where the surplus funds of the comparatively stronger mills are invested with the weaker mills under the same management, with the result that when the latter collapse they drag the former also down with them in a common ruin. Again, there are cases where the managing agents do not always pass on the sale proceeds to the mills concerned at once, but retain them for themselves for a considerable time. Thus in one particular case brought to the notice of the Tariff Board, the fact that the sale proceeds had remained with the managing agents was discovered only after that mill had gone into liquidation.[2]

It is difficult to think of any remedy, short of the complete abolition of the managing agency system, that will eradicate the serious evils noticed above. Nevertheless, so long as that institution remains in vogue, it is probable that the abuse of powers on the part of the managing agents could be considerably checked if the shareholders were able to secure a proper constitution of the Board of Directors, with a due proportion of their own nominees.[3]

13. SUMMARY AND CONCLUSIONS

Our survey of the development of the Cotton-mill Industry of India from the middle of the nineteenth century down to the present time and our examination of its conditions in recent

[1] It may perhaps be mentioned that the managing agents in the Cotton Industry are predominantly Indian.
[2] *Report of the Tariff Board*, Vol. I, pp. 89–90.
[3] Perhaps this reform should be ensured by means of a regulating Act.

years point to certain broad conclusions which may be summarised as follows:

(*a*) That throughout the whole course of its history, the industry has registered steady, continuous, and sometimes even marked, progress.

(*b*) That up to 1921–22, the import duty, being either altogether non-existent or very nominal, played little part in promoting that development.

(*c*) That both the spinning and the weaving branches of the industry had been able to capture a substantial and increasing share of the home market before obtaining the differential advantage under the tariffs of 1921–22 and 1930–31.

(*d*) That the steady expansion of output and the predominant position in the home market continued during the general trade depression that had set in in 1922–23, and that the comparative data regarding output and imports in recent years do not show in any way that the progress of the Indian industry was being hampered by any unusually severe foreign competition.

(*e*) That considering the severe world-wide and prolonged nature of the depression in trade and industry, the financial condition of the efficiently managed mills has been fairly good[1] in recent years and hardly called for support at the expense of the tax-payers.

(*f*) That the critical financial condition of a great many of the Bombay mills and some of the up-country mills is due to incompetence, inflation of capital, extravagant dividend payment, grave labour unrest, inelastic wage-rates, and serious, and sometimes fatal, defects in the institution of managing agency, which practically controls the Cotton Industry in Bombay and elsewhere.

(*g*) That the financial difficulties of the weaker and comparatively inefficient mills are due in a great measure to the existence of keen and growing competition within the country, and much less to the severity of foreign competition.

(*h*) As we saw in the previous chapter, the high revenue tariff of 1921–22 had already enabled the mill-owners of India to levy a considerable tribute from the consumers of cotton cloth in the country. We also saw that the Government of India by abolishing the cotton excise duty in 1925 had sacrificed an appreciable amount of legitimate

---

[1] A competent investigator states that though the Indian Cotton-mill Industry, in common with that in the rest of the world, has not had a very remunerative period of late, yet the return on the capital invested in it, on the average of the last ten years, has been higher than that of any country in Europe or America, and that the only country where the Cotton Industry has fared better than that of India is Japan. (Vide *The Cotton Industry of India*, by A. S. Pearse, p. 64.)

revenue in order to enable the cotton manufacturers to still further increase their gains at the cost of the general tax-payers. The analysis of the financial condition of a large number of mills in the period 1926–28, which we made in an earlier section of this chapter, showed that a considerable group of well-managed mills up-country and a somewhat smaller group in Bombay were able, in spite of the prevailing conditions of general depression, to pay reasonable dividends to their shareholders. On the other hand, our examination of the present condition of the Cotton-mill Industry as a whole in Bombay enabled us to see that the financial crisis of a large number of mills there was due to grave defects in organisation, financial mismanagement, and disturbed industrial relations, leading to higher costs of production, on account of which Bombay mills were increasingly unable to hold their own against the severe and growing competition of up-country mills. These facts would make it clear that, if the Bombay mill-owners had thoroughly reorganised and reconditioned the industry as a whole so as to bring it up to the level of the most efficient units in Bombay as well as up-country, they would not have required the artificial assistance from the general consuming public over and above what had been already secured to them by the high revenue tariff. The Government of India, thoroughly cognisant of these basic facts, rightly refused the aid of protective tariff to the Cotton Industry for three years, 1927–30. But, partly due to the persistent and vigorous propaganda carried on by the Bombay Mill-owners' Association, partly on account of the bad state of their own finances, and partly also with a desire to rally the business community to the support of the Government in a period of grave political unrest,[1] they had at last to enact the Cotton Industry (Protection) Act of 1930. Under these circumstances, naturally, very scanty consideration was given either to the merits of the case or to the interests of the consumers, on whom a considerable burden of taxation was placed under that Act.

(*i*) Again, this protective measure of 1930 was enacted for a period of three years.[2] But is there any guarantee, or at least assurance of any kind, that the tax-payers will be relieved at the end of the three years of the extra burden entailed by protection? In other words, is there any strong probability that the Cotton Industry will be thoroughly reorganised and reconditioned within the period and thus justify the sacrifice made by the consuming public in India, the vast majority of whom, we must remember, are exceedingly poor,

---

[1] i.e., Mr. Gandhi's Civil Disobedience movement.

[2] It may be noted that the rates of duty fixed under the Cotton Industry Protection Act of 1930 have been twice enhanced during the last twenty months, first, by a general surcharge of 5 per cent in March, 1931, and second, by another surcharge of 6¼ per cent in the emergency budget of September, 1931.

and only with difficulty able to meet the barest needs of life? So far as we are able to gather from the Debates in connection with the passing of the measure, the consumers have no stronger or more solid security against the continuation of the burden of the protective duty beyond the three years than the mere pious hope expressed by the Government of India that the Bombay mill-owners should reorganise their industry in the meantime and their announcement that the whole question of protection to the Cotton Industry would be reopened and investigated afresh by the Tariff Board at the end of the period.[1] It is needless to point out that the security thus given to the consumers is of a most intangible nature, and may easily prove to be no security at all in the face of timely and well-organised propaganda in the country[2] and judicious and skilful alliances in the Legislature.

---

[1] Vide the speech of Sir George Rainy, *Assembly Debates*, March 13, 1930; also Budget Statement, 1930–31.

[2] In June, 1932, the Tariff Board was again engaged in the enquiry into the Cotton Industry, and there was, again, the inevitable demand for the continuance of protection, backed by intensive propaganda. Great stress was laid upon the recent depreciation of the Japanese exchange. There was a demand for the prohibition of, or at any rate a 100 per cent additional duty upon, the imports of Japanese piece-goods.

On the recommendation of the Board, the duty on non-British piece-goods has been raised from 20 per cent to 50 per cent, as from August, 1932, with a view to counteracting the so-called exchange-dumping by Japan. This remains in force up to March 31, 1933, when the whole question of protection to the Cotton Industry will be reopened.

CHAPTER IV

THE INDIAN IRON AND STEEL INDUSTRY

1. THE INDIGENOUS IRON AND STEEL INDUSTRY OF INDIA

The art of smelting and fashioning iron seems to have been known to the people of India from very early times, and it is probable that the art was borrowed from China. It is the opinion of many historians that the earliest weapons that figure in the half-mythological records of the Mediterranean peoples came from India. The wonderful collections of ancient arms still found in India were made of the steel known as 'wootz' produced in Hyderabad. They indicate that the art of damascening upon soft steel was widely practised in India chiefly in connection with arms, and bear testimony to a high degree of skill and excellence attained by Indian workers. It may also be mentioned that the famous iron column at the Kutab Minar near Delhi, believed to be between 1,500 and 3,000 years old, represents a forging weighing between seven and eight tons, while the method by which it was produced is still a mystery to this day.[1]

Another kind of evidence shows that the art of smelting was practised as an indigenous industry in widely scattered areas. There is hardly a district away from the great alluvial tracts in which large and numerous slag heaps are not to be found. Even to this day there are in existence large numbers of diminutive blast furnaces in the wilder parts of India, particularly in the Central Provinces and Orissa, which continue to produce by wasteful methods small blooms of soft iron used chiefly for axe-heads and ploughshares. Thus, for example, in 1916 in the Central Provinces alone nearly 4,500 tons of iron ore were smelted in as many as 300 native furnaces.[2]

[1] *Life of J. N. Tata*, by F. R. Harris, pp. 155–56.
[2] *Indian Munitions Board Handbook*, p. 124.

It is, however, needless to point out that the modern Iron and Steel Industry which may be said to have been originated and developed in England during the eighteenth and first half of the nineteenth century, and later on transformed and enlarged in Europe and America in the last fifty years, is altogether a new industry based upon the scientific discoveries of the last 200 years. It was, therefore, inevitable that the ancient Iron-smelting Industry of India, still clinging to wasteful methods of consuming ore and charcoal, would rapidly disappear in the face of competition with the imports from Europe and America.

2. INTRODUCTION OF MODERN PROCESSES OF IRON MANUFACTURE: EARLY FAILURES AND RECENT SUCCESS

The earliest attempt to introduce modern processes for the manufacture of pig-iron and steel in India was made by Mr. Josiah Marshall Heath of the Madras Civil Service in 1830. Heath resigned the service of the East India Company and secured the exclusive privilege of manufacturing iron on a large scale in the Madras Presidency. Furnaces were set up at Porto Novo in South Arcot, and were subsequently maintained with financial assistance from the East India Company. In 1833 the business was taken over by the Porto Novo Steel and Iron Company, and additional furnaces were started at Beypur on the Malabar Coast. In spite of various concessions granted to Mr. Heath and the succeeding Company, the enterprise proved a complete failure. In 1853 a new association, known as the East India Iron Company, was started with a capital of £400,000. This Company obtained various concessions from the Government and erected two blast furnaces, one in the South Arcot district and another on the Cauvery River in the Coimbatore district. These furnaces were stopped in 1858, while operations at Porto Novo ceased in 1866, and at Beypur in 1867. Similar attempts to introduce modern processes were also made in the Birbhum district of Bengal, and the Kumaon district of the United Provinces, but these too ended in failure.[1]

These early failures in the production of pig-iron led to the tardy recognition of the fact that to be successful an Iron Works must be situated as near as possible to the rich coal-fields of Bengal and Behar. We, therefore, find that the very first blast furnaces, the Barakar Iron Works, set up in the Ranigunge Coal-fields in 1875, ultimately became a commercial success. These also, however, had to pass through a long series of vicissitudes of fortune before their establishment as a paying proposition. Started in 1875, recurring losses led to their being closed down in 1879. The Government took the factory up again in 1881 and handed it over as a going concern to the Bengal Iron and Steel Company in 1889. It took another ten years to demonstrate the profitableness of the enterprise, and it was in 1899 that the shareholders were able to get their first dividends. In 1919 a new Company called the Bengal Iron Company was incorporated with a capital of £2·5 million, and this new Company enlarged and modernised the works. The present pig-iron capacity of this plant is approximately 200,000 tons.

The Discovery of the 'Iron Belt' and the opening up of a New Epoch for the Iron Industry in India

The prospecting operations conducted by the late Mr. J. N. Tata under the directions of Mr. C. M. Weld, a mining engineer from America, in 1903–5 led to the commercial recognition of the now famous Iron Belt of India,[2] which contains some of the richest iron ore deposits known to the modern world. As an expert of the Geological Survey of India writes: "This tract extends from the deposits of Gurumaishini in Mayurbhanj State westwards through the Keonjhar and Bonai areas to the subdivision of Kolhan in Singhbhum. Both

[1] *Records of the Geological Survey of India*, Vol. XXXIX, pp. 101–2.

[2] The actual discovery of the Iron Belt had been made by Mr. P. N. Bose, of the Geological Survey of India (then in the service of the Mayurbhanj State), and it was he who persuaded the Tatas to take it up for commercial exploitation.

in quality and quantity these ores are thought to exceed any other ores of the same kind, including the great American occurrences of Minnesota, Wisconsin and Michigan."[1] This iron ore range rises to heights of 2,000 to 3,000 feet above the sea-level, and runs almost continuously for 40 miles.

India becomes an Exporter of Pig-iron

The epoch-making discovery of the 'Iron Belt' in 1905 led to the formation of two more big companies in the next fifteen years for the manufacture of iron and steel on a large scale. These are the Tata Iron and Steel Company (1907) and the Indian Iron and Steel Company (1918). As a result of the operations of these firms, India has become in recent years the seat of a considerable Iron Industry, and also a large exporter of pig-iron. In the three years, 1927–28, 1928–29, and 1929–30, the output of pig-iron in India amounted to 1,162,000, 1,050,000 and 1,376,000 tons respectively, while the corresponding figures for the exports were 393,000, 449,000 and 569,000 tons. In the last year of the series, i.e. 1929–30, the shipments of Indian pig-iron were as follows: Japan 350,000 tons, U.S.A. 86,000 tons, the United Kingdom 71,300 tons, Germany 14,700 tons, Italy 11,800 tons, China 13,100 tons, and the Argentine Republic 8,000 tons.[2] It is, therefore, clear that the manufacture of pig-iron in India, regarded as a separate industry complete by itself, has reached a high state of efficiency and compares very favourably with the corresponding manufacture in the oldest and most successful iron-producing countries of the world.

3. THE BEGINNINGS OF STEEL PRODUCTION IN INDIA

The Army Department of the Government of India set up a metal and steel factory at Ishapore near Calcutta in 1892 and

[1] Report on the Mineral Resources of India for a Domestic Steel Industry, by Dr. C. S. Fox. (*Report of the Indian Tariff Board* regarding the grant of protection to the Steel Industry, 1924, pp. 91 et seq.)

[2] *Review of the Trade of India*, 1929–30, pp. 34, 115, 116.

has been since producing acid steel out of imported iron,[1] the present capacity of the factory being rated at 10,000 tons of bars a year. In 1898, the East Indian Railway (now a State Railway) established two 15-ton furnaces, both basic-lined, and three mills for rolling ingots into billets, bars and small structural sections. In this factory the charge consists mainly of the scraps produced in the workshops of the railway at different centres. The factory is situated at Jamalpur, and rolls 6,000 tons of steel and 300 tons of castings.

These two steel factories, however, it should be noted, are very special cases, firstly because they are not run on strictly commercial principles under competitive conditions, and secondly because they are not based upon the use of Indian pig-iron as their principal raw material. The earliest attempt to manufacture steel out of native pig-iron on a commercial scale was made by the Bengal Iron Company in 1905–6. This experiment, however, resulted in heavy losses, the causes of the failure being: (1) the low price of imported steel at that time; (2) the fact that the orders received were for small quantities of steel of numerous sections instead of being confined to large orders for a few sections; (3) the inferior quality for steel-making of the pig-iron then produced (the excellent ores of the Iron Belt being available only since 1910); and (4) the necessity then existing of imported fire-bricks and ferro-manganese.[2]

At this point there came upon the scene a great Indian, the late Mr. J. N. Tata, who combined in himself the instinct and vision of a born industrialist with that infinite capacity for taking pains on details that characterises a man of science. It appears that the idea of utilising on the largest possible scale the iron deposits of India had been simmering in the mind of Mr. Tata since the early eighties of the last century. In 1882,

[1] Indian pig-iron contains an excessive degree of phosphorus and so cannot be treated by the acid process.

[2] Article on "Metallurgical Industries of India," by Dr. L. Leigh Fermor of the Geological Survey of India, in the *Indian Munitions Board Handbook*, p. 139.

the perusal of a Government document called *Report on the Financial Prospects of Iron-working in the Chanda District*, and written by a German expert named Ritter von Schwarz, who was then and for many years afterwards under state employment for the investigation of the iron and coal deposits of India, started Mr. Tata on an active, laborious and prolonged enquiry regarding the commercial prospects of a large-scale Iron Industry in India. He found that there were at that time two serious barriers to the success of an Iron Industry in the country. In the first place, Schwarz's Report had failed to solve the problem of accessibility to good coking coal, for the iron ore of Chanda in the Central Provinces was several hundred miles distant from the coal-fields of Jharia and Ranigunge, where alone coking coal of the requisite quality could be procured. He had suggested the use of charcoal from the surrounding forests. Mr. Tata, however, was too practical a man to start a modern Iron Industry on the basis of charcoal that was confined to a radius of 20 miles and that could yield fuel for only 32,000 tons of pig-iron each year.[1] A second barrier was found in the old, antiquated, and in many ways stupid, mining regulations of the Government of India. Under those rules the issue of a prospecting licence could be made only to an individual, but not to companies or associations. Again, when the commercial possibilities of any mining area had been ascertained by the prospector, the Government could step in and put up the whole of the mining rights for sale by auction.[2] These rules, evidently, could hardly encourage large-scale prospecting operations such as are needed to lay the foundations of an Iron and Steel Industry in modern times.

The year 1899, however, proved a turning-point. Lord Curzon swept aside the old mining regulations and introduced liberal rules. Thus was removed a tremendous handicap in the way of prospecting operations. Secondly, in that year General R. H. Mahon, an artillery officer who had been superintendent

[1] *Life of J. N. Tata*, by F. R. Harris, pp. 158–60.
[2] *India under Curzon and After*, by Lovat Fraser.

of the Government Ordnance Factories at Cossipore, issued a memorable report on the manufacture of iron and steel in India. It was he who pointed out for the first time that the Jharia coal-field of Behar contained sufficient quantities of good coking coal for a large-scale Iron and Steel Industry in India. Furthermore, he insisted that Calcutta or its neighbourhood, in the vicinity of the coal areas and in command of large markets, would prove to be the most suitable centre for the industry. And lastly, he laid down three excellent rules for the guidance of the promoters of an Iron and Steel Industry in India. These rules were: first, the works must be thoroughly up to date in every respect; second, the management must combine expert knowledge and local experience; and third, utmost economy should be observed in the collection and assembling of raw materials.[1]

This Report gave Mr. Tata a more definite idea regarding the commercial prospects of an Iron and Steel Industry in India. During 1902 he undertook an extensive tour in the iron districts of Great Britain and U.S.A., consulted iron- and steel-masters and mining experts, and finally secured the services of a firm of consulting and mining engineers in America. At this stage Mr. Tata retired from business, but his successors took up the work where he left it. Throughout the next three years, with the help of American engineers, they carried on extensive prospecting operations from the Central Provinces eastwards through Chota Nagpur into the Mayurbhanj State, and as already noticed, finally came upon the famous 'Iron Belt' area of India. The discovery of this extensive area, rich in high-grade iron ore, immediately decided the Tatas on taking in hand the twenty-five-year-old project for the establishment of a large-scale Iron and Steel Industry in the country. In the spring and summer of 1906 they appealed for funds to the great finance houses in London, but the response of the London money-market was disappointing, and for the moment the project appeared to have fallen through. In the next summer

[1] *Life of J. N. Tata*, by F. R. Harris, pp. 158–59.

(1907), however, an unexpected situation arose in India. The Swadeshi movement was at its climax and all around was evidenced a desire for the encouragement of indigenous enterprises. A new prospectus was issued by the Tatas in August, 1907, and the entire capital required, £163,000, was subscribed within three weeks.[1]

Having thus obtained the capital, the Tatas now appointed Messrs. Julian Kennedy, Sahlin & Co., a well-known firm of Pittsburg in America, as construction engineers. The years 1908, 1909 and 1910 were taken up with the building up, out of a primitive jungle village, of a most up-to-date industrial city with broad and straight roads, water-works, electric lighting, residential houses and schools and clubs,[2] the assembling and erection of the necessary plant and machinery, and the collection of a large number of technicians and skilled steel-workers from Great Britain, Germany and America, and also a large labour force from all over India. By 1912, Jamshedpur became an extremely cosmopolitan place. The staff included, besides members of various Indian races, Englishmen, Americans, Germans, Austrians,[3] Italians, Swiss and Chinese. At the same time the necessary command over the raw materials was secured by the acquisition of extensive collieries, iron ores, and limestone and dolomite quarries.

4. STEEL PRODUCTION AT JAMSHEDPUR

Pig-iron was first produced in December, 1911, and steel in 1913. In the second year of production, July, 1913, to June, 1914, the output of pig-iron was 155,383 tons, and of finished steel 48,872 tons. We have no definite information regarding the comparative costs and the commercial success or failure of the

[1] *Life of J. N. Tata*, by F. R. Harris, pp. 184–203.

[2] It would be interesting to note that the city planning and welfare committee appointed by the Tatas for laying down a programme of development on scientific lines included Mr. and Mrs. Sidney Webb, and Professors Hobhouse and Urwick of the University of London.

[3] During the war, however, Germans and Austrians were eliminated, and at present the superior technical staff includes only Englishmen and Americans besides a certain number of Indians.

steel produced by the firm before the war. Substantial dividends were earned for the shareholders for the first time in 1913–14 and 1914–15. During these two years the sale of pig-iron by the Tata Iron and Steel Company amounted to 106,795 tons and 97,698 tons respectively.[1] And as pig-iron had been from the very beginning a great commercial success, it is reasonable to presume that all the profit was earned only on pig-iron.[2] On the other hand, since most of the comparative disadvantages of steel-production in India, e.g. the necessity of importing expensive technical and skilled labour from abroad, the lack of experience of steel-making under Indian conditions, and the extreme temperature of the summer months, which have been given as reasons for the present inability to compete on equal terms with foreign steel, existed also in the pre-war years, it may be taken for granted that steel was a source of great loss to the Company in the initial years of trials and experiments. Accordingly, so far as steel production was concerned, the Company must have foreseen the inevitable losses of this early period and must have been ready to follow one of the only two alternative courses that lay before them. On the one hand, it was open to them to experiment with steel for a few years, and then give it up as a commercial failure and concentrate instead on the highly profitable pig-iron. On the other hand, if they had decided to carry on the production of steel till its final commercial success after fifteen or twenty years, they would have to be prepared to enlarge their resources very considerably so as to meet the unavoidable initial loss on the manufacture of steel. For, at the time when they commenced the manufacture of steel, there was not the least hint or offer of the grant of public assistance of any kind, either tariff or bounty, and therefore there is no reason to suppose that the promoters of the project, having presumably foreseen the certain losses

[1] Report of the Tariff Board regarding the grant of protection to the Steel Industry (1924), *Minutes of Evidence*, Vol. I, pp. 29, 69.

[2] It may be noted that even in the recent years of acute depression, pig-iron has been a source of profit to the Tata Iron and Steel Company.

of the initial years, were not prepared to meet them out of their own resources, but descending to the level of pure gamblers, merely banked upon the possibility of relief at the expense of the public.[1] It seems that this point needs to be sufficiently emphasised, because the position of the Tata Iron and Steel Company *vis-à-vis* the grant of public assistance remained exactly the same in 1922–24 when the campaign for protection was initiated, as it had been in 1913–14 when it had been the traditional policy in India to let private enterprise look after itself and not be encouraged to become a burden upon the none too plentiful public revenues of the country. And yet this important fact was either wholly ignored or utterly forgotten in all the public discussions that preceded the grant of protection to the Steel Industry in June, 1924. But before we proceed any further with our examination of the case for protection, we must acquaint ourselves with the course of development of the Steel Industry in India from 1914 onwards.

5. THE EFFECT OF THE WAR; HIGH PRICES AND BIG PROFITS; THE EXTENSION PROJECT; HEAVY BURDEN OF FIXED CHARGES; THE SEED OF FINANCIAL WEAKNESS

It has been again and again stated by the representatives of the Tata Iron and Steel Company as well as by the spokesman of the Government of India that the manufacture of steel at Jamshedpur was of great assistance to the Government in the supply of steel requirements for the prosecution of the war in Palestine, Mesopotamia, East Africa and Salonica. Thus, for instance, it is pointed out that during the war the Company supplied to the Government of India 290,000 tons of steel rails at an average base price of Rs. 150 a ton at a time when the supply from Europe was almost entirely cut off and the importation of steel rails from America would have cost at least Rs. 200

[1] The policy of protective tariff as a method of industrial development was adopted in India in 1923. The only help that the Government of India offered at the inception of the project was the promise to buy 20,000 tons of steel rails annually for ten years at import prices.

a ton more in price and freight and also involved inordinate and dangerous delays. It is, therefore, claimed that there was thus a saving of no less than Rs. 600 lakhs to the Government. It is also contended that "the strategic advantage of basing the campaigns in Mesopotamia and East Africa on steel supplied by India far outweighed any money-saving, and could not be estimated in terms of money."[1] As we shall see later on, this fact that the steel works at Jamshedpur were very serviceable to the Government of India during the war has been urged as a special ground for the grant of public assistance for the steel producer in recent years.

But we may well ask ourselves the question, what would have happened to the steel manufacturer of India had not the war come as a great boon to him in the most critical years of early experiments and initial losses? Had it not been for the almost complete and highly profitable monopoly of the home market during the war, it is very much to be doubted whether the Steel Industry would have survived till 1924, when it asked for and obtained public assistance in the form of protective tariff as well as bounty. However, as it happened, the war came as a manifold blessing to the infant Steel Industry of India. The infant had the extraordinary good luck to secure all the advantages and privileges of an adult almost at once. Under the stimulus of enlarged demand and high prices, production was speeded up, and the output of rolled steel rose from 48,872 tons in 1913–14 to 123,890 tons in 1917–18,[2] and this was the maximum capacity of the open hearth furnaces then in existence at Jamshedpur. Under the same stimulus, the output of pig-iron was also greatly increased. In consequence, the years 1915–16 to 1920–21 proved to be a period of large profits and satisfactory dividends. The extent of improvement in the financial position of the Company will be apparent in the following table:

[1] Report of the Tariff Board regarding the grant of protection to the Steel Industry (1924), *Minutes of Evidence*, Vol. I, p. 17. [2] Ibid., p. 69.

TABLE XIV

FINANCIAL POSITION OF THE TATA IRON AND STEEL COMPANY

1912–13 TO 1921–22*

1 Year	2 Capital Paid-up (000 omitted) Rs.	3 Gross Profits, Including Depreciation (000 omitted) Rs.	4 Depreciation (000 omitted) Rs.	5 Percentage of Dividend on Ordinary Shares	6 Percentage of Dividend on Deferred Shares
1912–13	231,75	8,59	2,00	nil	nil
1913–14	231,75	22,64	3,50	6	—
1914–15	231,75	24,83	5,00	8	25
1915–16	231,75	68,30	10,70	15	180½
1916–17	231,75	110,77	35,00	20	291
1917–18	256,81	105,70	47,81	20	291
1918–19	350,55	67,18	24,90	7	—
1919–20	398,05	115,31	61,45	16	202¾
1920–21	631,80	116,95	64,52	16	202¾
1921–22	946,80	88,37	41,00	4	—

* Report of the Tariff Board regarding the grant of protection to the Steel Industry (1924), *Minutes of Evidence*, Vol. I, pp. 26, 29, 222.

It will be seen from the table that as a result of the favourable conditions created by the war and the post-war boom, the Tata Iron and Steel Company were able to earn large sums by way of gross profits out of which, after laying aside reasonable amounts to depreciation account, they were able to distribute satisfactory dividends on the ordinary shares and very high ones on the deferred shares. Thus, while on the one hand the spectacular dividends paid on the deferred shares acted as strong inducement to the public to invest in the shares of the Tata Iron and Steel Company, on the other hand the highly profitable opportunity brought about by the war and realised in the shape of gratifying balance sheets for successive years led the Company to take in hand the project of considerably enlarging and extending the iron and steel works at Jamshedpur.

It appears that the proposal for the extension of the works was first mooted early in 1915 at the instance of their consulting engineer. Examination of the scheme in its various aspects took about three years. The available evidence on the subject shows that the project was originally taken in hand owing to the exceptionally favourable prospects of manufacturing steel at a profit, and not at the suggestion of the Government of India. But as the war advanced and India became the base of operations in East Africa, Palestine and Mesopotamia, the military and civil authorities in India naturally became interested in the extension scheme. On the other hand, owing to the difficulty of securing freight space for the importation of tools and machinery from overseas, the Company also had to seek the advice and help of the munitions departments in England and India for obtaining the necessary shipping facilities from the Government of the U.S.A., where the orders for the plant and machinery had to be placed. Furthermore, on account of the restriction then in force in India on the raising of capital by private individuals or Companies, they also obtained the special sanction of the Government of India for raising the necessary capital. From these instances of indirect help given to the

Company, we are likely to get an impression that the Government of India committed themselves to extend financial assistance to the Company in case of need in the future. The correspondence on the subject, however, clearly shows that, although the Government of India considered some parts of the project as calculated to help in the prosecution of the war, and, therefore, gave the Company the necessary facilities in many directions, their attitude throughout the entire period of discussion and consultation was one of simple approval and moral support, and did not in any way amount to a promise of financial assistance in any shape or form. On the contrary, we find that from beginning to end the Government of India deliberately and systematically refused to undertake any financial obligations at the expense of the public revenues in support or furtherance of the particular project.[1]

The original capital of the Company was Rs. 232 lakhs. In 1917, it was raised to Rs. 352 lakhs. Towards the close of 1918, again, a new issue of Rs. 700 lakhs was placed upon the market, and the total share capital was thus raised to the high figure of over Rs. 1,050 lakhs. At the same time, to ensure a regular market for the various kinds of rolled steel proposed to be manufactured at their works, they established a number of subsidiary companies at Jamshedpur and also entered into sale contracts with the Railway Companies as well as with the more important engineering firms.

Now, although the orders for the necessary tools, plant and machinery were placed in America in 1917 and 1918, due to the shortage of freight space, only small quantities were actually delivered during the war. Even after the cessation of hostilities, the American firms, caught in the short post-war boom, made unusual delays with the deliveries, with the result that the complete installation of the necessary plant and machinery took the abnormally long period of six years, 1918–24. This

[1] Cf. statements (*b*) to (*m*) submitted by the Tata Iron and Steel Company to the Tariff Board (1924) regarding the Greater Extensions, *Minutes of Evidence*, Vol. I, pp. 79–97.

inordinate interval between the initiation and the completion of the project proved to be a source of great financial weakness and embarrassment to the Tata Iron and Steel Company. For, on the one hand, the purchase and importation of large plant and extensive machinery at a time of high prices and costly freights resulted in burdening the industry with permanently high overhead charges by way of interest and depreciation on capital,[1] and thus undermined its competitive power from the outset. On the other hand, the post-war depression having set in in India in 1921–22, the difficult years of initial trials and experiments coincided with a period of severe external competition. In consequence, the Company found itself in the unenviable and dangerous position of being faced with an acute financial crisis at the very commencement of the new undertaking. As we shall see later on, it was at this stage that the Tata Iron and Steel Company succeeded in evoking the special sympathy of the Fiscal Commission and securing the recommendation of the Tariff Board for protective support.

6. QUANTITY OF OUTPUT AND VARIETY OF PRODUCTS

The extension scheme of 1917–24 included new blast furnaces, steel furnaces and rolling mills. As a result of these changes, the output capacity for finished steel increased from 126,000 tons to 420,000 tons. By 1926–27 it was found that the new plant was ill-balanced in certain respects. The capacities of the coke ovens and the steel furnaces proved too small, while those of the blast furnaces and the rolling-mills turned out to be too large. In that year, therefore, a further extension was decided upon at a cost of Rs. 270 lakhs, and it is estimated that the proposed additions to the plant due to be completed by 1931–32 will increase the capacity of the plant to 600,000 tons

[1] The share capital of the company is Rs. 1,050 lakhs. Of this, Rs. 775 lakhs consists of first and second preference shares with cumulative fixed dividends, and only Rs. 275 lakhs of ordinary and deferred shares. Besides, the Company is also burdened with a heavy debenture loan, which was just over Rs. 300 lakhs in 1929–30.

of finished steel.[1] The highest output so far reached is 428,654 tons (1927–28). The finished products consist of rails and fishplates, bars and structural sections, plates and sheets, tin-bars and sleepers. Although the proportions of the different kinds of products vary to a certain extent from year to year, it appears that on an average of years, 40 per cent of the total output of finished steel would be rails and fishplates, 32 per cent structurals and bars, 15 per cent plates and sheets, 10 per cent tinbars, and 3 per cent sleepers.[2] So far as tinbars are concerned, the Company has entered into a long-period contract with a subsidiary company, namely, the Tinplate Company of India, for the sale of practically the entire output. Out of the remaining 90 per cent, 43 per cent can be sold only to the state and company railways, 32 per cent to the engineering firms and 15 per cent to miscellaneous industries and general consumers.

7. DIFFERENT BRANCHES OF THE STEEL INDUSTRY IN INDIA

When the impurities in the pig-iron have been removed in the open hearth or tilting furnaces, the product is steel ingot. It is the usual practice in modern times that the conversion of pig-iron into steel ingots and the rolling of the ingots into convenient shapes and sizes are carried on in the same works. Thus, as we have already seen, in India the manufacture of steel ingots and the rolling of the ingots into rails and fishplates, bars and structurals, etc., are carried on as associated processes in the same works. For the purpose of convenience, we would use the term 'Steel Industry' to consist of the processes indicated above.

It would be observed that the 'Steel Industry' as defined above is not altogether a self-contained industry by itself. While some of the products of the rolling mills, such as rails and fishplates, sleepers and galvanised sheets, are ready for their

[1] Vide the Representation submitted to the Indian Tariff Board by the Tata Iron and Steel Company Ltd., Statutory Enquiry (1926). *Minutes of Evidence*, Vol. II, pp. 29–34.

[2] *Report of the Tariff Board*, Statutory Enquiry (1926), Vol. I, p. 39.

respective final uses, others among them, e.g. structurals and plates, have often to be subjected to further processes of alteration through fabrication, bending, machining, drilling, etc., so as to be suitable for building houses and bridges, wagons and carriage-underframes, and ships and launches, and manufacturing machinery and boilers, etc. All these operations are carried on in large workshops separate from the general steel works and may be regarded as constituting what is called the Engineering Industry.[1] Although all these processes may be and sometimes are carried on in the same workshops, large and continuous demand may necessitate some special branches of the Engineering Industry being organised separately on a comparatively large scale. Under such circumstances it is usual to call these special branches by distinctive names, e.g. the Ship-building Industry. In India in the past, due to the lack of sufficiently large and continuous demand for any of the special products of the Engineering Industry, there was an absence of specialisation. In recent years, however, on account of the initiation of the policy of state encouragement of native manufactures, one branch of the Engineering Industry has attained a sufficient degree of specialisation and importance to deserve being placed in a separate class by itself. This is the Wagon-building Industry.

Thirdly, again, we have in India a small number of subsidiary industries that use some types of rolled steel as their principal raw material. Among these may be mentioned the Tinplate Industry and the Wire and Wire-nail Industry.

[1] This is only a convenient, though perhaps somewhat arbitrary, description, and not in any way a precise definition. In the above description the writer has closely followed the Indian Tariff Board.

CHAPTER V

FACTORS AFFECTING THE COMPETITIVE EFFICIENCY OF THE STEEL INDUSTRY IN INDIA

I. GENERAL

The Indian Fiscal Commission in their Report issued in September, 1922, recommended a policy of discriminating protection and suggested that the Steel Industry should be the first case to be referred to the Tariff Board for investigating the suitability of that industry for protection. The Government of India, in accepting that policy, constituted the Tariff Board in July, 1923, and directed that body to examine the question of extending protection to the manufacture of steel. As a result of the findings of that Board, the Steel Industry (Protection) Act was passed in June, 1924. The scheme of protection adopted under that Act embraced the Steel Industry (rolled steel), the Engineering Industry, the Wagon-building Industry, the Tinplate Industry and the Wire and Wire-nail Industry. While the protection granted to the last-named industry was withdrawn in 1928,[1] all the other four branches of the Steel Industry are still under protection. Here it will be sufficient for us to note that the central object of steel protection in India has been the development of the manufacture of rolled steel, and that the extension of protection to the other branches of the Steel Industry has been mainly in furtherance of that primary object. Before entering upon an investigation of the principles and methods of protection as applied to the case of the Steel Industry, therefore, it is necessary for us to examine the factors that affect the competitive efficiency of the manufacture of rolled steel in India. These factors fall conveniently under four heads: (A) Raw Materials, (B) Power, (C) Market, and (D) Labour.

[1] It has once again come under protection for the period March, 1932, to March, 1934.

2. RAW MATERIALS: IRON ORE; FLUXES; REFRACTORY MATERIALS

(1) IRON ORE

There are four different kinds of iron ore in India—magnetite, laterite, clay iron-stone, and hematite. Magnetite deposits estimated in thousands of millions of tons exist in the Salem district of Madras, but they are not at present worked to any large extent owing to the great difficulty of securing fuel at a reasonable cost. Laterite ores also exist in enormous quantities, but they are low-grade and therefore not utilised under present circumstances. Clay iron-stone is generally found among the coal-bearing strata of the Indian coal-fields. The Bengal Iron and Steel Company had used this ore, which contains 46 per cent Fe. (iron), from 1889 to 1910, when they discontinued its use and began to draw upon the hematite deposits of Singhbhum. This clay iron ore also occurs in the coal-fields of Upper Assam and Auranga in Behar and Orissa, but this ore is not likely to be used so long as the better hematite deposits are available. The most important hematite deposits are those of Singhbhum and Orissa in what is known as the Iron Belt. As we have already noted in the previous chapter, the discovery of the iron ore deposits in the Iron Belt in the year 1910 is regarded as an epoch-making event in the history of the Indian Iron and Steel Industry.[1] According to an estimate made by Dr. C. S. Fox of the Geological Survey of India, the deposits in this belt hold reserves amounting to 2,830 million tons, while the ore contains 60 to 68 per cent Fe. (iron), 0·08 per cent phosphorus, and 0·06 per cent sulphur. His conclusions with regard to the adequacy of the iron ores for an Indian Iron and Steel Industry are that the deposits of the Iron Belt exceed any other ores of the same kind, including the great American occurrences of Minnesota, Wisconsin and Michigan, and that they alone will be sufficient to satisfy the requirements

[1] Vide *Indian Munitions Board Handbook*, p. 140.

of the Indian iron-masters for one thousand years at the rate of 1½ million tons of pig-iron annually.

Besides the reserves in the Iron Belt, there occur several other important hematite deposits of good quality, though these are not at present utilised to any large extent due to the difficulty of obtaining fuel at a reasonable cost. The Lohara deposits of Central Provinces contain at least 100 million tons of reserves with a composition of 61 to 67 per cent Fe., the Rajara hills of Central Provinces 10 million tons with a composition of 66 per cent Fe., while the Bababudan hills of Mysore contain 25 to 60 million tons with a composition of 42 to 64·5 per cent Fe., and the Ramgarh and Dechauri deposits of Kumaon an unknown quantity with a composition of 39 to 60 per cent Fe. Taking all these areas together, we may put the hematite reserves of India approximately at some 3,000 million tons.[1]

Again, in so far as the iron content of the ore is concerned, it appears that the Indian ore compares favourably with that used in the great iron- and steel-producing countries of the world. Thus, while the percentage of iron content in the Indian hematite ores may be taken to be 55 to 70, that of British ores is 30 to 35, French ores 40, Belgian ores 35, German ores 40, U.S.A. ores 50 to 60, Swedish ores 60 to 70, and Spanish ores 50 to 60.[2]

On the other hand, we have to observe that there is at least one important respect where the composition of the Indian iron ore tends to the disadvantage of the iron and steel manufacturers of the country. While, due to the low percentage of lime in the composition of the Indian ore, large quantities of limestones have to be used as flux in the blast furnaces, some of the ores in Great Britain as well as on the Continent contain a large percentage of lime, and are therefore self-fluxing.

[1] Dr. C. S. Fox's Report on the Mineral Resources of India for a Domestic Steel Industry (vide *Report of the Tariff Board* regarding the grant of protection to the Steel Industry (1924), pp. 89–94.

[2] *The Engineering and Mining Journal* (New York), July 17, 1926, quoted by the Balfour Committee on Industry and Trade, *Survey of Metal Industries*, p. 124.

Besides these questions of quantity and quality, there are other factors such as depth of ores, facilities for economical transport, and efficiency of mining labourers, which count for a good deal in determining the comparative advantage of the ores as of other things. Judging, however, from the fact that India has been now for some years exporting considerable quantities of pig-iron to such distant markets as the West Coast of America, the Argentine Republic, Japan, the United Kingdom, Germany and Italy, we may infer that the Indian pig-iron manufacturer on the whole enjoys some advantage in respect of his iron ore.

(2) FLUXES

(a) *Limestones and Dolomites*

In order to remove the impurities in the iron ore so as to produce pig-iron, basic fluxes are required, and of these, limestones and dolomites are commonly used. The limestone should be as pure as possible and uniform in quality. Although the quantity of limestone to be used as flux is comparatively small, the existing iron and steel works of India can secure a supply of good quality limestone only from an inconveniently great distance. Thus, for instance, the Tata Iron and Steel Company obtain their limestone from Katni, a distance of nearly 500 miles from the steel works at Jamshedpur. This firm owns some limestone quarries in Panposh (Gangpur) which, though considerably nearer the works site, are not so good in quality.[1] Dr. C. S. Fox is of opinion that the best quality of limestone would be those obtainable from Assam which, however, owing to the high cost of freight, are placed beyond the reach of the existing ironworks. There is an occurrence on the eastern edge of the Auranga coal-field, which requires further examination before being established as an economical source of supply. There are also several occurrences in the Central Provinces, which are fairly good in quality, but which

[1] Vide Oral Evidence of Mr. T. W. Tutwiler (the General Manager, Tata Iron and Steel Company), during the Tariff Board's Enquiry regarding the grant of protection to the Steel Industry (1924), *Minutes of Evidence*, Vol. I, p. 278.

must still be regarded as an uncertain quantity.[1] It would, therefore, appear that, although sufficient quantities of limestones exist in different parts of India, the comparatively richer sources of supply are at a considerable distance from the existing iron and steel works of the country.

When true limestones of high quality are not obtainable, the ironworks often use dolomite limestones. These do not produce so fusible a slag and therefore require a somewhat higher temperature in the furnace. Although sufficient supplies of dolomite limestones are obtainable within a reasonable distance of the present iron and steel works, in quality they are held to be distinctly inferior to those available in foreign countries. The result is that there is a comparatively larger volume of slag, which means unnecessary strain on the furnace and a greater consumption of coke owing to the greater length of time each heat has to be run.

(*b*) *Fluorspar*

A third fluxing material used in Indian steel-making is fluorspar which increases the fluidity of the charge. The Tata Iron and Steel Company use some 400 tons of fluorspar in their furnaces. Although several deposits of this material have been known, none has been found so far which may be regarded as economically workable. There is an occurrence at Barla in Kishengarh State (Rajputana) which was sought to be worked by the Tata Iron and Steel Company, but the quantity proved unattractive and the cost unremunerative. So the attempt was a short-lived one, and the Indian iron and steel manufacturers at present obtain their supplies from abroad.[2]

(*c*) *Modifying Metals*

In order to produce the necessary mechanical properties in the finished steel, modifying metals are added to the steel in the form of alloys, those chiefly used in India being manga-

[1] Dr. Fox's Report, op. cit. [2] Ibid.

nese ores and silicon. India is one of the largest manganese-producing areas in the world. In 1926, the total output for the whole of India was just over a million tons and the figure for exports was 613,535 tons. The consumption of manganese ore at the works of the three principal iron and steel companies of India in the same year was only 40,000 tons, or 4 per cent of the total output.[1]

There is also plenty of quarts rocks at Kumardhubi and other places from which ferro-silicon of the necessary composition may be obtained in any quantity.[2]

(3) REFRACTORY MATERIALS

The open hearth furnace is built of fire-bricks and silica bricks, while for the basic lining of the furnace magnesite and dolomite are used.

(*a*) *Fireclay*

There are beds of fireclay throughout the country. But in the absence of any comprehensive survey, no definite ideas as to the quantities and qualities of various fireclays can be formed. Fireclay suitable for the manufacture of fire-bricks is found around the coal seams in the Gondwana area, and good fire-bricks are now manufactured in the Bengal coal-fields by Messrs. Burn and Company, the Kumardhubi Fireclay and Silica Works, and the Reliance Fireclay and Pottery Company, and at Jubbulpore by the Perfect Pottery Company.[3] Although considerable quantities of fire-bricks are now manufactured in India, it appears that the iron smelters and steel manufacturers of India still show a distinct preference for well-known brands of British fire-bricks, the annual import of fire-bricks during the five years, 1925–26 to 1929–30, ranging between 1½ and 2 millions.[4]

[1] *Records of the Geological Survey of India*, Vol. LX, p. 223.
[2] Dr. Fox's Report, op. cit.
[3] *Indian Munitions Board Handbook*, p. 132.
[4] *Annual Statement of the Sea-borne Trade of British India*, 1929–30, Vol. I, p. 30.

(*b*) *Silica Bricks*

Siliceous materials (sand, sandstone, quartzite and quartz) are used for the manufacture of silica bricks and for lining furnace bottoms. Silica bricks are now being manufactured in continually increasing numbers by Messrs. Burn and Company and by the Kumardhubi Fireclay and Silica Works. The various raw materials of good quality for the manufacture of silica bricks occur in abundant quantities in almost every province of India, and there is no reason to apprehend any shortage in the future.

In point of quality, however, it appears that the Indian silica bricks are distinctly inferior to those used in America, Germany and England. The Indian steel manufacturer, therefore, gets much less life out of his furnace than his foreign competitor. Thus, we are told that while the furnaces in foreign countries run about 200 heats on an average, the Indian furnaces last only 125 heats. This shorter duration of the Indian furnace is due partly to the inferior quality of the bricks used in the building of the furnaces and partly to the heavier volume of the slags. This difference in the number of heats that can be run by different furnaces means a corresponding difference in the number of stoppages and repairs. Moreover, owing to the poor quality of the refractories, holes occur constantly on the banks of the furnace bottoms, and in order to facilitate the removal of the steel worked out from the holes several hours have to be wasted by the stoppage of heat. And lastly, it also necessitates a dozen men standing only six feet away from the furnace door and working the metal out by using long rabbles. To stand in close proximity to the furnace for using the rabbles for several hours at a time is a severe strain upon the men working there, specially in the hot weather.[1] All these difficulties arising from the inferiority of the refractory

[1] Vide Oral Evidence of Mr. T. W. Tutwiler, Report of the Tariff Board on the grant of protection to the Steel Industry (1924), *Minutes of Evidence*, Vol. I, pp. 408, 413, 415, 418 and 422.

material used in India are undoubtedly contributory causes of the higher cost of the manufacture of steel in the country, and this disadvantage can only be eliminated by a gradual process of improvement in the quality of the bricks produced.

3. POWER: COKING COAL—SERIOUS LIMITATIONS IN QUANTITY AND QUALITY

The estimated reserves of coal of all grades in India are approximately 54,000 million tons. The output in 1929–30 was about 23½ million tons. The exports in that year amounted to 1,618,000 tons, out of which 933,000 tons were bunker coal.[1] These figures would indicate that the Indian iron and steel producers can rely upon a sufficient supply of many ordinary grades of coal as a source of power. But when we turn to examine the question of the available supply of good quality coking coal for the blast furnaces, we find that the outlook is somewhat serious. The existing data on the subject tend to show that the supply of coking coal is likely to fall far short of the supply of high-grade hematite and other iron ores in India.

The Indian Industrial Commission of 1916–18 summarised the coal position as follows: "For metallurgical purposes the supplies of suitable coal are greatly restricted. The Tertiary coal of north-east Assam produces an excellent coke, but its situation naturally limits its use; there are also similar coals in some of the smaller Assam fields, like Daranggiri, which are not yet served by railways; but the only large supply of good coking coal so far established, and within an area suitable for industrial development on modern lines, is that of the Gondwana fields of Bengal and Behar. Even in these Gondwana coking coals, the high percentage of ash and the correspondingly low calorific value reduce their radius of economic use under conditions of railway transport, and it will be still further diminished, as the shallow seams are exhausted and the deeper coal is worked at higher cost."[2]

[1] *Review of the Trade of India*, 1929–30, p. 120.
[2] *Report of the Indian Industrial Commission*, p. 58.

Dr. C. S. Fox of the Geological Survey of India, after a careful study of the records available on the subject, has given us a fairly trustworthy estimate of the reserves of coking coal in the country. According to this estimate, the coal-fields of Bengal, Behar and Orissa, and Assam contain coal reserves amounting to 54,000 million tons. Of this huge total, however, only a small fraction, less than 5 per cent, is suitable for conversion into good quality coke. The Bengal, Behar and Orissa coal-fields which make up what is known as the Gondwana region contain only 2,180 million tons of coking coal, while the upper Assam coal-fields contain another 220 million tons, the two areas together giving a total of 2,400 million tons.[1] On the other hand, as we have already noticed, the known reserves of hematite in the Iron Belt of Singhbhum and Orissa alone are estimated at 2,830 million tons, and to smelt this into pig-iron India will require a minimum supply of good quality coking coal amounting to 3,000 million tons. We must, therefore, accept the finding of the Industrial Commission that the quantity of suitable fuel for an extensive Iron and Steel Industry in India is strictly limited.

In point of quality, again, the Indian coking coal seems to be distinctly inferior to the British coal. It is characteristically high in phosphorus and moderately high in ash. The phosphorus from the coal finds its way into the pig-iron, and this necessitates the use of the comparatively more expensive basic process for the conversion of the pig-iron into steel. Further, due to the high ash content of Indian coal, the percentage of tar obtained is lower than that in foreign countries. The coal tar, itself a marketable product, gives rise to many valuable chemicals such as disinfectants and dyes. The high percentage of these by-products confers a distinct advantage on the foreign manufacturers as compared to the Indian iron and steel producers. And lastly, on account of the high phosphorus percentage in the coking coal, the ferro-manganese obtained from the Indian blast furnaces contains more than 0·3 per cent of phosphorus—the limit fixed by the European makers.[2]

[1] Dr. Fox's Report, op. cit.

[2] Ibid.

The capacity of the existing blast furnaces in India is approximately 1½ million tons of pig-iron, while that of the only steel works in the country is 600,000 tons of rolled steel. The quantity of coking coal required for these furnaces may be approximately placed at 3½ million tons. So long, therefore, as the output of iron and steel in India remains at or near the present level, there can be no difficulty with regard to the supply of the necessary coking coal for many centuries. Even if the present output of both pig-iron and steel be doubled, which is all that is likely to take place in the near future, the supply of coking coal will be adequate. On the other hand, should there be an unexpected development of steel consumption and steel production in the next thirty or forty years so as to raise the steel output of India to anything like that of the United Kingdom or Germany or U.S.A.,[1] the problem of an adequate supply of coking coal would at once become serious. Thus, if the output were to increase to the size of that of the United Kingdom, the known coking coal reserves of India would last only 130 years, provided all the coking coal were used only for the blast and steel furnaces. Again, if it should rise as high as that of the U.S.A., the proved coking coal reserves of India would be entirely used up in less than thirty years.

We, therefore, find that, although the supply of coking coal in India will undoubtedly be adequate to the needs of an Iron and Steel Industry of a moderate size, it will be utterly insufficient for the requirements of a gigantic Steel Industry of the same size as exists in the United Kingdom, Germany and the U.S.A. Evidently it is of the utmost importance that India should exercise the most rigid economy in the use of her coking coal by adopting the most up-to-date technological improvements in the matter of fuel economy such as have been effected in some of the Continental iron and steel works, specially in those of Germany.

[1] The steel ingot capacity of these three countries has been estimated at 12, 13 and 53 million tons respectively (vide Report of the Balfour Committee on Industry and Trade, *Survey of Metal Industries*, pp. 18, 88, 89).

4. MARKET: AN ESTIMATE OF THE CONSUMPTION OF STEEL IN INDIA

Modern experience shows that, due to the technological conditions of steel production, a steel works, to be commercially successful, must be set up on a large scale or not at all. According to the Balfour Committee on Industry and Trade, the economical size for a steel plant in Great Britain would be a capacity of 300,000 tons of finished steel.[1] On the Continent of Europe and in U.S.A., however, where standardized production is the dominant note in steel as in many other branches of industry, the size of steel plants is much larger. In so far as India is concerned, experience in steel production is so short and limited that we cannot fix with any degree of confidence the minimum size for an economical plant. The Tata Iron and Steel Company started in 1911–12 with a plant capable of producing only 126,000 tons, but by 1916–17 it became clear that the plant was too small to be commercially successful. Accordingly, they extended the plant to a capacity of 400,000 tons. In 1923, the Tariff Board, on the evidence of the representatives of steel trades, stated that a plant with a capacity of 400,000 tons would be economical. By 1927, however, the Tata Iron and Steel Company found that their new plant was ill-balanced in many directions, and that to restore the necessary balance between the coke ovens, the blast furnaces, the steel furnaces, and the rolling mills, the capacity of the plant would have to be raised to 600,000 tons. The available evidence so far, therefore, suggests that under Indian conditions a steel plant, to be economically successful, must have a capacity of between 400,000 and 600,000 tons. Perhaps we would not be far wide of the mark if we were to put the size at 500,000 tons.

Now, in order that the establishment and growth of an industry under new environment may be facilitated, it is advantageous, if not essential, to have a sufficiently large

[1] Report of the Balfour Committee on Industry and Trade, *Survey of Metal Industries*, p. 8.

home market. It is also important that the home market should be extensive enough to afford scope for the establishment of a large number of independent plants of the minimum size so as to ensure competition and promote efficiency. We have, therefore, to enquire what is the capacity of India in the matter of steel consumption.

Imports

The articles of imports into whose costs and composition steel enters as a principal material are classified in the latest foreign trade statistics of India (1929–30) into four groups:

I. Iron and steel and manufactures thereof.
II. Cutlery, hardware, implements and instruments.
III. Machinery of all kinds.
IV. Vehicles excluding locomotives and tractors for railways.

For classes II, III and IV, the trade statistics record only values, and not quantities. It is, however, evident that the type of steel used in these three classes is often of a special quality. It should also be noted that the cost of steel forms only a very small part of the total cost for the great majority of articles enumerated in these groups. In estimating the quantity of imports of ordinary steel, therefore, these three classes should be excluded.

For articles under class I, however, the quantitative measurements (weights) are given. This class includes (*a*) steel, (*b*) iron or steel, (*c*) railway materials such as rails, fishplates, chairs, bridge-work and steel sleepers. The imports of these materials in the five years, 1925–26 to 1929–30, averaged 1,105,693 tons. In this class are included many articles made out of cast or wrought iron as well as of special steel such as high-speed steel, spring steel, etc. The trade statistics do not indicate the exact material of composition, and so we cannot find out the exact quantitative figure for the importation of ordinary steel as a separate item. Nevertheless, we may perhaps assume, as a guesswork, that about 10 per cent of the quantity shown under the group 'iron or steel manufacture' would consist of cast and wrought iron as well as of special steel. Eliminating this, therefore, we may put the quantity of steel imports into India during the period in question at approximately 1,000,000 tons.

To this must be added the figure for the output of indigenous steel. The average annual quantity of finished steel produced by the Tata Iron and Steel Company in the five years, 1925–26 to 1929–30, was 360,000 tons. Actual figures for the output of steel at the Government Ordnance Factory at Cossipur and the small East Indian Railway Factory at Jamalpore are not available. Their combined capacity is 16,000 tons, and we may take their output in the period at 15,000 tons. The total production of steel in India, then, may be put at 375,000 tons.

Adding up, we arrive at a figure between 1¼ and 1½ million tons for the consumption of steel in India. On the assumption that an output capacity of 500,000 tons is the minimum size for an economical steel plant in India, we may, therefore, state that so far as the present standard of steel consumption in India is concerned, there is room in the country only for two or three plants of an economical size. It is, therefore, clear that the extent of the home market in India is not so wide as to offer scope for the establishment of a sufficiently large number of independent plants so that competition may be stimulated and efficiency promoted. On the contrary, as long as the domestic market remains as small as it is, there can be only two or three producing units in the country; and it will be a comparatively easy and simple matter for them to enter into monopolistic agreements of some kind or other so as to exploit the full possibilities of the tariff by raising the price for the consumers. This is a danger which has been abundantly illustrated in European and American experience and will need to be fully guarded against in India.

5. LABOUR; TECHNICAL ABILITY AND SUPERVISION; CLIMATIC HANDICAP

(a) *Ordinary Skilled and Unskilled Labour* [1]

There hardly exists in India any class of labour which might be called purely industrial in the modern sense of the term. Most of the workers who drift into industrial life are drawn from off the land, and generally speaking, they represent the lowest strata of agricultural population. The majority of these workers alternately work on the field or in the factory according as there is busy or slack season in agriculture. It may, therefore, be stated that the Indian industrial worker is an agriculturist by heredity and preference, and a factory operative only by the compulsion of pecuniary embarrassment. Hence we find that the supply of industrial labour in the country is unsteady and intermittent and shows alternate periods of superabundance and scarcity. Another characteristic of the Indian labourer is his ignorance, his conservatism, his lack of ambition, and his easy contentment with a low standard of comfort. Hence arises one of the paradoxes of Indian economics that, contrary to the general experience of modern industrial countries, in India an increase in wages is followed by a decline in the supply of labour. If higher wages gave him the opportunity of earning just enough for his customary standard of life, he would work for fewer days, because he has no desire to earn more money by working more regularly or by improving his own efficiency. And thirdly, owing to his poor physique, the Indian labourer cannot stand the strain of hard and monotonous work in the factories for hours at a stretch, and is therefore accustomed to work in an easy-going, leisurely fashion with frequent breaks in his day's work.

[1] For fuller information on the conditions of factory labour in India, read the *Report of the Royal Commission on Labour in India* (1931), specially Chapters II–IV, XII–XV.

All these deficiencies in the quantity and quality of the labour supply are a source of special handicap to the Steel Industry of India. For, the steel manufacturer in India, unlike those of foreign countries, has to devote a considerable part of his time and energy, and spend a good deal of money, in collecting large numbers of agricultural workers and training them into skilled and well-disciplined industrial operatives. And furthermore, in order to ensure permanence of supply and growth of efficiency, he has to make the conditions of life for the workers as attractive as possible by providing decent houses at low rents, and establishing schools, gymnasiums, clubs, hospitals and dispensaries. In this way the manufacture of steel in India is saddled with the cost of maintaining an elaborate municipal administration, which in other places is shared by the general public. The annual municipal cost of the city of Jamshedpur to the Tata Iron and Steel Company, including hospitals, schools, etc., but excluding housing, is stated to be in the neighbourhood of Rs. 12 lakhs (in 1923). It is of course likely that the establishment of allied and associated industries, and the general expansion of the population, will in the course of a few decades reduce the expenses of the Company on account of municipal administration. Meanwhile, however, the fact remains that this extra element in the cost of production will continue to be a special handicap in their competition with the steel producers of foreign countries.

(*b*) *Technical Ability and Supervision*

When we pass on to examine the conditions of the supply of higher grades of labour required for technical work as well as for expert direction and supervision, we come upon what might perhaps be regarded as the greatest comparative disadvantage of the Indian Steel Industry. There being little local supply of men with the necessary training and experience in the difficult and highly technical processes of steel manufacture, the Indian manufacturer has to import them from Europe and America. Over and above high salaries, they are also paid considerable bonuses on production and handsome travelling allowances. The representative of the Tata Iron and Steel Company stated before the Tariff Board in 1923 that the wages and salaries given to these employees were at least 50 per cent higher than what they would have got in Europe. If we add bonuses and allowances, it becomes clear that the cost of technical labour and supervision in India is about double that in foreign countries. In 1925–26, the total wages bill at the Jamshedpur Steel Works amounted to Rs. 146·7 lakhs; and the sum paid to the covenanted (imported) hands Rs. 34·20 lakhs, Rs. 23·73 lakhs in salary and Rs. 10·47 lakhs in bonus. If the entire staff consisted of Indians, there would be a saving of Rs. 11·87 lakhs in salary (50 per cent reduction) and Rs. 10·47 lakhs in bonus, as Indians are given no bonus. The total saving in the cost of production on this one item alone would thus be Rs. 22·34 lakhs.[1] In the year 1925–26 the output of finished steel at the Jamshedpur works was 320,000 tons. The extra cost due to the necessity of importing expert supervision and technical ability from abroad, therefore, was approximately Rs. 7 a ton.

It is obvious that as long as there is not available to the steel manufacturer of India an adequate supply of local men with the necessary degree of training and experience so as to enable him to dispense with the highly expensive services of the imported hands, his item of cost under direction and supervision is bound to remain appreciably higher than that of his competitor in other countries. In order to eliminate this disadvantage, the Tata Iron and Steel Company have established a Technical Institute at Jamshedpur for the training of suitable Indian young men in the different branches of metallurgy. But, mainly because of the traditional aversion of Indian youths for manual work, the results achieved so far have been disappointingly poor. Thus during the five years, 1921–25, only twenty-five students of the Institute were found adequately fit for employment at the Steel Works. Apart from the recruit-

[1] Vide *Minutes of Evidence*, Tariff Board, Statutory Enquiry (1926), Vol. II, pp. 210–11, 224–25; Vol. III, pp. 91–93.

ment of Indians through the Institute, there is also occasional recruitment by the promotion of ordinary local labourers who gradually acquire the necessary training, skill and experience at the works.[1] When, however, we remember that it takes at least three to four generations to make efficient steel workers even in western countries, and further that it will necessarily be an exceedingly slow process to overcome the traditional divorce between the intelligentsia and manual occupations, we cannot help thinking that the Indian manufacturer will suffer from this handicap, though in diminishing degrees, for at least the next thirty or forty years.

(c) *Climatic handicap*

In connection with labour, it is also important to note that the comparatively high temperature of the summer and autumn months in the iron districts of India is a further disadvantage to the steel manufacturer of the country. The temperature is much higher during March, April, May, June and October than at any time of the year in the corresponding districts of Europe. In the hot weather, the temperature at Jamshedpur frequently exceeds 110° F. and sometimes even 120° F. During July, August and September as well, the temperature is high as compared to that in the European iron areas, and moreover the atmosphere is excessively moist. In such circumstances, iron and steel making becomes a very arduous operation and calls for special provisions in the lay-out of the works or in the details of the equipment.[2] Furthermore, on account of the excessive physical strain involved in working at the furnaces in the exceedingly high temperature, the imported labourers cannot work as steadily and as long as in European countries, and they have also to be assisted by a large number of Indian artisans. The result is that in the Indian open hearth furnace they have

[1] Vide *Minutes of Evidence*, Tariff Board, Statutory Enquiry (1926), Vol. II, pp. 158–63; Vol. III, pp. 91–93.

[2] Paper by Mr. R. Mather, late Metallurgical Inspector to the Government of India, published in the *Journal of the Royal Society of Arts*, Vol. LXXV, pp. 600–24.

to employ as many Europeans or Americans as there are in a European or American furnace of the same size, and in addition a large number of Indian workers as well. This inevitably makes for a higher cost of production, and since this is mainly due to the climatic conditions, the handicap must be regarded as a permanent one.[1]

[1] Statement No. C. submitted by the Tata Iron and Steel Company to the Tariff Board (1924), *Minutes of Evidence*, Vol. I, p. 223.

CHAPTER VI

THE PROTECTION OF THE INDIAN STEEL INDUSTRY[1]

1. REASONS FOR THE SPECIAL SUPPORT OF PUBLIC OPINION

The Indian Steel Industry has been veritably the prize-boy of the Government and the Legislature of India ever since their adoption of the policy of protection in 1923. The Fiscal Commission of 1921–22, which had been appointed to advise on a suitable tariff policy for the Government of India, had specially commended the case of the Steel Industry as an appropriate one for state assistance. The first investigation of the Tariff Board, therefore, was concerned with the conditions of the Steel Industry, and the first protective measure passed by the Indian Legislature was designed to help that industry. During the seven years, 1924–31, no less than six successive investigations have been followed by six consecutive legislative and administrative measures for the benefit of this one single industry, which is so far identified with the varying fortunes and misfortunes of one single firm.

For this special devotion to the cause of this particular industry, several reasons may be assigned. In the first place, the steel works at Jamshedpur, representing as they do the largest single modern factory in India, with its huge capital, elaborate organisation, stupendous machinery and gigantic furnaces, have been from the outset regarded by the Indian public as a matter of special national pride and glory. It is not too much to say that Jamshedpur has been looked upon during the last fifteen years almost as a place of pilgrimage by all those who are interested in the industrial progress of India, while the name of Jamshedji Nusserwanji Tata has become a house-

[1] The term 'Steel Industry' is used in the narrower sense of the manufacture of rolled steel, and as such is to be distinguished from the Engineering Industry, the Ship-building Industry, etc.

hold word. Secondly, during the war, when India was almost cut off from foreign supplies of iron and steel, the necessary extensions and replacements of industry and transport were found to be exceedingly difficult and sometimes even impossible. Thus was brought home to the Government and the people alike the great weakness in the economic position of India due to the absence of steel manufacture within the country itself. Thirdly, in supplying rails for the theatres of war east of the Suez, the steel works at Jamshedpur proved of much assistance to the Government of India, and accordingly have ever since been certified by the military as well as the civil administrations as an industry of military necessity. And lastly, when once a policy of economic nationalism to be promoted by protection was adopted, the Steel Industry, already in high favour with the public as well as the Government, proved to be the one industry that answered satisfactorily to all the ordinary protectionist pleas, such as infant industry, basic industry and military industry. It is, therefore, no wonder that the Steel Industry should have so far suceeeded in overshadowing all others in the matter of public assistance by way of import duties, bounties and state purchases.

2. THE SEQUENCE OF EVENTS THAT LED TO THE DEMAND FOR, AND GRANT OF, PROTECTION

Now, although the history and the conditions of the Indian Steel Industry are very different from those of the Cotton Industry, the circumstances under which public assistance in the shape of protective measures was asked for were somewhat similar in the two cases. Exceptionally favourable prices and markets, large profits, extension of plant and machinery under the stimulus of high profits, and liberal payments of dividends, during the war and the post-war boom, followed by falling prices, diminishing profits, mal-adjustments between costs and prices, and increasing embarrassments in securing working capital and meeting fixed charges, and last of all, the inevitable request for financial relief at the expense of the general public—

this has been the invariable order of happenings leading ultimately to the adoption of protectionist measures in both these, as well as in nearly all other cases of state assistance to industries in India. In both cases, again, the real issue, which was nothing more and nothing less than imposing special taxation upon the people of the country so as to help particular firms or companies to increase their profits or avoid their losses at the expense of the public, was greatly obscured by the far too familiar method of employment of psychologically effective phrases and arguments such as 'the national industry in danger,' 'the wickedness of the foreigner in selling his goods at a low price with a view to killing the indigenous industry,' 'the right of the home industry to supply the home market,' and so on. And, so far as the special case of the Steel Industry was concerned, there were also the additional arguments of 'infant industry,' 'military necessity,' and 'basic industry,' set forth in elaborate detail.

As these arguments, for what they are worth, are already familiar to students of economics, it would not be profitable for us to stop to examine them. The real point involved in this particular case of protection can be elucidated only if we trace the actual sequence of events that brought the Indian Steel Industry to its critical phase leading to the demand for protection. The Tata Iron and Steel Company was incorporated in 1907 with a capital of £1,630,000; iron was first produced in 1911, and steel in 1913. While pig-iron became a paying proposition from the outset, steel never arrived at a stage where it combined satisfactory quality with economic costs. Luckily for the Company, the war supervened as a natural protection guaranteeing to the manufacturer a semi-monopoly of the home market with high prices and large profits. The result was that the small and experimental steel plant, now called the old plant, reached its full capacity of 125,000 tons in 1917–18. Under the stimulus of the abnormally favourable circumstances of the moment, the Company took in hand a very large scheme of extensions (known as the Greater Extensions). Originally it was hoped that the extensions would be carried through by

1920 or 1921, but due to special governmental restrictions on shipping during the war, and on account of the delays in the delivery of the machinery in the period of the post-war boom, some parts of the plant could be put into operation as late as 1922–23 and 1923–24, while other parts were started only in 1924–25.[1]

It should also be noted that the purchases of the tools and machinery for the Greater Extensions having been contracted for in the period of high prices towards the close of the war, the capital cost of the plant became abnormally high. It was also natural that in the initial stages of inexperience, trials and errors, the efficiency of labour and the effectiveness of the plant would be comparatively low, and the costs of production correspondingly high. On the other hand, with the advent of the trade depression in India in 1921–22, the prices at which steel could be sold began to fall rapidly, with the result that the pioneer steel manufacturer, even before he had started, was faced with increasing financial embarrassment on account of the widening gap between costs and prices. As is well known, due partly to the enlarged productive capacity of the world in steel, partly to the great technological improvements introduced in the steel works in Germany, Belgium, France and to a certain extent in Great Britain, and partly also to the general monetary and economic conditions, specially the rapid depreciation of the foreign exchanges, in Continental Europe, the slump as well as the competition in the iron and steel trades became particularly severe. Under such circumstances it was inevitable that the steel manufacturer of India would find it impossible to continue producing steel at competitive prices. A further and no less serious difficulty was that, having practically exhausted all their credit in the money market in raising the huge capital for their new extensions and having had no accumulated reserves to fall back upon, the Steel Company found it exceedingly difficult to meet their overhead charges, including interest on

[1] Report of the Tariff Board regarding the grant of protection to the Steel Industry (1924), p. 8.

debenture loans, and to raise the necessary working capital. From 1921–22 onwards, therefore, they were rapidly approaching a point where they would be forced to close down the works. It was at this stage that they applied for public assistance in the shape of protection.

The Tariff Board was constituted in July, 1923, to examine the question of extending protection to the Steel Industry of India. After due investigation, it came to the conclusion that the Steel Industry was essential for self-defence and also important as a basic industry; that the natural advantages of India in respect of the more important raw materials as well as the home market were favourable to the development of a Steel Industry; that due to the very wide gap between the prices of imported steel and the internal cost of production, steel was being produced in India at a loss; and finally, that without protection, the production of steel was likely to cease and the development of the industry be indefinitely postponed.[1]

As already mentioned, in February, 1923, the Government of India, on the recommendation of the Fiscal Commission and in concurrence with the Legislature, had adopted a policy of protection with a view to fostering the development of industries in the country. It was in pursuance of that policy that the Tariff Board was appointed. The task before the Tariff Board, therefore, was to decide whether the Steel Industry deserved to be promoted by means of protection, and if it did, to indicate the amount and the method of protection. As a matter of fact, however, the issue before the Board was much narrower still, for, after the definite crystallising of responsible opinion in India during the war to the effect that the Steel Industry was of great importance as a basic as well as an essential military industry, it had to be taken for granted that the Steel Industry must be fostered in India. And since it had become certain that the steel manufacturer would be forced to stop running the steel works if no public assistance were forthcoming, the

[1] Report of the Tariff Board regarding the grant of protection to the Steel Industry (1924), pp. 10–17.

case for protection had been already established. The real question before the Board, therefore, was to find out what was the amount of assistance required, and to suggest an appropriate method for administering that amount.

3. THE FORMULA FOR THE TARIFF RATE

Students of American tariff history are familiar with the fact that in that country attempts have been made from time to time to devise a simple formula to express the tariff policy of the Congress. The high-tariff policy of the Republican Party, for example, has often been expressed by the formula 'equalising costs of production,' while the low-tariff policy of the Democrats has sometimes been phrased as 'equalising conditions of competition.'[1] Although it is true that the interpretation and the application of a simple formula like either of the above to the infinite complexity, intricacy and indeterminateness of the facts of economic life are found in practice to involve almost endless difficulties, experience shows that a formula, however incomplete and unsatisfactory, serves as a convenient starting-point in analysing the conditions of competition and fixing the rate of the tariff. The formula adopted by the Indian Tariff Board is that the amount of protection should be equal to the margin of difference between the 'fair selling price' of Indian steel and the price of imported steel. The exact meaning and implication of the formula will be unfolded to us when we have studied its actual application.

Definition of 'Fair Selling Price'

The 'fair selling price' is defined as "the price at which the Indian manufacturer can sell steel at a reasonable profit," and is taken to consist of the following three elements:

(*a*) Works costs;
(*b*) Overhead charges; and
(*c*) Manufacturers' profit.

[1] Thomas Walker Page, *Making the Tariff in the United States*, pp. 68 et seq.

It is obvious that this statement of the definition of 'a fair selling price' is a simple enough matter and may be accepted as adequate and satisfactory. But when we get down to details and proceed to lay hold of the concrete facts and figures relating to the three constituent items of 'fair selling price,' we come up against serious difficulties arising out of the inadequacy, discontinuousness and indeterminacy of the essential data. The investigation of the Tariff Board was taking place in 1923–24, and that year was a transitional year for the steel manufacturer in more ways than one. The new plant had not yet been completed, and consequently the estimates of costs of production for maximum output could not be anything better than a guesswork. The old plant, for which the costs sheets were available, was a comparatively small one, and moreover, the costs figures for 1922–23, the latest year for which the data were available, were vitiated by a six weeks' stoppage of the plant due to a strike. Under such circumstances, the Board took the costs of production for 1921–22 as their starting-point, and after examining the different items in detail both with reference to the actuals for 1916–17 and the estimates for 1924–25 onwards, arrived at what has been called the 'fair selling price' of Indian steel during the period of protection.[1]

4. THE 'FAIR SELLING PRICE' OF INDIAN STEEL IN 1921–22

(a) *Works Costs*

	Works Costs per Ton, 1916–17 Rs.	Works Costs per Ton, 1921–22 Rs.	Percentage of Increase
Pig-iron	18·54	34·47	86
Steel ingots	41·13	68·82	67
Rail mill products ..	75·17	116·00	54
Average cost of all finished steel	77·23	120·41	56

The reasons for the great increase in the costs of 1921–22 over those of 1916–17 as given by the Company and accepted by the Tariff Board were briefly as follows:

[1] Report of the Tariff Board regarding the grant of protection to the Steel Industry (1924), pp. 28–64.

(i) The rise in the price of coal with a simultaneous deterioration in the quality of the coal used. This was responsible for a rise of Rs. 8·4 in the cost of pig-iron per ton, and Rs. 18 in the cost of rails per ton.

(ii) An increase of between 40 and 50 per cent in the wages of labour.

(iii) A general increase in the price of all purchased materials and stores.

(iv) A fall in the average output of steel furnaces from 34,750 tons to 26,000 tons or about 25 per cent per furnace, due to the attempt at improving the quality even at the cost of quantity.

The Tariff Board were on the whole satisfied with the above explanation for the striking increase in the costs of production, and concluded that the costs were reasonable and could not have been substantially lower. Accordingly they accepted the Company's figure of Rs. 120·41 as the works costs of steel per ton in 1921–22.[1]

(b) Overhead Charges

(i) *Interest on Working Capital.*—According to the Company's figures, while the output of finished steel had gone up by only 27 per cent between 1916–17 and 1921–22, the amount of working capital required had increased from Rs. 100 lakhs to Rs. 600 lakhs. The Tariff Board, however, allowed an increase of 100 per cent only, about $33\frac{1}{3}$ per cent for increase of output and the balance for the general increase in prices. The interest allowed on the working capital (i.e. Rs. 200 lakhs) at $7\frac{1}{2}$ per cent per annum was Rs. 15 lakhs.

(ii) The Tata Iron and Steel Company is under the managing agency of the firm of Tata Sons, Ltd., with their Headquarters at Bombay. The Headquarters expenses together with the managing agents' commission in 1921–22 amounted to Rs. 7·31 lakhs.

(iii) *Depreciation.*—The fixed capital expenditure on the old plant together with the capital expenditure on the town and the Company's ore mines and limestone quarries was Rs. 400

[1] Report of the Tariff Board regarding the grant of protection to the Steel Industry (1924), p. 35.

lakhs in 1921–22. In view of the rise in the price of tools, machinery, etc., since the pre-war days, the replacement value of the old plant in 1921–22 was estimated at Rs. 600 lakhs. The allowance for depreciation at 6¼ per cent amounted to Rs. 37·5 lakhs.

Incidence.—The total overhead charges in 1921–22 thus amounted to Rs. 59·81 lakhs. This was distributed between 125,873 tons of finished steel and 107,000 tons of surplus pig-iron in proportion to the total works costs of the two joint products. On that basis, the incidence of overhead charges per ton of finished steel was Rs. 38·24.

(*c*) *Manufacturers' Profit*

Here the Board allowed 10 per cent on the ordinary and deferred shares, and the rates actually paid by the Company in raising the capital on the first and second preference shares, the details of which were as follows:

	Amount, Lakhs of Rupees	Rate of Interest, Per Cent	Interest Payable, Lakhs of Rupees
Ordinary and deferred shares	156·75	10	15·67
First preference shares ..	75·00	6	4·50
Second preference shares ..	168·25	7½	12·63
Total	400·00	8·2	32·80

Here, again, the total amount of profit was distributed between the surplus pig-iron and finished steel in the ratio of the total works costs of the two products, the incidence per ton of steel being Rs. 20·96.

The three elements in the 'fair selling price' of steel per ton of steel as calculated by the Board were thus as follows:

	Rs.
(i) Works costs	120·41
(ii) Overhead charges	38·24
(iii) Manufacturers' profit	20·96
Total	179·61, say 180

The Board, therefore, held that in 1921–22 Rs. 180 per ton was the 'fair selling price' of Indian steel, and that, as the price actually realised by the Tata Iron and Steel Company was only Rs. 159 a ton, steel was being produced in India at a loss.[1]

5. THE LIMIT OF 'FAIR SELLING PRICE' DURING THE PERIOD OF PROTECTION

As already noted, the investigation of the Tariff Board was carried out in 1923–24. It involved forming an estimate of the future costs of production as well as of the future price of imports. The new steel plant at Jamshedpur had not yet been completed, and, therefore, the estimates of costs of production in the years to follow could not be anything more than a guess-work. On the other hand, due to the extreme fluctuations in the prices of steel in Europe and America, any accurate anticipation of the course of steel prices was exceedingly difficult. Realising, therefore, that the necessary data for determining the margin between the 'fair selling price' and the future price of import were scanty and unascertainable, the Board wisely decided to limit the protective measure to be proposed to a period of three years, 1924–25 to 1926–27.[2]

The procedure followed by the Board in estimating the future costs of production of steel was an interesting and peculiar one in certain important respects. The works cost per ton of steel, which had risen from Rs. 77·23 in 1916–17 to Rs. 120·41 in 1921–22 (i.e. 56 per cent), increased further to Rs. 130 in 1922–23, as well as 1923–24, mainly on account of a rise in the price of coal, which was based upon a twenty-five-year contract with the coal companies, the price to be paid by the Tata Iron and Steel Company being 8 annas a ton higher than the price paid by the Railway Board. The price paid by the Railway Board in its turn was fixed by a contract for the three years, 1922–25, and according to this contract, the price fixed for the first year was considerably higher than those paid previously, and was, moreover, to be increased by 12 annas a ton in each of the second and third years. It happened that the contract

[1] Report of the Tariff Board regarding the grant of protection to the Steel Industry (1924), p. 40.

[2] Ibid., p. 57.

price paid by the Railway Board subsequently proved to be appreciably higher than the market prices.[1] As each ton of steel required four tons of coal, and since the price of coal under the ill-judged contract was automatically to increase in each succeeding year by 12 annas a ton, the works costs of finished steel would also go on rising as long as the contract lasted. It was, therefore, clear that so far as the old plant was concerned, the works costs could not be brought appreciably below Rs. 130 a ton (the figure for 1922–23), because the old plant having reached its maximum output for some years past had little scope for further economies. On the other hand, although considerable economies were expected in the long run out of the operation of the much larger new plant, those economies could not be appreciable in the two or three years immediately following, because the plant involved an altogether new and untried process (i.e. the Duplex process) in India. In other words, so far as a general consideration of the available data showed, the likelihood of the works costs rising was much greater than that of their falling. Faced with the somewhat paradoxical situation that the costs of production in 1924–25 to 1926–27 might be higher rather than lower than those of 1921–22, the Board took the almost desperate step of deciding that the fair selling price of steel during the period of protection could not be taken at a higher figure than that of 1921–22, i.e. Rs. 180 a ton.[2]

Having in this somewhat arbitrary fashion fixed the selling price that should in fairness be guaranteed to the Indian steel manufacturer, the Board proceeded to justify that price by examining the effects of the price in relation to (*a*) the manufacturers' profit, (*b*) the overhead charges and (*c*) the works costs, during the successive years of protection.

[1] Evidence of the Chief Mining Engineer, Railway Board, before the Tariff Board, during the enquiry into the Steel Industry (1924), *Minutes of Evidence*, Vol. III, pp. 291 et seq.

[2] Report of the Tariff Board regarding the grant of protection to the Steel Industry (1924), p. 52.

(*a*) *The Manufacturers' Profit*

According to the books of the Company, the fixed capital expenditure amounted to Rs. 21 crores—Rs. 4 crores on the old plant, Rs. 2 crores on the collieries, and Rs. 15 crores on the Greater Extensions. As the Company's collieries had not yet been sufficiently developed to pay their own way, the Board excluded the expenditure on them out of the capital account for the steel works. Since the old plant had been bought at comparatively low pre-war prices, its replacement value on the basis of post-war prices was estimated at Rs. 6 crores, i.e. Rs. 2 crores higher than the purchase price. On the other hand, as the old plant had a comparatively small productive capacity (130,000 tons), it was not quite economical and up to date in the light of post-war technological development. A somewhat arbitrary deduction on that account reduced the replacement value to Rs. 5 crores. Out of the Rs. 15 crores shown against the Greater Extensions, Rs. 2½ crores were deducted on account of expenditure from the depreciation fund, and another Rs. 2½ crores on account of reduction in the replacement value of the plant which had been bought in America at comparatively high prices during the war and the post-war boom. The total replacement value of the old and the new plant thus came to Rs. 15 crores. To allow for a return at a flat rate of 8 per cent on the fixed capital, a sum of Rs. 120 lakhs was required. This had to be earned from the sale of surplus pig-iron and steel. Now, with regard to the probable profit from the sale of pig-iron all previous experience pointed to the fact that the pig-iron capacity of the plant was much greater and would be reached much sooner than its steel capacity. Thus, in one single year, 1921–22, there had been no less than 107,000 tons of surplus pig-iron, and the sale of pig-iron alone had brought in a profit of over Rs. 50 lakhs. Subsequent experience also showed that the quantity of surplus pig-iron available for sale was about 150,000 tons a year.[1] Nevertheless, the Board, on what would appear to be insufficient grounds, assumed that the Company

[1] *Report of the Tariff Board*, Statutory Enquiry (1926), Vol. I, p. 15.

during the period of protection would be able to sell surplus pig-iron to the extent of 40,000 tons only a year, and estimating an average profit of Rs. 20 a ton, debited surplus pig-iron with only Rs. 8 lakhs, so that the balance of Rs. 112 lakhs was to be earned by finished steel. On an estimated output of 420,000 tons when full production would be reached, the incidence of the charge on account of profit would work out to Rs. 26·67 per ton of steel.[1]

(*b*) *Overhead Charges*

(i) Interest on working capital: the estimate of working capital submitted by the Company was as follows:

	Lakhs of Rupees
Stores and spare parts of all kinds	180
Raw materials and refractory bricks ..	75
Outstandings and stocks of finished steel ..	190
Total	445

The figure under the second item was based upon the estimate of the quantities of materials required, and the Board left it intact. The estimate under item one was based upon the assumption that on account of the difficulty and delay in securing supplies from abroad, the Indian manufacturer must have in hand stocks at least equal to eighteen months' supply. The Board held the view that six months' supply was adequate, and so reduced the amount under stores and spare parts to Rs. 110 lakhs. Under the third item, again, a reduction to Rs. 25 lakhs was made on account of the fact that the Company had valued the stocks of finished goods at the selling price instead of at cost price. Deducting for the reductions under these two items, the estimate for working capital necessary for full production was reduced from Rs. 445 lakhs to Rs. 350 lakhs. At 7½ per cent per annum, the amount of interest required to be met would be Rs. 26·25 lakhs.

(ii) Allowing at a rate of 6¼ per cent on Rs. 15 crores, the sum required for depreciation amounted to Rs. 93·75 lakhs.

[1] Report of the Tariff Board regarding the grant of protection to the Steel Industry (1924), p. 45.

(iii) The expenses of the Headquarters at Bombay were estimated at Rs. 4 lakhs, and the managing agents' commission under the terms of their contract at Rs. 8·4 lakhs.

Adding up all the items, we get a sum of Rs. 132·40 lakhs as the estimated amount of total overhead charges. Out of this, only 2½ per cent was deducted on account of surplus pig-iron, and the balance of Rs. 128 lakhs spread over 420,000 tons of finished steel gave an incidence of Rs. 30·70 per ton.

(*c*) *Works Costs*

The incidence of manufacturers' profits and overhead charges per ton of steel thus amounted to Rs. 57·37 a ton. As the Tariff Board had at the outset decided to fix the upper limit of the 'fair selling price' to be allowed at Rs. 180 a ton, the works costs per ton of steel had to be limited approximately to Rs. 123.[1]

6. CRITICAL EXAMINATION OF THE TARIFF BOARD'S ESTIMATE OF 'FAIR SELLING PRICE'

The estimated 'fair selling price' has been a central feature in the protective measures with regard to steel as well as other articles. It is, therefore, necessary to examine critically the several stages involved in estimating the 'fair selling price' and indicate important gaps and defects in that estimate which our examination may bring out.

At the outset we should mention that the task of the Tariff Board was rendered exceedingly difficult by at least two important factors. Firstly, there was only one firm engaged in the manufacture of steel, and, therefore, the Board had no effective and satisfactory way of checking the actuals and estimates of costs of production submitted by that firm. In the absence of comparable data relating to the production of steel under identical conditions, the Board could not reasonably have gone far in forming an independent estimate materially different from that of the manufacturer. And in the second

[1] Report of the Tariff Board regarding the grant of protection to the Steel Industry (1924), pp. 41–54.

place, as the enquiry regarding the future costs of production was conducted in a period of great fluctuations of prices, wages, exchanges, etc., many of the elements in the estimate could not be better than conjectures. That, in the face of these difficulties, the Board succeeded at all in giving some sharpness and mathematical precision to the several elements in the solution of the problem of fixing the 'fair selling price,' must indeed be regarded as a creditable performance.

It may also be admitted that the refusal of the Tariff Board to allow a selling price above Rs. 180 per ton, which had been the figure for 1921–22, in spite of a strong probability of the rise in the cost of production due to the rise in the price of coal, the reduction in the output of steel furnaces unavoidable in experimenting with a new process under Indian conditions (i.e. the Duplex process), and the continuation of comparatively high labour costs in a period of training and apprenticeship, laid upon the manufacturer the duty of effecting all-round improvement in efficiency, so that full production might be quickly reached and works costs reduced to a definite figure, i.e. Rs. 123 a ton; for, as long as the output remained below the maximum possible and the works costs above the figure laid down, the margin allowed for overhead charges and profits would be considerably absorbed by the excess of works costs and by the necessary overhead charges, and thus leave a very inadequate balance for a reasonable return on capital. Thus, according to the scheme outlined by the Board, in 1924–25, the first year of protection, with an estimated output of 250,000 tons, the overhead charges alone would approach Rs. 50 a ton, and would thus leave Rs. 130 for works costs and profits together. And since the works costs alone in 1923–24 had been Rs. 130, the amount of profit that could be earned by the manufacturer in 1924–25 would depend upon the margin by which he could effect economies and reduce costs in that year. In this way the scheme was so devised that if the manufacturer wanted to earn a reasonable margin of profit on his capital, he could do so only by progressive reductions in his works costs. Hence, by somewhat arbitrarily fixing a sufficiently low figure as the 'fair selling price,' the Board provided a strong incentive to the manufacturer to increase his output and bring down his costs of production as far and as fast as possible. And lastly, we may also indicate that on account of the fall in the price of the imports much below the level anticipated by the Board, the protective assistance actually realised by the Company did not result in bringing even a reasonably satisfactory return on the capital.[1]

While fully acknowledging that the enquiry of the Board was surrounded with unusual difficulties and admitting that the degree of protection actually realised by the steel manufacturer was considerably minimised by the unexpected fall in the price of imported steel, it is nevertheless permissible to point out that the procedure followed was somewhat defective and that the estimate of the 'fair selling price' of Indian steel was appreciably higher than was warranted by the available data. The criticisms on the score of wrong procedure and defective analysis are indicated in the following paragraphs:

(*a*) *Capital Account*

As already noted, the fixed capital expenditure of the Company was estimated by the Board as follows:

	Lakhs of Rupees
(i) Original cost of the old block	400
Add for the increased cost of replacing the old block at the current price of 1923–24	100
Replacement value of the old block in 1923–24 ..	500
(ii) Original expenditure on the Greater Extensions ..	15,00
Deduct for expenditure from the depreciation fund ..	250
Deduct for excess expenditure on American purchases and freights	250
Replacement value of the Greater Extensions ..	10,00
Total replacement value of the old and the new blocks	15,00

[1] In 1923–24, the year before the passing of the Steel Industry (Protection) Act, no dividends were paid. During the three years of protection, 1924–27, only 1½ per cent dividends were paid on ordinary shares and none on deferred shares; full dividends were earned on 6 per cent first preference shares alone and only partial dividends on 7½ per cent second perference shares.

This estimate is subject to two serious criticisms. The rolling mills of the old block established before the war had, in spite of considerable renewals and improvements, definitely become out of date and uneconomical as compared to the corresponding mills in the Greater Extensions. Thus in 1925–26, the second year of protection, while the cost of rail per ton in the old rail mill was Rs. 102, the corresponding figure for the new rail mill was Rs. 96 only. Similarly, in the same year, while the cost of the old bar mill product per ton was Rs. 111, the corresponding figure for the new mill was Rs. 105.[1] The Board, instead of directly reducing the value of the old block by the sums spent on these antiquated and inefficient mills, which should have been scrapped in the interest of efficiency, reduced the capital value of the Greater Extensions by the amount of money that had been spent on them out of the depreciation fund of the old block. Although we cannot measure with certainty the effect of this wrong procedure on the estimate of the replacement value of the entire steel plant, there can be no doubt that the defective procedure itself vitiated the estimate to a considerable extent. The same conclusion will be forced on us if we examine the capital account in 1923–24 from another point of view. In that year, the company's share and debenture capital amounted to Rs. 1,652 lakhs.[2] Deducting Rs. 200 lakhs for expenditure on the collieries, we are left with Rs. 1,452 lakhs as the amount of capital expenditure on the iron and steel works. The greater part of the money was raised and spent in the purchase of tools and machinery in the boom period. Due to the subsequent depression, the earning capacity of the capital must have fallen appreciably, and consequently the sum of Rs. 1,452 lakhs should have been considerably reduced by way of devaluation. Instead, we find an inflation of the capital to Rs. 1,500 lakhs under the estimate of the Board.

[1] Vide Representations submitted to the Tariff Board by the Tata Iron and Steel Company, *Minutes of Evidence*, Statutory Enquiry (1926), Vol. II, pp. 86, 87, 89, 90.

[2] Report of the Tariff Board regarding the grant of protection to the Steel Industry (1924), p. 45.

Another point which seems to invite criticism is that the expenditure incurred by the Company in converting a primitive Santal village into an up-to-date modern city with its fine residential buildings, lighting, etc., has been allowed in its entirety to swell the capital account. The capital expenditure debited to the town development work up to the 31st of March, 1922, amounted to about Rs. 120 lakhs.[1] In their estimate of the fixed capital expenditure of the Company, the Board included the whole of the amount spent on general town development. At a rate of 8 per cent, the annual amount of profit on this sum would be Rs. 9,60,000, and with an output of 420,000 tons, the incidence of this item of expenditure would be over Rs. 2 per ton of steel. The important question of principle as to how far the capital expenditure on the town development may be allowed to overload the capital account of the iron and steel works has been left undecided. The major part of the capital expenditure on the town development was incurred on residential buildings for the employees, and it represents a progressively revenue-yielding investment. It would, therefore, appear that it would have been quite proper and reasonable to treat the town development as an altogether separate investment and consequently to eliminate the capital expenditure on that account from the block account of the iron and steel works. The failure of the Tariff Board to do so has resulted in adding an unnecessary element to the cost of production of steel and has to that extent increased the degree of protection granted to it.

(b) Manufacturer's Profit

We have just seen that the estimated figure for the 'fair selling price' might have been reasonably reduced by making the necessary debit against the town expenditure. We have also noticed that the Tariff Board made an insufficient allowance for profit

[1] The Representations submitted by the Tata Iron and Steel Company to the Tariff Board, *Minutes of Evidence*, Statutory Enquiry (1926), Vol. II, pp. 261–62.

on the sale of surplus pig-iron, in which the Jamshedpur works have been eminently successful both in point of output as well as costs. And lastly, we may mention that the Board also omitted to debit a sufficient amount for profit as well as depreciation allowance against two of the important by-products, tar and sulphate of ammonia, for which the new plant has been fully equipped. According to the estimate submitted by the Company, the selling value of these two would be 2·93 per cent, of pig-iron 3·23 per cent, and of steel 93·84 per cent of the total sale proceeds of all the products.[1] It is, therefore, obvious that about 3 per cent of the necessary return on capital as well as depreciation allowance might have been reasonably debited to tar and sulphate of ammonia.

(*c*) *Interest on Working Capital*

Both the Company's as well as the Tariff Board's estimates of working capital were based upon full output. But the full output was due to be reached by progressive stages in the course of three years. The necessary reductions from the estimates of working capital and the interest thereon should, therefore, have been made for the first and second years.

(*d*) *Depreciation*

The Board's estimate of capital expenditure in 1923–24 was Rs. 15 crores. At an all-round rate of 6¼ per cent, they allowed a sum of Rs. 93·75 lakhs on depreciation account for each of the three successive years, 1924–25 to 1926–27. Here the mistake was that they failed to note the automatically progressive reduction in the capital value of the plant due to depreciation from year to year. If this fact had been fully allowed for, in the second year the block value of the plant and the depreciation allowance thereon would have come down to Rs. 14·06 crores and Rs. 88 lakhs respectively, and in the third

[1] Evidence recorded by the Tariff Board during the Enquiry into the Steel Industry (1924), *Minutes of Evidence*, Vol. I, p. 101.

year the corresponding figures would have been Rs. 13·18 crores and Rs. 82 lakhs respectively.

(*e*) *Works Costs*

As already observed in an earlier section, the Board's estimate of works costs and 'fair selling price' were somewhat arbitrary in character. All that they did was to fix sufficiently low figures for both these items so as to lay upon the manufacturer the obligation to reduce the costs as far and as fast as possible in order that he might earn a profit. Although this was undoubtedly to a certain extent an ingenious way of saving the consumer from an excessive burden of high prices, nevertheless it would perhaps have added greatly to the authority of the figures if the Board had been more precise and definite in stating the grounds on which these figures were based.

7. ESTIMATED IMPORT PRICES; THE EXTENT AND FORM OF PROTECTION; PROVISION FOR A FLEXIBLE TARIFF

According to the formula adopted by the Tariff Board, the extent of protection to be given was to be measured by the margin of difference between what they called the 'fair selling price' of Indian steel and the probable prices of imports. We have seen that the ascertainment of the 'fair selling price' of Indian steel was an exceedingly difficult business. Those who have followed the extraordinary fluctuations of prices in the post-war period will easily realise that the forecasting of the future prices of steel in 1923 was hardly a less difficult task. After briefly noticing the diverse factors likely to affect the future prices of steel, some tending to lower and others to increase the price of imported steel, the Board decided to take the prices prevalent in the latter half of 1923 as the basic prices for the purpose of determining the margin of protection to be accorded to Indian steel. These were as follows:[1]

[1] Report of the Tariff Board regarding the grant of protection to the Steel Industry (1924), pp. 23–27.

	C.I.F. Landed Price of Steel per Ton without Duty Rs.
Steel bars and rods	140
Structurals, i.e. angles and beams, channels, etc.	145
Rails, 30 lb. and over	140
Plates, ordinary	150
Sheets, black	200
Sheets, galvanised	300

Having thus estimated the probable import prices, the Board now proceeded to examine the question of the form and extent of protection to be given for different kinds of steel. With regard to the form of protection, while fully admitting that the best method of protecting a basic industry like the Steel Industry was the grant of a bounty, they ruled a bounty out on account of the fact that the Government of India had been passing through years of budget deficits and could not possibly spare the funds needed for a bounty. Moreover, as we shall presently see, the Board apprehended a probable fall in prices of Continental steel due to any further depreciation of exchange,[1] and indeed provided for a flexible tariff under which the amount of protection was to be increased so as to compensate for any substantial decline in the import prices below the basic prices. Under such circumstances, it was realised that to recommend an all-round bounty scheme would be to commit the state funds to an indefinite and unlimited liability, and that, too, at a time of large and successive budget deficits.[2] Accordingly, they recommended the protection of all kinds of steel except rails and fishplates by means of import duties, while in the case of rails and fishplates, on account of special circumstances to be noticed later, a graduated scheme of bounties was preferred.

[1] The Report of the Board was issued in March, 1924, and protective legislation passed in June, 1924. The three Continental countries which export steel to India are Germany, Belgium and France. None of these had stabilised their currencies by that time, the actual dates of currency stabilisation being: Germany, August, 1924; Belgium, October, 1926; and France, June, 1928.

[2] The total budgetary deficits of the Government of India during the five years, 1918–19 to 1922–23, amounted to over Rs. 98 crores. Small surpluses began to reappear from 1923–24 onwards. (See Budget for 1927–28.)

Rates of Duties

Bars and rods, and plates.—In the case of bars and rods, and plates, the rates of duty recommended were only the simple difference between the fair selling price (Rs. 180) and the estimated import prices (Rs. 140 for bars and rods, and Rs. 150 for plates). These rates were Rs. 40 a ton on bars and rods, and Rs. 30 a ton on plates.

Structurals

The estimated import price for structurals was Rs. 145 a ton, and the rate, according to the formula, should have been Rs. 35. In view of the fact that the engineering industries and the Railways are the principal consumers of structurals, they recommended a rate of Rs. 30 a ton only on this class of steel materials.

Sheets, black and galvanised.—At the time when the Board wrote their report (February, 1924), the Tata Iron and Steel Company had not yet commenced operations on their sheet mills. The mills were actually due to be started in September, 1924. Accordingly, here the estimates were based upon absolute guess-work. It is, however, necessary to point out that the estimates given by the Company were so incredibly low that the Board considered it necessary to reject them altogether. The estimated figures for works costs submitted by the Company were Rs. 149 a ton for black sheets and Rs. 194 a ton for galvanised sheets.[1] The then current prices of imported black sheets and galvanised sheets (with the 10 per cent revenue duty then in force) were Rs. 220 and Rs. 330, and these would have left margins of Rs. 71 and Rs. 136 respectively over the works costs—margins much bigger than those provided for other kinds of steel under the protective scheme. Therefore, had the Board seen their way to accept the over-sanguine and

[1] The actuals for 1924–25 were Rs. 204 and Rs. 357, and for 1925–26 Rs. 181 and Rs. 314, and these would show that the Company's estimates given to the Board in 1923 were worse than useless (vide Statutory Enquiry, 1926, *Minutes of Evidence*, Vol. II, pp. 92–93).

ill-considered estimates of the Company, no additional duty by way of protection would have been necessary. The Board, however, assumed that it was exceedingly unlikely for the manufacture of sheets to be established without some degree of protection, and without taking the trouble of estimating the 'fair selling price,' simply adopted the rule-of-thumb method, and recommended that the duty on black sheets should be raised from Rs. 20 to Rs. 30, and that on galvanised sheets from Rs. 30 to Rs. 45. (In both cases, in terms of *ad valorem* rates, the increase was from 10 to 15 per cent.)

Rails and Fishplates

The Tata Iron and Steel Company had already entered into contracts with the Railway Board as well as with certain Railway Companies[1] to supply rails at fixed prices.

These contracts were as follows:

Name of Railway Administration	Duration	Price per Ton, Rs.	
(*a*) Bengal Nagpur Railway	Five years till March 31, 1925	Rails ..	110
		Fishplates	140
(*b*) Palmer Railways[2] ..	Six years till March 31, 1926	Rails ..	122·8
		Fishplates	152·8
(*c*) Railway Board ..	Seven years till March 31, 1927	Rails ..	130
		Fishplates	160

The contract with the Bengal Nagpur Railway was made in 1915, that with the Palmer Railways in 1918, and that with the Railway Board in 1919. The evidence on the subject shows that, in fixing the terms of each one of the contracts, the Company made serious errors of judgment with regard to both the future market prices of rails in India as well as their own cost of production. Thus, when the contract with the Bengal Nagpur Railway was made in 1915, the wholesale market price of rails

[1] In India, while most of the railways are actually operated by the Railway Board, there are a few lines still managed by Companies.

[2] Palmer Railways include the Bombay, Baroda and Central India Railway, the Madras, Southern Mahratta Railway, the Nizam's Guaranteed Railways, the Bengal and North-Western Railway, the Burma Railways, and the Assam Railways and the Trading Company.

in India was Rs. 150, while Tatas' cost of production of steel per ton was between Rs. 120 and Rs. 130; in 1921–22, while the contract price received by them was only Rs. 110 a ton, the wholesale market price was Rs. 132, and their own cost of production Rs. 180. Large discrepancies of the same kind to the disadvantage of the Company are also found in respect of all the other rail contracts.[1] While the Railway Board which is responsible for the State Railways made certain concessions in prices later on, the Company Railways refused to pay anything beyond the contract prices. If the full difference between the wholesale market prices of rails and the contract prices received by the Company from the various Railway Administrations be regarded as the measure of the loss sustained by the Company due to their ill-judged rail contracts, then the loss would amount to over Rs. 142 lakhs in the two years 1920–21 and 1921–22. The importance of the sum will be realised when we see that in those two years, the total quantity of finished steel produced at Jamshedpur was only 248,000 tons, so that the incidence of the loss due to the rail contract was no less than Rs. 57 a ton.

The Tariff Board, in view of the fact that the prices that would be received by the Company for their rails had been already fixed under the contracts, rightly concluded that the proper method of assistance for rails was a bounty and not import duties. The landed price of steel rails including the 10 per cent revenue duty was Rs. 154, and the difference between the 'fair selling price' and the import price Rs. 26. The Board recommended that this difference should be made up by a sliding scale of bounties on rails, Rs. 32 a ton in the first year, Rs. 26 in the second year and Rs. 20 in the third year.

Provision for a Flexible Tariff

In the post-war years we have become familiar with what is called the flexible tariff under which the executive is authorised to modify the statutory rates of duty in order mainly to counter

[1] Statement No. XXIII submitted by the Tata Iron and Steel Company to the Tariff Board (1924), *Minutes of Evidence*, Vol. I, pp. 140–41.

the fluctuations of import prices due to dumping, depreciating exchange, etc. The best known recent instance of a flexible tariff is the American Tariff Act of 1922, which authorised the President, after due investigation by the Tariff Commission, to make changes in the statutory rates of duty by not more than 50 per cent in order to 'equalise' the difference between foreign and domestic costs. The experience of U.S.A. shows that the flexible provision is generally used for increases in duties rather than for decreases. Thus under the Tariff Act of 1922, up to June, 1929, the discretionary powers of the President were used in 37 cases, out of which 32 were cases of increase of duties, and only 5 of decreases.[1]

The Indian Tariff Board also, in view of the uncertainty of import prices in a period of far-reaching changes in economic and monetary conditions, foresaw the necessity for some limited degree of flexibility in the protective tariff in order to ensure that the degree of protection intended to be granted to the Indian manufacturer was not rendered ineffective by a decline in foreign prices. Accordingly, they recommended that the Act should confer special discretionary powers on the Governor-General in Council to vary the rate of duty from time to time. The exercise of discretionary power on the part of the Executive was, however, to be limited only to cases where the change was necessitated by a serious and continuous fall of import prices, but did not extend to cases where the modification might be called for either by the rise of import prices or by the fall of internal costs of production.

8. SUPPLEMENTARY PROTECTION FOR STEEL

The Steel Industry (Protection) Act, incorporating the protective measures recommended by the Tariff Board, was passed in June, 1924. Scarcely a quarter of a year had passed when in September, 1924, the Tata Iron and Steel Company applied for supplementary protection in view of the heavy

[1] Cf. article on the American Tariff Act of 1930 by Abraham Berglund in the *American Economic Review*, September, 1930.

decline in the prices of imported steel below the base prices assumed by the Board in their First Report. The matter was referred to the Board for enquiry in October, 1924. They found that while the prices of British bars and plates had not varied much in the preceding twelve months, the prices of British structural sections (beams, angles and channels) had fallen appreciably. Again, due to the collapse of the Belgian and French exchanges, there had been also a sharp fall in the price of all Continental steel. Moreover, on account of the heavy importation of bars and structurals in the early part of the year and the consequent over-accumulation of stocks, the importers had to sell those sections at a heavy loss. Furthermore, since there had been meanwhile a large substitution of Continental for British steel, the base prices, in which British steel had been given a much greater weight than Continental steel, needed to be considerably modified. And, lastly, due to the rise in the rupee—sterling exchange from 1s. 4d. to 1s. 6d., there was an automatic temporary fall of 12½ per cent in the rupee prices of British steel. As a result of the operation of all these factors, the average prices actually realised by the Tata Iron and Steel Company for their steel had fallen short of the assumed import prices by Rs. 22 a ton for bars, Rs. 19 a ton for structurals, Rs. 20 a ton for plates, and Rs. 30 a ton for light rails. There had been, moreover, a heavy accumulation of stocks at Jamshedpur which could not be cleared except at a great loss. The Board, therefore, concluded that, in order to ensure to the steel manufacturer the 'fair selling price' intended under the Act of 1924, substantial increases in duties were called for. It was accordingly recommended that the duty on steel bars be raised from Rs. 40 to Rs. 75, iron bars from Rs. 25 to Rs. 55, structurals from Rs. 30 to Rs. 65, plates from Rs. 30 to Rs. 65, black sheets from Rs. 30 to Rs. 52, galvanised sheets from Rs. 45 to Rs. 78, rails and fishplates, heavy and medium, from Rs. 14 to Rs. 30, and rails and fishplates, light, from Rs. 40 to Rs. 75.[1]

[1] Report of the Tariff Board regarding the Increase of the Duties on Steel (1924).

It would be noticed that in less than six months the extent of protection necessary was found to be between 70 and 105 per cent higher than was originally granted.

In giving effect to the recommendations of the Board, the Government of India preferred bounties to import duties as a measure of additional protection for steel. Under the Government scheme, the bounty was to be paid at the rate of Rs. 20 a ton on 70 per cent of the total weight of the ingots manufactured in each month, and the amount of the bounty was to be limited to a sum of Rs. 50 lakhs and to a period of twelve months ending the 30th of September, 1925. In explaining the reasons for preferring bounties to import duties, Sir Charles Innes, the Commerce Member of the Government of India, set forth the following arguments: In the first place, the imposition of additional duties would place an excessive burden on all the consumers of steel which was an article of common use and which was so essential to the Railways, the Mining Industry, the Port Trusts and all the other important industries of India. As a matter of fact, it was in view of the extreme importance of the Steel Industry as a basic industry that the Fiscal Commission of 1921–22 had expressed its preference for a bounty. It was estimated that the burden of these additional duties would be about Rs. 2 crores, while the additional benefit that was intended to be conferred upon the Company was only Rs. 50 lakhs, so that the grant of supplementary protection by means of import duties would have involved a much greater burden upon the consumers than was necessary to meet the needs of the case. Secondly, due to the heavy accumulation of stocks in the hands of merchants, increased duties would fail to raise the price to the full extent of the duty, and therefore the Company would not be able to reap the full advantage of higher prices contemplated by the Board. And lastly, it was pointed out that while in June, 1924, Sir Charles had opposed a bounty on the ground of financial stringency, the situation had changed very materially since then. The increased duties sanctioned in the preceding June had exceeded the estimated revenue by Rs. 71 lakhs, and this amount was available for the grant of the proposed bounty. In answer to the objection on the ground of the very short duration of the measure, Sir Charles stated that the imposition of additional duties by the exercise of discretionary powers on the part of the Executive was meant to meet an emergency, on the expiry of which the additional duties might be taken off. At the same time, he announced the decision of the Government that the whole matter would be taken up for review at the expiry of a year, and if necessary, fresh measures would be taken.[1]

In accordance with the announcement noted above, the Government of India instituted a third enquiry by the Tariff Board in June, 1925, as to the necessity of modifying or extending the supplementary protection for a further period. On a careful forecast of future prices of steel and re-examination of the 'fair selling price,' the Board recommended a bounty of Rs. 18 a ton for the period of eighteen months ending the 31st of March, 1927, subject to a maximum of Rs. 90 lakhs.[2] The Government of India, however, on an independent review of the position, came to the conclusion that a somewhat lower rate of bounty would be both feasible and adequate and sanctioned a bounty at the rate of Rs. 12 a ton for a period of eighteen months, subject to a maximum of Rs. 60 lakhs.[3]

[1] Assembly Debates, January 26, 1925; and also the Government of India Resolution No. 260T (15), dated November 27, 1924.

[2] Report of the Tariff Board regarding the grant of supplementary protection to the Steel Industry (1925).

[3] Assembly Debates, September 15, 1925.

CHAPTER VII

THE PROTECTION OF THE STEEL INDUSTRY

(Continued)

I. CONTINUANCE OF PROTECTION FOR STEEL; THE DIFFERENTIAL DUTIES; THE PERIOD OF FURTHER PROTECTION

It will be remembered that the reason for limiting the Steel Industry (Protection) Act of 1924 to a short period of only three years, 1924–27, was the instability and uncertainty of both internal and external conditions with regard to the steel trades, and not any false hope entertained by the tariff-makers that the Indian Steel Industry would achieve the miracle of becoming independent of tariff assistance within so brief a space of time. Moreover, the two supplementary enquiries of November, 1924, and June, 1925, had brought out the fact that the Steel Industry was still far from showing anything approaching a state of independence. Accordingly, in the second half of 1926, the Tariff Board were asked to examine the conditions of the Indian Steel Industry once again and to report as to the necessity of the continuance of protection.

According to the formula laid down by the Board in their First Report of 1924, if there is an appreciable difference between the 'fair selling price' of Indian steel and the prices of imported steel, then the case for protection is automatically established. As there was an undoubted margin of difference between the two, the real question that the Board were called upon to answer was not whether protection should be continued or not, but what was the minimum degree of protection that could tide the steel manufacturer of India over his financial difficulties for a reasonable period of time. In providing an answer to this question, the procedure followed by the Board was the same as in 1924. In the first place, they took the data supplied by the manufacturer regarding the estimated costs of production, examined them in a broad and general way, and reduced the figures to a certain extent. In the second place, by reviewing the state of the steel trades and the course of the steel prices during the preceding three years, they adopted two sets of prices as the probable import prices of British and Continental steel respectively. And finally, after balancing the arguments for and against uniform versus differential duties, they concluded that the interests of producers as well as those of consumers could best be reconciled by adopting two different scales of duties: there was to be, first, a lower scale of basic and minimum rates to be applied to all imported steel and to remain in force for the entire period of the Act; and second, there was to be a flexible scale of additional duties applicable to non-British steel only and variable from time to time so as to meet changes in the level of import prices. As we have already examined in detail the procedure followed by the Board in connection with the Steel Industry (Protection) Act of 1924, we need now only touch very briefly upon those salient features of the Report of 1926, on which the Steel Industry (Protection) Act of 1927 was based.

The Period of Protection.—The Tariff Board found that although the Tata Iron and Steel Company had effected substantial reductions in the works costs by 1926–27, there was still large room for further and appreciable economies in many directions in the years ahead. For, apart from the fact that many parts of the more modern and efficient plant known as the Greater Extensions had been operated for too short a period to yield the benefit of maximum efficiency, there had also been meanwhile revealed a certain lack of balance between the different branches of the works. Thus, for example, it had been found that the capacities of the coke ovens and the steel furnaces were too small relatively to those of the blast furnaces and the rolling mills respectively. Furthermore, the old plant as a whole, specially the old rolling mills, had become obsolete and uneconomical, and their works costs were really rising instead of falling. To eliminate those elements of weakness in the plant as a whole, therefore, the Company had adopted in

1926 a development programme estimated to cost Rs. 2·68 crores in order, first, to round off the plant, and second, to increase output to the technically possible maximum by fitting up the plant with auxiliary machinery here and there. This development programme was to be realised in full by 1931–32 and was expected to lead to maximum efficiency by 1933–34. The Board, therefore, decided that the next instalment of protection should cover a period of seven years, 1927–28 to 1933–34. Hence their task was to find out the 'fair selling price' of Indian steel and the probable price of imported steel during the seven-year period.

2. ESTIMATE OF 'FAIR SELLING PRICE' OF INDIAN STEEL; CRITICISM

(*a*) WORKS COSTS

With regard to the works costs, what the Board did was to take the actuals under the main heads for 1925–26 and then, mainly with reference to the anticipated output of 1933–34, to estimate the principal items of works costs for the latter year. In scrutinising the costs figures, however, although some deductions were made for possible economies in labour, coal, stores, etc., the Board do not appear to have gone as far as they might have done on the basis of the data at their disposal. On the contrary, instead of insisting on the most rigid and rapid exercise of economy in the matter of works costs, they took a halting and apologetic attitude, and in many instances based their estimates of works costs, not on what appeared possible in the light of the available data, but on what the Tata Iron and Steel Company suggested as the limits of economy likely to be realised by themselves.

These comments on the Board's analysis of the works costs would find particular support in the following instances:

(i) *Labour.*—In their First Report of 1924, the Board had already commented upon the fact that the labour cost per ton of steel at Jamshedpur was much higher than the corresponding cost in western countries, partly on account of the higher wages of the imported skilled labour but partly also on account of the excessive numbers of unskilled and semi-skilled labourers employed at the works. This matter was thoroughly examined in 1926, and it was found that the Tata Iron and Steel Company had been strikingly extravagant in respect of the numbers of labourers employed at their works. Thus, for instance, in 1925–26 the number of labourers in the coke ovens and blast furnaces was found to be excessive to the extent of 2,000 in comparison with the number employed by the Indian Iron and Steel Company for a proportionate output. Similarly, the other departments also showed a total redundance of 4,350 beyond the necessary number for the given output. Hence the Board found that the 1925–26 scale of operations could have been easily carried on with a total labour roll of 19,940 instead of the 26,290 actually employed by the Company. The excess amounted to 30 per cent. Even after allowing for an increase of output by about 90 per cent, from 320,000 tons in 1925–26 to 600,000 tons in 1933–34, the Board found that the number of labourers could reasonably be reduced by 11 per cent, from 26,290 to 23,440. In so far as this proposal for the reduction in the number of labourers was concerned, the Board were quite right. Strangely enough, however, no proportionate reduction at all was made in the estimated cost of labour. The actual for 1925–26 was Rs. 148·4 lakhs. The Board allowed the same figure for 1933–34 as well in spite of the fact that they had themselves indicated a reduction in the number of labourers to be employed by at least 11 per cent.[1] It should also be noticed that no reductions at all were made on account of the progressive substitution of native for imported labour at increasingly lower costs. On both these counts, a total reduction of at least 20 per cent might perhaps have been reasonably made from the labour costs of 1925–26. Instead of definitely insisting on the necessary reductions in the labour costs as indicated by the available data, the Board simply expressed a pious hope that undoubtedly "the Steel Company so far as is compatible with

[1] *Report of the Tariff Board*, Statutory Enquiry (1926), Vol. I, pp. 22–26.

smooth and efficient working, will take steps to counteract any tendency towards overstaffing the various departments."

(ii) A second point where the Board's treatment of the question of works costs seems to be open to criticism arises in connection with the consumption of coal. The actual consumption of coal in 1925–26 had been 4·09 tons per ton of finished steel. The Board were convinced that a consumption of less than 3 tons of coal per ton of finished steel should ultimately be sufficient. Nevertheless, because the Company proposed a reduction to 3·14 tons only, the Board accepted the Company's figure instead of their own, and added that they could not reasonably insist on a lower consumption than the 3·14 tons suggested by the Company within the seven-year period. It is really difficult to understand why the economy in the use of coal that is held to be ultimately possible should not be capable of realisation within so long a time as seven years.

The estimated incidence of the works costs for various steel products:

The incidence of the estimated works costs per ton of finished steel in 1933–34 was Rs. 78·8 as against Rs. 111·7 a ton, the actual for 1925–26. This meant a reduction of Rs. 32·9 a ton, or nearly 30 per cent. A substantial part of this reduction from the costs of 1925–26 had been already realised in August, 1926, when the works costs showed a reduction of no less than Rs. 13·3 a ton, so that there now remained only the balance of Rs. 19 a ton to be reduced within the seven-year period. Due, however, to the fact that the different mills in the plant had reached different stages of efficiency, the average reduction of Rs. 19 a ton was distributed in unequal proportions among the different products. Thus, the estimated reduction under works costs varied from Rs. 16 a ton in the case of tin bars to Rs. 63·7 a ton in the case of galvanised sheets.

The average works costs assumed for each different product during the period 1927–28 to 1933–34 was the mean between the actual costs for August 1926, and the estimated figures for 1933–34.

(*b*) OVERHEAD CHARGES, consisting of

(i) depreciation,
(ii) interest on working capital, and
(iii) agents' commission and head office expenses.

A lump sum of Rs. 10 lakhs was allowed for agents' commission and head office charges, while the Company's estimate of Rs. 3½ crores for working capital was reduced to Rs. 2·2 crores, partly on account of the estimated reduction in works costs and partly on account of the fact that the anticipated improvement in the financial position of the Company would enable them to draw upon the various reserves and undistributed profits for an appreciable proportion of the running expenses. These estimates do not seem to call for any comment.

But, if in estimating the working capital the Board exercised a severe scrutiny, they do not appear to have been equally careful in their estimate of the allowance for depreciation on the fixed capital of the steel works. The estimated value of the block in 1924 had been Rs. 15 crores. The task before the Board was to find out the replacement value of the plant during the period of protection, 1927–34. What they did was to split up the sum of Rs. 15 crores into two parts: Rs. 3 crores as the expenditure incurred in India on labour and local materials in the erection of the works, the development of the ore, limestone and dolomite quarries, the preparation of the works site, and the construction of houses, etc.; and Rs. 12 crores as the price of imported machinery and tools. While, in view of the fall in the rupee prices of imported materials, the sum of Rs. 12 crores was reduced by about 20 per cent to Rs. 9½ crores, no reductions for the fall of Indian prices and Indian costs were made from the sum of Rs. 3 crores. Nor were any reductions made on account of the expenditure on the general town development, which is and should be regarded as an altogether separate and independent business proposition.

On the estimated replacement value of the plant in 1926, i.e. Rs. 12½ crores, a flat rate of 6¼ per cent was allowed for depreciation; the annual amount allowed for depreciation was thus Rs. 78 lakhs for each of the seven years to be covered by protection. As was pointed out in the last chapter, this simple way of calculating the depreciation allowance seems to be based on a certain amount of confusion. Assuming that the replacement value of the plant in 1926–27 was Rs. 12½ crores, there should have been made an annual reduction in that replacement value on account of the depreciation of the plant from year to year. Thus, for instance, the replacement value of the plant in 1927–28, after the depreciation of the previous year, would be Rs. 11·72 crores (i.e. Rs. 12½ crores—Rs. 78 lakhs). Annual reductions on account of depreciation should thus have cumulative effect on both the capital value as well as the depreciation charges. If this method were followed, our calculation shows that the capital value of the plant and the depreciation allowance thereon in 1933–34 would have been about Rs. 8 crores and Rs. 50 lakhs respectively. On this basis, the average capital value of the plant and the depreciation allowance thereon during the whole period, 1927–28 to 1933–34, would be Rs. 9·86 crores and Rs. 61·62 lakhs respectively. On an average output of 500,000 tons of finished steel, the incidence of overhead charges per ton would have thereby come down to the extent of about Rs. 3·7. On this showing, therefore, it would seem clear that the Board's estimates for the plant and the depreciation allowance thereon erred considerably in the direction of excess.

(*c*) MANUFACTURERS' PROFIT

Here the Board allowed a flat rate of 8 per cent profit per annum on the whole of the 12½ crores. Our criticism of the Board's estimates of the capital value of the plant and depreciation allowance thereon is, it is obvious, fully applicable in this case as well.

Distribution of the incidence of overhead charges and profit among the different steel products:

The estimated annual average output of finished steel during the proposed period of protection was 500,000 tons. The amount of money required for overhead charges and profit, however, was distributed not at a flat rate over all the different kinds of rolled steel manufactured at Jamshedpur, but in unequal proportions on the basis of different works costs and the different capital values of the several plants in use. It may also be noted that, for the purpose of calculating the incidence of overhead charges and profits per ton, the total output of finished steel was assumed to consist of definite quantities of diverse products. On these assumptions, the incidence of overhead charges and profits on tin bars was as low as Rs. 24 a ton, while that on galvanised sheets was as high as Rs. 51 a ton.

Adjustments for losses on second-class materials as well as for internal freight:

According to the formula adopted by the Board, the 'fair selling price' of different products might be regarded as equivalent to works costs plus overhead charges and profits. In order, however, that every plausible ground for adding to the margin of protection might be exploited, the Board also added varying sums for different products in order to compensate the manufacturer for loss on the sale of inferior materials. Moreover, considerable adjustments were also made by adding to or subtracting from the so-called 'fair selling price' of each different product according to its freight advantage or disadvantage relatively to the imports in the several parts of the home market. In this way, while on the one hand Rs. 8 a ton was added for rails and fishplates, and Rs. 5 a ton for sleepers, on the other hand Rs. 7 a ton was subtracted for galvanised sheets, Rs. 2 for black sheets, and Re. 1 for plates.[1] These adjustments led to the addition or a total sum of Rs. 15 lakhs, or Rs. 3 a ton, to the 'fair selling price.'

[1] *Report of the Tariff Board*, Statutory Enquiry (1926), Vol. I, pp. 39, 40.

Criticism

The assumptions on which these considerable adjustments were made for the benefit of the Company would seem to call for serious criticism. In the first place, it is a dangerous principle to hold that the manufacturer, instead of being left to suffer for the inferior quality of part of his output, should be fully compensated for the same at the expense of the general tax-payer. And secondly, if the unwise location of the plant is responsible for relative freight disadvantage in the home market, it is the business of the manufacturer to make up for the deficiency by economies in other directions or by cultivating those parts of the home market where he enjoys a comparative freight advantage. The adjustments made on both these counts would, therefore, seem calculated to perpetuate inefficiency and reward mistakes.

The Board's estimates of 'fair selling prices' after the final adjustments may now be tabulated as shown on page 222.

3. PRICES OF IMPORTED STEEL AND THE METHOD AND AMOUNT OF PROTECTION

In view of the fact that the prices of British steel were seriously affected after April, 1926, by the coal dispute, the Board adopted the import prices of the first four months of 1926 as the basis of their recommendations.[1] Now, of the seven classes of imported steel which compete against Indian steel, three, namely, rails, fishplates and galvanised sheets are imported almost entirely from Great Britain; one, namely, sleepers, only from the Continent; while the remaining four, namely, structural sections, bars, plates and black sheets are imported both from Great Britain and the Continent. With regard to the first four classes, it is obvious that the determination of the margin of protection required was simply a question of finding the difference between two sets of prices. With regard to the other four classes, however, the wide gap between

[1] *Report of the Tariff Board*, Statutory Enquiry (1926), Vol. I, pp. 39–41.

ESTIMATED 'FAIR SELLING PRICE' OF VARIOUS STEEL PRODUCTS

(1927–34)

Products	Average Output, Tons	Average Works Costs, Rs. per Ton	Overhead and Profit, Rs. per Ton	'Fair Selling Price' F.O.R. Works, Rs. per Ton	'Fair Selling Price' After Adjustments, Rs. per Ton
Rails	195,000	71	39	110	118
Fishplates	7,000	103	45	148	156
Structural sections	70,000	81	39	120	120
Bars	90,000	88	41	129	129
Plates	30,000	92	42	134	133
Tinbars	50,000	63	24	87	87
Black sheets	13,000	143	42	185	183
Galvanised sheets	30,000	232	51	283	278
Sleepers	15,000	74	36	110	115
Total	500,000	88	38·83	126·83	129·80

the British and Continental prices made the problem of the rate of duty an extremely complicated one. The Board were faced with two alternative solutions: a system of differential duties or a single scale of uniform duties based on the weighted average price of British and Continental imports. Both these systems had their relative merits and demerits, and in order to understand where the balance of advantages lay, we have to examine the implications of these two systems very briefly.[1]

(a) *Uniform Duties based on the Weighted Average Prices of British and Continental Steel*

The weights were determined by the proportions which the the Steel Company's sales of standard material (i.e. up to British Engineering Standard specifications) were expected to bear to their sales of non-standard steel, it being assumed that all imports from Great Britain were standard steel and all imports from the Continent non-standard. The difference between the 'fair selling price' of Indian steel and the weighted average price of British and Continental steel would, then, be the measure of protection to be extended to Indian steel.

The scale of duties required under the system would be as follows:

	'Fair Selling Price,' Rs. per Ton	Weighted Average Import Price without Duty, Rs. per Ton	Duty Required, Rs. per Ton
Structural sections	120	95	25
Bars	129	94	35
Plates	133	107	26
Black sheets ..	183	128	55

Under this system of uniform duties, the three sets of prices would be as follows:

	'Fair Selling Price' of Indian Steel, Rs. per Ton	Duty-Paid Price of British Steel, Rs. per Ton	Duty-Paid Price of Continental Steel Rs. per Ton
Structural sections	120	129	111
Bars	129	143	125
Plates	133	141	118
Black sheets ..	183	208	177

[1] The data used in the following four tables are from the *Report of the Tariff Board,* Statutory Enquiry (1926), Vol. I, pp. 53–55.

Merits and Demerits of Uniform Duties

There were only two advantages in favour of the system of uniform duties. In the first place, there was the simplicity of administration. Secondly, there was the benefit of lower prices to the consumers of Continental steel. The debit side of uniform duties was, however, much heavier than the credit side. In the first place, as the experience of the previous three years of steel protection had shown, the assumptions as to the relative proportions of standard and non-standard steel on which the weighted average price was based might be falsified to a very great extent by the substitution of Continental steel for British steel, and thus the scheme of protection might entirely break down. In the second place, a system of uniform duties would unduly raise the price of British steel and thus excessively penalise the consumers of standard steel. This consideration, it should be noted, was extremely important because, in all public utility undertakings, large construction works, and general engineering industries, the use of standard steel was essential. And since the general economic prosperity of the country as a whole was ultimately bound up with the rapid development of these undertakings, a wise policy demanded that the price of standard steel should be kept as low as possible consistently with the requirements of protection. And lastly, as the system of uniform duties would not fully cover the margin of difference between the 'fair selling price' of Indian steel and the price of Continental steel, there was a serious danger that the increasing competition of the latter might compel the Indian manufacturer to lower the quality of his steel. From these considerations, it would be clear that the balance of arguments lay overwhelmingly against the system of uniform duties.

(b) The System of Differential Duties

Under this system, the scales of duties required to cover the margin of difference between the 'fair selling price' of Indian steel on the one hand and the prices of British and Continental steel on the other would be as follows:

	British Steel Rs. per Ton	Continental Steel Rs. per Ton
Structural sections	19	30
Bars	26	37
Plates	20	36
Black sheets	35	59

And the 'fair selling prices' of Indian steel as against the duty-paid prices of British and Continental steel would be as follows:

	Average Fair Selling Price of Indian Steel Rs. per Ton	British Steel Rs. per Ton	Continental Steel Rs. per Ton
Structural sections	120	123	116
Bars	129	134	127
Plates	133	135	128
Black sheets ..	183	188	181

Merits and Demerits of Differential Duties

A little reflection would make it clear that the arguments for and against a scale of uniform duties would be exactly reversed when applied to differential duties, and that, therefore, the balance of the arguments we have already examined would be preponderatingly in favour of the latter. With regard to the difficulties involved in the administration of the differential duties, the customs officials were of opinion that though the difficulties were real, they were not insuperable. And finally, the system had the great practical advantage of making it possible to guarantee to the Indian steel manufacturer a certain amount of minimum protection based upon the lower scale of duties and at the same time to provide for some degree of flexibility in the additional duties so as to meet changes in prices.

Now, although the balance of the economic arguments was thus clearly in favour of a system of differential duties, there was a serious obstacle of a political character in the way of its adoption in that the Nationalist Party in the Legislature had been known to be consistently opposed to any scheme of duties that had any element or even semblance of Imperial Preference.

The Tariff Board, however, as a body of expert advisers, rightly decided not to allow its conclusions to be influenced by non-economic considerations, and recommended the adoption of the differential duties. As was anticipated, strong opposition to the differential scales was offered by the members of the Nationalist Party.[1] Nevertheless, the Steel Industry (Protection) Act of 1927 as finally passed was based upon the principle of differentiation.

A Fixed Scale of Basic Duties and a Flexible Scale of Additional Duties

In view of the fact that the prices of British Steel had been in the preceding three years, and were also likely to be in the subsequent period, comparatively more stable than those of Continental steel, the Board recommended that the scale of duties to be applied against British steel should be regarded as basic and minimum, and not alterable during the period of protection. On the other hand, as there was every probability of wide fluctuations in the prices of Continental steel, they suggested that in the case of all non-British steel, the basic duties should be supplemented by variable additional duties to be increased or decreased according as there was fall or rise in the import prices. This scheme, however, had one obvious defect: while it fully provided against the upward and downward movements in the prices of non-British steel, it took no account of the possibility of a decline in British prices. The Select Committee of the Assembly, therefore, amended it to the effect that although the lower scale of duties could in no case be decreased, it might be increased if there was an appreciable fall in the prices of British steel.[2]

4. ADDITIONAL PROTECTION FOR GALVANISED SHEETS

As noticed above, the Steel Industry (Protection) Act of 1927 authorised the Government of India to vary the rate of

[1] *Assembly Debates*, January 26 and February 14, 16, 18 and 21, 1927.
[2] The Steel Industry (Protection) Act, 1927.

duty on different kinds of steel in order to meet large changes in the prices of imported steel. The Tata Iron and Steel Company in September, 1930, applied to the Government of India for an increase in the duty on galvanised sheets on the ground that the price of imported sheets had fallen much below the figures on which the rates of duty under the Act of 1927 were based. The Tariff Board found that, while in 1926 the margin between the 'fair selling price' of Indian sheets and the price of imported sheets had been calculated to be Rs. 30 a ton, towards the close of 1930 the margin of difference had become widened to Rs. 67 a ton, due mainly to the fall in the price of the imported sheets. It was therefore recommended that the import duty be raised from Rs. 30 to Rs. 67 a ton.[1] Effect was given to the proposal in December, 1930, by an administrative notification of the Government of India.

Further Financial Assistance in the Shape of Increased Prices for Rails

It would be recalled that the Tariff Board's calculation of the 'fair selling price' of different kinds of rolled steel in India was based upon a rigid assumption as to the quantities of the output of different products at the Jamshedpur plant. It was assumed that out of an average annual output of 500,000 tons of finished steel during the period of protection, the output of rails would be approximately 195,000 tons or about 40 per cent of the whole. It was further assumed that the rail requirements of the different Railway Administrations in India would always be large enough to absorb the entire rail output of the steel works at Jamshedpur. On the basis of these assumptions, the fair selling price of rails f.o.r. Jamshedpur was calculated to be Rs. 110 a ton. Following a suggestion of the Tariff Board that all orders for rails should be placed in India, i.e. with the Tata Iron and Steel Company, the Government of India entered into a seven-year contract with that Company for the supply of

[1] Report of the Tariff Board on additional protection for galvanised sheets (1931).

rails at Rs. 110 a ton, the quantity of purchase to be determined from year to year according to the state of the Government finances. The actual purchases in the three years 1927–28 to 1929–30 were 435,000 tons; while, due to a considerable deterioration in the budgetary position of the Government of India, the estimated purchases for the next following four years, 1930–31 to 1933–34, were put at a maximum of 360,000 tons only. The average annual purchase of rails during the seven-year period would thus be only 113,000 tons as against a maximum output capacity of 195,000 tons. On account of this unexpected contraction in the demand for rails, the rail mill was actually operated at much below the maximum capacity. Consequently, the incidence of works costs as well as overhead charges per ton of steel was higher than what was assumed in 1926. The Tariff Board estimated that this reduction in the output of rails raised the 'fair selling price' from Rs. 110 to Rs. 130 a ton. The Government accepted the suggestion and agreed to raise the contract price for rails accordingly. On the estimated purchases of rails for the four years 1930–31 to 1933–34, this meant an additional assistance of Rs. 72 lakhs or Rs. 18 lakhs per annum. Due to the reduction in the output of rails, the figure for average annual output of finished steel fell from 500,000 tons to 410,000 tons.[1] The additional assistance given in the shape of increased prices for steel rails, therefore, amounted in effect to a bounty of Rs. 4·4 per ton of finished steel produced at Jamshedpur.

5. GENERAL CONCLUSIONS AND SUGGESTIONS

A. There is considerable room for improvement in the efficiency of organisation.

While examining the sequence of events that led to the demand for, and grant of, protection to the Indian Steel Industry, we found that the real purpose of protection was to help a particular firm to tide over the financial difficulties that had been brought about largely, if not wholly, by its own

[1] Report of the Tariff Board on steel rails (1931).

mistakes, miscalculations and misfortunes. The Tariff Board in their first Report of 1924 were at considerable pains to argue the point that the protection of steel was not really intended to rescue the Tata Iron and Steel Company out of their financial distress, but to promote the establishment of the Steel Industry in India.[1] But whatever the intentions or the arguments behind the protective measures might be, the fact remains that the extent and even the form of protection have been largely designed to meet the requirements of this one firm. Thus, for example, its ill-judged coal contracts and its particular freight advantages and disadvantages in the different markets have been regarded as constituent elements in calculating the 'fair selling price' of steel in India. Similarly, the reason for the grant of bounty on rails and fishplates under the Act of 1924 was that the Company had already entered into fixed-price contracts with the Railway Administrations of the country. Then, again, the calculation of the works costs, the overhead charges and the fair selling prices of different kinds of steel for the purpose of the Act of 1927 were based upon the relative quantities of the different products that could be turned out at the Jamshedpur works. These instances would show that, whatever the theoretical aspects of the protective measures might be, in practice they are intended as well as designed to meet the difficulties of one particular firm. It is, therefore, essential to examine whether that firm is endowed with a sound organisation and efficient management.

The machinery that controls and manages the steel works at Jamshedpur falls into three parts: first, the General Manager and his technical staff at the works who are responsible for the technical management of the factory; second, the ornamental Board of Directors that pass the annual accounts; and third, the familiar Managing Agents, in this case the Tata Sons, Ltd., who decide the larger questions of business and finance. The connection between the Technical Staff at Jam-

[1] Report of the Tariff Board regarding the grant of protection to the Steel Industry (1924), p. 61.

shedpur and the Managing Agents at Bombay is at best a loose and ineffective one, for while the former are altogether innocent of any appreciation of the general commercial and financial aspects of the business, the latter are equally lacking in a proper acquaintance with the technical problems of the industry. Neither among the Board of Directors nor among the Managing Agents is there a single gentleman who has had a first-hand knowledge of the intricate details of organisation and costs in a gigantic steel factory of modern times. The result is that the business and financial heads of the steel works are absolutely powerless in checking the costs of production.[1] This ineffectiveness of control over the costs of production is also due to the fact that not even one member of the Managing Agents or the Board of Directors is resident at Jamshedpur. There is hardly any need to stress the point that it is absurd to expect any effective exercise of control over a vast and complicated steel works from a distance of over 1,000 miles only by means of long dispatches backwards and forwards, specially on the part of persons who are untrained and inexperienced in the technique of steel production. It is, therefore, clear that the organisation of the Steel Industry in India violates the excellent dictum laid down by General Mahon in his famous report of 1899 that the management of a steel factory should combine expert knowledge and local experience.

In the same connection, it may also be pointed out that, due to the multiplicity of business interests controlled by the firm of Managing Agents[2] (i.e. Tata Sons, Ltd.) as well as by

[1] This statement finds full confirmation in the following criticism reported to have been made by Sir M. Visweswaraya, one of the new Directors of the Tata Iron and Steel Company and one who has had a unique reputation for constructive ability both as an administrator as well as an engineer. He publicly stated that there were many directions in which technical improvements could be made and where technical advice was needed; that there was no budgetary system at the works; that there was too much secrecy in the figures given to the Board; that the system of management at the steel works at Jamshedpur was antiquated; and that the Board had no control over it. (As reported in the *Statesman*, Mail Edition, October 9, 1930.)

[2] The firm of Tata Sons, Ltd., are the Managing Agents for no less than fourteen large-scale industrial concerns: one Iron and Steel Company, four Power

most members of the Board of Directors, neither the Managing Agents nor the Board have a single member who is a whole-timer for the steel works. To remedy these defects, a competent critic has made the excellent suggestion that there should be at least two whole-time Directors on the Board, who should be experienced iron-masters skilled in the administration and technical management of great iron works and mostly resident at Jamshedpur, where their status would give them the necessary authority to exercise effective control over the costs of production.[1]

B. Data of foreign costs of production necessary.

In briefly describing the procedure followed by the Tariff Board in determining the amount of protection to be given to the Indian Steel Industry, we had occasion to point out certain serious defects in that procedure. Most of these defects might be traced to the fact that there was only one firm producing steel in India. The result was that, in calculating the different elements that constitute what the Board called the 'fair selling price' of steel, they had to base their conclusions largely on the costs figures supplied by the Tata Iron and Steel Company. A moment's reflection will make it clear that the enactment of protective measures on the basis of data supplied by the beneficiary alone is open to serious objections, for, however careful and competent a body of outside experts might be, it

Supply Companies, four Cotton Mills, two Cement Companies, one Hotel Company, one Oil Mills Company, and one Electro-Chemicals Company. Some of these concerns, again, e.g. the Iron and Steel Works, and two of the Cotton Mills, are far away from Bombay. It is also worthy of note that as against these fourteen major concerns, the firm has only nine Directors in all, of which at least five (possibly six) appear to be blood relations. (*Times of India Directory of Bombay City and Presidency*, 1930.) Although the House of Tatas have undoubtedly a great number of remarkable business successes to their credit, we must not forget the warning lesson of experience that the hereditary control of business inevitably tends to lead to stagnation and decay.

[1] *Times of India*, Bombay, Mail Edition, September 20, 1930, Editorial comments on the meeting of the shareholders of the Tata Iron and Steel Company. (Since the above was written, a gentleman with experience of municipal administration has been appointed as a whole-time Director for the steel works, to be ordinarily resident at Jamshedpur. This, however, obviously does not meet the point of the criticism noticed above.)

would be impossible for them to determine how far the high figures of costs were due to external causes beyond the manufacturer's control and how far they were the result of incompetence and inefficiency on the part of the management. A very illuminating instance of the difficulty referred to here was found in the course of the investigations of the Tariff Board in 1926. Both in 1924 as well as in 1926 the Board expressed the very generous opinion that they had no fault to find with the technical management of the steel works at Jamshedpur. Nevertheless, in 1926 it was discovered that the Tata Iron and Steel Company employed at least 40 per cent more labourers in the coke ovens and blast furnace departments than the Indian Iron and Steel Company.[1] As soon as this point was brought out, the Company admitted that it was so, and agreed to substantially reduce the number of labourers in the subsequent years. In order to provide against this very real danger of the costs figures being unduly inflated on account of the incompetence of the manufacturer, it is suggested that the data of costs should be checked, wherever possible, by reference to similar data from competing firms within the country. But whether comparable internal data are available or not, there should always be a thorough comparison with the costs of production in foreign countries. For it is only by such a comparison that we can determine where exactly the inferiority of the native producer lies, find out whether that inferiority is organic or functional, and estimate the probabilities of the future. In this connection it is also important to enquire whether the technical efficiency of the plant as a whole is up to the highest standard attained in any part of the world. In the post-war period, very great progress has been attained, specially in Germany, in introducing technological improvements, particularly in respect of fuel consumption.[2] The Reports of the Tariff Board on the Indian Steel Industry give

[1] *Report of the Tariff Board,* Statutory Enquiry (1926), Vol. I, pp. 23–24.

[2] Cf. Balfour Committee on Industry and Trade, *Survey of Metal Industries,* p. 92.

us no information as to how far the most recent technological improvements realised in foreign countries have been introduced into the Indian Steel Industry. The available evidence, on the contrary, tends to show that the Indian steel manufacturer, partly no doubt due to lack of financial resources, has been exceedingly slow in discarding antiquated machinery and introducing the most up-to-date plant. Thus, for instance, although the old rolling mills, set up before the war, were found to be inefficient and uneconomical as early as 1923, they have not been discarded even to this day (1931). It is only by an elaborate comparison of foreign costs of production with internal costs that the functional inferiority of the native manufacturer may be brought into sharp relief. This will also indicate the lines along which progress can be made in order to place him in a position of equality with his competitor in foreign countries. The data of costs in foreign countries will, moreover, considerably help judgment in fixing the replacement value of the plant, depreciation charges and debits for by-products, in respect of all of which the analysis of the Tariff Board has been undoubtedly incomplete and unsatisfactory.

C. There should be greater flexibility in the tariff.

The Steel Industry (Protection) Act of 1927, as we have noted, contains certain elements of flexibility. Under that Act, the Governor-General in Council is authorised to both increase or decrease the additional duties on non-British steel, but only to increase the basic duties which are applicable to British as well as non-British steel. No provision is made in the Act for a reduction of the basic duties under any circumstances whatever. This limitation of the flexibility was based upon two assumptions: firstly, that the estimated average costs of production for the Indian manufacturer would remain unaltered, and secondly, that the prices of imported steel would never rise beyond the level of the British steel prices of 1926.[1] While undoubtedly there is justification for the second assumption in that there has been on the whole a continuous downward

[1] *Report of the Tariff Board*, Statutory Enquiry (1926), Vol. I, pp. 48–62.

tendency of prices since 1921, the first assumption would seem to be somewhat gratuitous in nature, since it makes no allowance for possible new economies or for a rapid fall in the prices of raw materials, stores and supplies. If it was likely that the intended degree of protection might be rendered ineffective by a fall in the price of imports, it was also nearly equally probable that the realised degree of protection might become excessive owing to the reduction in the internal costs of production, specially in a period of general fall of prices all the world over. It is, therefore, suggested that if flexibility is introduced in the tariff law, that flexibility should be complete, and not partial, so as to make the rates variable not merely in the upward but also in the downward direction. But a mere nominal provision for flexibility in the rate will not be adequate. For, as the experience of the administration of the American Tariff Act of 1922 shows, the flexibility is in practice used almost entirely for increases in the rates and very rarely for decreases, because, as a competent American observer puts it, the pressure to make use of the flexible provision comes mainly from those who want to have increase in rates, while the people who are interested in the decrease of rates, i.e. the consumers, have no means of effectively securing their interests by demanding reductions in rates.[1] In order to make the flexible provision fully effective, it is, therefore, suggested that the Tariff Board should secure and closely scrutinise the costs of production of the protected industries from year to year. This will familiarise them with the infinite intricacies of the problem of costs of production, increase their experience in and power of judgment on some at least of the technical aspects of their duties, and also help them to a certain extent in finding out when and whether the rates can be legitimately lowered.

D. The question of Bounties, versus Import Duties should be decided on its own merits, and not merely as a part of the general financial scheme of the Government of India.

[1] Abraham Berglund, 'Tariff Act of 1930,' the *American Economic Review*, September, 1930.

As rolled steel is the raw material of many fundamental industries, such as railways, engineering industries, ship-building, etc., the Fiscal Commission of 1921–22 recommended that the best way of assisting a basic industry like the Steel Industry was by a bounty rather than by import duties.[1] Since there has been only one firm manufacturing steel in India, and since the output so far has been comparatively small, the bounty method, over and above being obviously a cheaper method of protection, would also have been simple in administration. In fact, on account of its economy and simplicity, the bounty method has been partially tried in India in the case of rolled steel. Thus, under the Act of 1924, due to the fact that the Tata Iron and Steel Company had entered into long-period contracts with the Railway Administrations for the supply of rails at much less than cost prices, protection for rails was given by means of a bounty. Similarly, in granting the supplementary protection of 1924 and 1925, the Government of India preferred the bounty method to additional import duties on the ground that a bounty was much less expensive to the taxpayer than import duties. In spite of these known and admitted advantages of bounties over import duties, we find that the Tariff Board in both the Reports of 1924 and 1926 summarily dismissed the bounty method as impracticable on account of the financial position of the Government of India.[2] This objection to the bounty method is exceedingly vague, misleading, and far from decisive. If the bounty method is preferable on the ground of cheapness to the general taxpayer, its adoption means no greater difficulty than some alteration in the taxational system of the country so as to replace protective import duties by other, preferably direct, taxes as a source of revenue. Furthermore, we have to notice that the imposition of protective import duties on rolled steel also automatically involved the imposition of compensating duties on fabricated steel, and this in its turn led to the extension of

[1] *Report of the Indian Fiscal Commission*, p. 60.

[2] *Report of the Tariff Board*, Statutory Enquiry (1926), Vol. I, p. 52.

protection to various branches of the engineering industry, although the case for protection to these on independent grounds was scarcely established.[1]

The real reason why the Tariff Board as well as the Government of India have fought so remarkably shy of substituting the bounty system of protection for import duties is that the Government of India, having so far failed to sufficiently develop the direct taxes of the country such as the Income Tax and Death Duties, are compelled to augment the import duties under any plea whatsoever; and since the adoption of a protective policy by the Legislature, they have in the plea for protection a very helpful and popular pretext for increasing the revenues by means of import duties. Thus, while in the decade 1921–22 to 1930–31, the customs duties have been increased by 55 per cent from Rs. 34·41 crores to Rs. 53·40 crores, the yield of the income tax has so far remained at or below the level of 1921–22 (Rs. 18·74 crores).[2]

In order that the administration of protective measures may be in accord with the principle of economy, it is necessary to treat the question of bounties versus import duties, not merely as part of the general financial scheme of the Government of India, but also as an independent issue to be decided on its own merits. As it is, the consumer, due to lack of the necessary knowledge and organisation, has no effective way of safeguarding his position as against the strong, persistent and organised pressure of the manufacturer to the end that a part of the money in the former's pocket may be diverted to the capacious pocket of the latter. If, on the top of that, the financial system of the Government is organised in such a way as to coincide with the aims and purposes of the large-scale manufacturers, then the consumer and taxpayer would undoubtedly become absolutely helpless in protecting himself.

[1] The Engineering Industry has been in existence in India for over a hundred years. Although compensating protection could justly be claimed, the case for substantive protection was neither thoroughly investigated nor proved.

[2] Cf. *Report of the Indian Statutory Commission*, Vol. II, Part VIII (Indian Finance, Layton Report).

E. The question of capital value and depreciation allowance needs further examination.

We found that the question of the estimated replacement value of the plant and the depreciation allowance thereon was somewhat superficially handled by the Tariff Board. The annual allowance for depreciation automatically reduces the original value of the plant from year to year. The profit on the replacement value of the plant and the amount of depreciation allowance thereon, therefore, should, it would seem, be cumulatively reduced in successive years. This important matter, however, is a subject for expert opinion, and it is suggested that the question should be authoritatively decided in the light of expert advice.[1]

[1] In this connection it would be interesting to note that since 1925 a few of the more conservative and financially orthodox companies have considerably reduced the nominal value of their capital due to the fall of prices: the Indian Iron and Steel Company from Rs. 3 crores to Rs. 1½ crores in June, 1925; the Indian Standard Wagon Company from Rs. 60 lakhs to Rs. 30 lakhs in 1926; the Scindia Steam Navigation Company from Rs. 4½ crores to Rs. 1½ crores in July, 1925; and the Tata Construction Company from Rs. 2 crores to Rs. 24 lakhs in 1925.

CHAPTER VIII

THE TARIFF IN RELATION TO THE SUGAR INDUSTRY

1. THE SUGAR TARIFF, FOR A LONG TIME AN IMPORTANT SOURCE OF REVENUE, HAS RECENTLY BEEN CONVERTED INTO A PROTECTIVE TARIFF; REASONS FOR THE CHANGE OF POLICY

A small revenue duty on imported sugar was a constant feature of the Indian tariff schedule before the war. From 1894–95 to 1915–16, the duty on sugar was only 5 per cent, which was also the general rate on cotton manufactures as well as other important articles of import. In March, 1916, in the course of a complete revision of the tariff, while the general rate was raised from 5 to 7½ per cent, the duty on sugar was enhanced to 10 per cent. In March, 1921, it was again raised to 15 per cent, and in the following March to 25 per cent. In June, 1925, the sugar duty was converted into a specific one, and the rate was raised to Rs. 4–8 as. per cwt. This remained in force for nearly five years. The average wholesale price of Java white sugar in Calcutta during those five years was approximately Rs. 14 per cwt.,[1] which is equivalent to a price of approximately Rs. 8–8 as. per cwt. c.i.f. (deducting Re. 1 for landing charges, traders' commission, etc.). The specific duty in force during the period would, then, work out to an *ad valorem* rate of over 50 per cent. In March, 1930, the duty was raised to Rs. 6 per cwt. and remained in force for one year. The average wholesale market prices of Java white sugar in Calcutta during 1930–31 hovered round Rs. 12 per cwt. This is equivalent to a c.i.f. price of approximately Rs. 5 per cwt. The rate of duty in 1930–31, then, would amount to 120 per cent. In March, 1931, the duty was again enhanced to Rs. 7–4 as. per cwt. The Calcutta sugar prices during April, May

[1] These prices are from the *Indian Trade Journal*. The quotations are for maunds (1 md. = 82·28 lb.).

and June of the current year (1931–32) have fluctuated very slightly from those of 1930–31, i.e. Rs. 12 per cwt. Deducting for the duty, landing charges, traders' commission, etc., we get a c.i.f. price of Rs. 3–12 as. per cwt. The *ad valorem* rate of the recent duty on the average prices of the last few months would, therefore, be over 190 per cent.[1]

It will thus be seen that from 1916 onwards, imported sugar has been an object of increasingly heavy taxation in India. The reasons for this special treatment of the import duty on sugar have been as follows: Firstly, due to the spreading habit of drinking tea, coffee and other beverages sweetened with sugar in the urban areas, the demand for crystalline sugar has been expanding at an appreciable rate during the last thirty years. Thus, while in 1900–1 the imports of sugar, refined and unrefined, amounted to only 200,000 tons, by 1909–10 they rose to 630,000 tons. There was a considerable drop during and after the war, but the tendency to expansion began again in 1923–24; the figures for the imports being 582,000 tons for the triennium 1923–24 to 1925–26, 793,000 tons for the triennium 1926–27 to 1928–29, and 940,000 tons for 1929–30.[2] It will be noticed that the recent increases in consumption have taken place in spite of a heavy import duty ranging from 50 to over 100 per cent. It was, therefore, natural for the Finance Member of the Government of India to turn his attention more and more to the import duty on sugar. These repeated increases in the duty on sugar together with the continuous expansion in its consumption have now raised the sugar duty to the first place among the import duties as a producer of revenue.[3] Whereas in 1900–1 the import duty on sugar

[1] In converting the specific duties into *ad valorem* rates, it has been assumed that the c.i.f. price is equal to the wholesale price minus the duty minus the landing charges and traders' commissions.

[2] *Review of the Trade of India.*

[3] Although it is true that the consumption of refined sugar is on a comparatively small scale among the rural agricultural population, it has nevertheless become a conventional necessary among the urban working classes who are increasingly acquiring the habit of drinking tea, coffee and other beverages sweetened with sugar. Therefore, the effect of the duty on sugar may be

yielded a revenue of only Rs. 53 lakhs, the amount produced by it in 1929–30 was no less than Rs. 870 lakhs.[1] In the latter year, the total customs revenue of India (excluding salt revenue)[2] amounted to just over Rs. 5,202 lakhs, and of this the import duty on sugar alone contributed nearly 17 per cent,[3] as against 12 per cent yielded by the duty on cotton manufactures. Secondly, it seems that in subjecting the consumers of sugar to this progressively heavy taxation, the Finance Member of the Government of India has been also influenced to a considerable extent by a similar tendency to be found in other progressive countries of the world. Thus, for example, Sir George Schuster, when proposing to raise the import duty on sugar from Rs. 4–8 as. to Rs. 6 per cwt. in his budget statement for 1930–31, invited the Legislative Assembly to note that the proposed duty of 9s. per cwt. on imported sugar in India compared quite favourably with the rates in force in England, U.S.A., Germany, France, Austria and Australia, the rates in these countries ranging from 8s. 6d. per cwt. in France to 12s. 7d. in Germany.[4]

Now, although the import duty on sugar has been increasingly utilised in recent years as a good revenue producer, the relation

taken to be mildly regressive, at any rate, as between the urban working classes, middle classes and upper classes. This is also the view taken by the Taxation Enquiry Committee (*Report*, pp. 120–21). Still, it would be proper to point out that, from the revenue point of view, a duty on sugar would clearly be less regressive in effect and hence less objectionable in principle than a duty on a common necessary of life like cotton piece-goods.

[1] *Statistical Abstract for British India.*

[2] The administration of the salt duty is separate from that of ordinary customs.

[3] It is interesting to note that the yield of the sugar duty in the U.S.A. in recent years has been estimated to be approximately 25 per cent of the entire customs revenue of that country. (Vide P. G. Wright, *Sugar in Relation to the Tariff* [1924], p. 235.)

[4] *Assembly Debates*, February 28, 1930. It is not known how the Honourable Members of the Assembly appreciated this comparison, but it is necessary to point out that the purchasing power and the taxable capacity of the consumers in India are much smaller than those in the countries mentioned by Sir George. According to Sir Walter Layton, the estimated annual per capita income in India is only £8 as against £100 in the United Kingdom. (Vide *Report of the Indian Statutory Commission*, Part VIII, Chapter I.)

between the import duty and the indigenous Sugar Industry was never considered or examined before 1930–31. Due to the recognition of the fact that the modern Cane Sugar Industry as it is carried on in Java, Hawaii and Cuba, depends for its success largely upon a highly developed system of agriculture and well organised and perfectly controlled processes of manufacture, the authorities in India during the last twenty years have devoted their main attention to researches in the various aspects of cane cultivation and sugar manufacture, and not relied upon the indirect, artificial, and uncertain effect of the tariff in helping to solve the major problems of the indigenous Sugar Industry of the country. Cane-breeding experiments with a view to evolving improved and suitable canes, researches into the diseases of the canes, propagation of new varieties through demonstration and propaganda, and encouragement of intensive cultivation through irrigation, manuring and rotation—these have been the main lines along which solid results have been obtained by the organised efforts of the Agricultural Departments in the Centre as well as the Provinces.[1] As we shall see later on, although a good deal has been done in these directions to improve the cultivation of cane in India, there is still a vast scope for the extension of these activities under Indian conditions, and therefore it was well within the bounds of probability that these direct measures of research and propaganda might have in course of time solved the major problems of the Indian Sugar Industry without the assistance of a protective tariff.

In this connection it is also noteworthy that a committee of experts[2] in 1920 thoroughly investigated the various aspects of the Sugar Industry in India and made as many as 435 specific recommendations embracing the cultivation of sugar-cane in

[1] The measures so far taken for the improvement of sugar-cane production in India have been briefly discussed in an article "The Indian Sugar Bowl and Agricultural Research in Connection Therewith," by Rao Bahadur T. S. Venkataraman, Government Sugar-cane Expert, Coimbatore, published in the *Agricultural Journal of India*, May, 1928.

[2] *Report of the Indian Sugar Committee* (1920).

the different provinces, manuring and irrigation problems, prospects of gur[1] and indigenous sugar manufacture,[2] manufacture of crystalline sugar with modern methods, sugar research and cane-breeding, and establishment of sugar schools. It appears that many of the major recommendations of that committee, based upon an elaborate examination of the conditions both in India as well as Java, have not so far been carried out by the Central or Provincial Governments. There are good grounds for believing that if the principal recommendations of that Committee had been given effect to, sugar-cane cultivation as well as the Sugar Industry in all its branches would have been by now placed on a fairly sound and stable position.[3]

During the last two years, however, there seems to have been going on a gradual reorientation of the governmental policy towards the promotion of the Sugar Industry of India. As a result of discussions between the Imperial Council of Agricultural Research and the Governments of the main sugar-cane producing provinces of India in the financial year 1929–30, the Government of India about the middle of 1930 came to the conclusion that the Indian Sugar Industry presented a suitable case for examination by the Tariff Board as to the desirability of protecting it by means of a tariff. The Board, after examining the different aspects of the Indian Sugar Industry, recommended that the revenue duty on sugar, already as high as 120 per cent at the close of the financial year 1930–31, should be transferred to the protective schedule for a period of fifteen years, the rate for the first seven years to be about 135 per cent and the next eight years approximately

[1] Jaggery. For a description of its manufacture, see below, section 6.

[2] Called 'bel' or 'khandasari' sugar. For a description of the process of manufacture, see below, section 7.

[3] Cf. the oral evidence of the representatives of Indian Sugar Producers' Association, Cawnpore, before the Royal Commission on Indian Agriculture, 1927 (*Minutes of Evidence*, Vol. VII, pp. 499 et seq.). These representatives of the Sugar Industry, among other things, complained that although the Sugar Committee had reported so long ago as 1920, the Government had done very little to further the measures advocated by the Committee.

101 per cent.[1] As already noted, in the current financial year the Government of India, without committing themselves to the conversion of the revenue duty into a protective duty,[2] have raised the rate from Rs. 6 per cwt. to Rs. 7–4 as. per cwt. (the rate recommended by the Tariff Board for the first seven years of protection).[3]

In the present chapter an attempt is made to analyse the reasons for this change of policy and to investigate how far the objective of the new policy is likely to be realised by the means of a protective tariff.

2. ANALYSIS OF THE ARGUMENTS FOR PROTECTION TO THE SUGAR INDUSTRY

The case for protection to the Sugar Industry has been founded on an elaborate series of propositions, which hang together, as it were, in a long chain of causation, and which may be briefly described as follows:

(*a*) The maintenance of the area under sugar-cane in India is extremely desirable for several important reasons. Firstly, as sugar-cane cultivation involves the use of irrigation water, manuring, and better ploughing, it helps to promote the spread of intensive agriculture and a better utilisation of the resources of the soil, so essential to the improvement of the economic condition of the ryot in India. Secondly, while the Government cannot do anything to arrest the decline of the prices of other staple crops like wheat, rice, jute and cotton, which depend on world conditions, they can help to keep up the price of sugar-cane by encouraging the manufacture of white sugar

[1] These percentages are calculated on the c.i.f. prices estimated by the Tariff Board. (Vide *Report of the Tariff Board on the Sugar Industry*, pp. 78–79.)

[2] The transfer of the duty from the revenue to the protective schedule would mean that the high rate of duty on sugar would remain in force for at least fifteen years irrespective of revenue considerations.

[3] The Sugar Industry (Protection) Bill was passed in April, 1932, and gives protection for fourteen years. The present rate of Rs. 7–4 as. will remain in force for six years, after which a fresh enquiry regarding the rate will be held. The present rate may, however, be enhanced at any time, if the existing protection is found to be ineffective, due to foreign sugar being imported at too low prices.

within the country so as to displace the approximately 1,000,000 tons of sugar which are now purchased from abroad. Thirdly, in view of the fact that the cultivator is now passing through a serious state of financial stress on account of the great fall in the prices of jute, cotton and rice, he ought to be helped, as a measure of relief, to realize a good price for his sugar-cane, which is the only other staple crop that is grown over large tracts of the country. Fourthly, since the harvesting of the sugar-cane crop commences in November and extends as a rule up to the middle of March and thus occupies the interval between the 'kharif' (autumn) and 'rabi' (winter) harvests, it serves to create employment for the agriculturist and his cattle at a time when other employment is scarce. Moreover, the tops and the edible leaves are an important additional source of cattle fodder in the country, where the under-feeding and under-nourishment of the cattle population has long since become a serious problem. And lastly (and here perhaps can be traced the most important reason for the initiative taken in the matter by the agricultural departments in the provinces), since the realization of land revenue and irrigation charges has been recently attended with increasing difficulties on account of the prevalence of acute agricultural distress all over the country, the Provincial Administrations hold that those difficulties would be considerably mitigated if the prices of sugar-cane and gur could be maintained at an artificially high level and the cash resources of the ryot strengthened thereby.

(*b*) Although during the last twenty years, 1908–09 to 1928–29, in spite of great ups and downs in the price of gur and sugar, the area under cane in India has remained fairly steady at between 2¼ and 3 million acres, it is feared that there may be a decline in the area in the near future due to the threatened over-production of sugar-cane and the consequent slump in the price of gur, which is the principal outlet for sugar-cane in India.[1] The great increase in the output of

[1] It is estimated that in 1928–29, out of a total cane output of 35·2 million tons, 25·45 million tons, or over 72 per cent, was turned into gur (jaggery),

sugar-cane in its turn is anticipated as a result of the spread of the cultivation of heavy-yielding types in the United Provinces and Behar and Orissa, where much progress has already been achieved in the replacement of inferior by improved types. In the United Provinces (which is by far the largest sugar-cane producing province in India, its share of the area under cane in the whole of India being approximately 50 per cent), out of a total of 1,357,000 acres under cane in 1928–29, 500,000 acres were under improved varieties. In Behar and Orissa, again, out of a total of 287,000 acres under cane in the same year, 70,000 acres were sown with superior canes. As it is in these two provinces that the spread of the cultivation of improved canes has been rapid and successful in the last few years, the Provincial Departments of Agriculture anticipate that the whole area under cane in each of these provinces will be placed under heavy-yielding canes in the next three years.

Now, the result of past experience in these two provinces shows that the substitution of heavy-yielding canes for light-yielding ones increases the yield of cane approximately by 50 per cent from an average of 10 tons per acre to an average of 15 tons per acre. On this basis it is estimated that the spread of heavy-yielding canes throughout the cane areas of these two provinces in the next three years will increase the production of cane by over 6 million tons and of gur by over 600,000 tons. Since these two are the main gur-exporting provinces of India, the anticipated increase in the output of gur in these two areas will lead to heavy exportation to the markets in the Punjab, Central India and Bombay and thus create a slump in the gur prices of these latter provinces, where the costs of production and consequently the prices of sugar-cane and gur are appreciably higher than in the United Provinces and Behar and

3·8 million tons, or under 11 per cent, into 'bel' or 'khandasari' sugar, only 0·75 million tons, or 2 per cent, into crystalline sugar in central factories, while 4·5 million tons, or 13 per cent, was eaten direct by chewing, and 700,000 tons, or under 2 per cent, was kept for setts. (Vide *Report of the Tariff Board on the Sugar Industry*, p. 44.)

Orissa.[1] If this slump in the price of gur in the unfavourably situated provinces should take place, the area under cane there would shrink and all the manifold advantages of cane cultivation, both to the cultivator and the provincial government alike, would be lost.

(*c*) In order that the large anticipated output of sugar-cane in the United Provinces and Behar may not lead to an overproduction of gur in that area and thereby bring about, as already noted, a slump in the gur markets of those cane-producing provinces which are less favourably situated in respect of costs of production, it is necessary to enlarge the alternative outlet for sugar-cane in the two northern provinces, which are already the seat of a modern white sugar industry in India.[2] India's import of sugar in 1929–30 was 940,000 tons. Assuming a minimum increase in the output of canes by 5 tons an acre, the 2 million acres of land now under the old indigenous varieties are expected to give an additional output of about 10 million tons of sugar-cane, and this will be adequate for the production of at least 900,000 tons of crystalline sugar.[3] The immediate object of the protective policy is, however, somewhat less ambitious than the supply of the whole of the demand for white sugar in the country from Indian factories, the idea being to ensure the expansion of the manufacture of white sugar to some 400,000 or 500,000 tons in the next ten or fifteen years. To the end that the object in view may be thoroughly realized, it is suggested that "any duty which is imposed on foreign sugar must be fixed at such a high level as to ensure not merely the continuance of existing factories but the establishment of new ones."

[1] The estimated cost of production of cane per maund is as high as 10·4 annas in Bombay and as low as 4·5 annas a maund in the United Provinces and Behar and Orissa. (Vide *Report of the Tariff Board on the Sugar Industry*, pp. 55–59.)

[2] In 1929–30 there were 29 central sugar factories in India with an output of 89,000 tons. Of these 29, 13 were located in the United Provinces, 11 in Behar, 3 in Madras and 2 in Bombay. The 24 factories of the first two provinces produced 80,000 tons of sugar in 1929–30.

[3] The percentage of sugar recovery to the weight of canes crushed is at present 9 in India.

3. WHITE SUGAR: COSTS AND 'FAIR SELLING PRICE'

As we have noticed in a previous chapter, the formula adopted by the Indian Tariff Board is that the difference between the 'fair selling price' of the indigenous product and the probable price of the competing import should be the measure of the duty. Now, under the ambitious and elaborate scheme drawn up by the Board for the protection of all branches of the Sugar Industry under the widely varying conditions of the different provinces, a 'fair selling price' is to be guaranteed to the producers of sugar-cane as well as to the manufacturers of sugar in its various forms.

(*a*) *Costs of Production and 'Fair Selling Price' of Sugar-cane*

According to the data collected by the Provincial Departments of Agriculture from selected areas and experimental farms, the cost of producing sugar-cane in 1930–31 was 7 annas per maund in Madras, 10·4 annas in Bombay, 7 annas in Bengal, 5·5 annas in the Punjab, and 4·5 annas in the white sugar belt of the United Provinces and Behar. Since the need as well as the probability of success of a modern sugar factory was greatest in Northern India, the Board took 4·5 annas as the estimated cost of raising sugar-cane. To this was added 2·5 annas per maund, partly to cover the cost of transport to the factory, and partly as an insurance against loss due to plant disease, depredations of wild animals and the vagaries of the seasons, and 1 anna as profit. The 'fair selling price' of sugar-cane which was to be secured to the cultivator in order to encourage him to continue the supply of cane was thus estimated to be 8 annas per maund.

(*b*) *Costs of Production of White Sugar*

The Board estimated the costs of production of white sugar both at the present day as well as at the end of the protective period of fifteen years. In support of the opinion that protection was needed for so long a period as fifteen years, the Board stated that, since the agriculturist was slow and conservative by nature and since the introduction of improved varieties of cane and more intensive methods of agriculture involved a prolonged period of research, experiments, demonstration and propaganda, an assurance of protection for a shorter period would not be sufficient for the purpose of promoting steady improvements in the agricultural and manufacturing branches of the Sugar Industry. The costs of production that were taken as the basis for determining the rate of protective duty were to be the mean of the present-day costs and costs at the end of the fifteen-year period.

Assumptions regarding the Economic Unit of Production

According to a well-known authority,[1] the average annual output of a sugar factory in different countries is as follows:

	Tons
Cuba	26,000
Hawaii	18,000
Philippines	17,000
Porto Rico	15,000
Australia	14,000
Java	12,500
South Africa	9,500
Mauritius	5,500

In view of the fact that sugar-cane is grown in India, not in compact and centralised blocks as in Cuba and Java, but in small and scattered holdings, and also on account of the absence of quick transport in the sugar-cane areas, the Board held the view that a factory with an output of 4,500 tons of sugar might be regarded as an economic unit in India. The estimates of costs of production, therefore, were based on the costs sheets of existing factories of that size in Northern India.[2]

[1] Francis Maxwell, *Economic Aspects of Cane-sugar Production* (1927), p. 104.

[2] According to the latest report of the Sugar Bureau of India, in 1930–31, while the biggest factories crushed as much as 90,000 tons of canes, the smallest ones crushed only about 10,000 tons of canes. The present sugar output capacity of the Indian factories, therefore, would seem to range from 900 tons to over 8,000 tons.

Assumptions regarding the Recovery of Sugar Per Cent of Canes Crushed

The sucrose content of sugar-cane in Northern India is 11·5 per cent as against between 13 and 14 per cent in Java. The average recovery of sucrose in the factories of Northern India is 78 per cent as against 85 per cent in Java. This gives a sugar recovery of 9 per cent in Northern India as against between 11 and 12 per cent in Java. The Board expect that at the end of fifteen years the percentage of sucrose recovery in India should reach 82 per cent, and sugar recovery increase to 9·4 per cent.

It is worth while noting at this point that even if this anticipated improvement should take place in the Indian sugar factories, their efficiency in the matter of sugar recovery at the end of the period of protection would still remain considerably below that of the Java factories, and since the Tariff Board hold the view that the average factory in India could not be expected to attain to an efficiency beyond the limit of 9·4 per cent of sugar recovery, the present difference in efficiency is likely to continue for an indefinite period of time.

Anticipated Economies in the Costs of Production during the Period of Protection

The experts of the Imperial Council of Agricultural Research estimate that in the course of fifteen years the cost of production of cane would come down by 2 annas per maund (25 per cent reduction) as a result of improvements in the methods of cultivation and introduction of better varieties of cane. The Tariff Board anticipate that during the same period improved practice and better control in the factories would raise the percentage of sugar recovery from 9 to 9·4 per cent. This would lead to the increase of sugar output in a typical factory from 117,000 maunds to 122,000 maunds, and thereby effect proportional economies in overhead charges and other general expenses per unit of product.

Details of Costs of Production of Sugar

According to the estimates based upon the costs data of average factories and making due allowance for the anticipated improvements noted above, the details of costs of production of white sugar in 1930–31 and 1945–46 (i.e. at the end of the proposed period of protection) would be as follows:[1]

	Costs per Maund of Sugar					
	1930–31			1945–46		
	Rs.	a.	p.	Rs.	a.	p.
1. Cane	5	8	10	4	0	0
2. Other raw materials	0	2	0	0	2	0
3. Labour	0	8	0	0	7	8
4. Power and fuel	0	1	3		nil	
5. Supervision, office charges, etc.	0	11	3	0	10	11
6. Current repairs	0	7	0	0	6	7
7. Packing	0	2	9	0	2	9
8. Miscellaneous	0	10	0	0	6	9
	8	3	1	6	7	6
Overhead charges, and profit at 10 per cent	1	13	4	1	11	8
	10	0	5	8	3	2
Credit for molasses	0	10	8	0	6	9*
	9	5	9	7	12	5

* The reduction in the credit for molasses is due to the anticipated fall in price from Re. 1–8 as. to Re. 1 a maund on account of increased output at the Indian factories.

The mean between these two costs is Rs. 8–9 as.–1 pie, and this is the figure for the 'fair selling price' of Indian sugar as estimated by the Tariff Board.

4. IMPORT PRICES AND THE AMOUNT OF PROTECTION

It has been the established practice of the Indian Tariff Board to accept the current landed price of imports as the price likely to remain in force during the period of protection. The lowest wholesale price of sugar in Calcutta in 1930–31

[1] *Report of the Tariff Board on the Sugar Industry*, pp. 65–69.

was Rs. 7–15 as. per maund. Deducting the current duty (Rs. 4–6 as. 5 pies per maund) and landing and clearing charges (3 annas per maund), the lowest c.i.f. landed price of Java sugar (25 Dutch standard and above) in 1930–31 was Rs. 3–5 as. 7 pies. But it was clear from the serious efforts at price stabilisation initiated by the principal sugar exporting countries of the world towards the close of 1930 that the sugar prices had fallen to an unremunerative level. As a matter of fact, the purpose of the International Sugar Conference held in Brussels in December, 1930, was to restrict production and export with a view to raising prices.[1] In view of the probability of an upward rise in prices as a result of the Conference, the Tariff Board checked the current c.i.f. price of Java sugar in Calcutta by an estimate of the average costs of production in Java in 1929. The estimate was based upon the figures for Java costs in 1926 supplied by Prinsen Geerligs in his memorandum to the Economic Committee of the League of Nations,[2] modified in the light of the available data regarding the improvements effected in the production of sugar-cane and manufacture of sugar in that country during the period 1926–29.[3] The estimated c.i.f. landed price of Java sugar on the basis of average Java costs of production without profit was Rs. 3–15 as. per maund in 1930–31.[4] The Board, therefore, took a c.i.f. landed price of Rs. 4 per maund as the probable price of imported Java sugar during the period of protection.

The estimated 'fair selling price' of Indian sugar, as already noted, was fixed at Rs. 8–9 as. 1 pie per maund. The margin of difference between the two prices was thus Rs. 4–9 as. 1 pie per maund, and this was the average amount of import duty proposed for the entire period of protection. This is equivalent

[1] The initiation, progress and final acceptance of the Sugar Export Restriction Scheme, known as the 'Chadbourne Scheme,' are described in the *International Sugar Journal*, issues for November, 1930, to June, 1931. An official summary of the Brussels Sugar Convention of 1931 is published in the same journal, May, 1931.

[2] League of Nations Publication No. C. 148, M. 57, 1929, II.

[3] These data are from the *International Sugar Journal*, 1929.

[4] *Report of the Tariff Board on the Sugar Industry*, pp. 74–76.

to a duty of Rs. 6–9 as. 3 pies per cwt. In view of the fact that the efficiency of the Indian factories would improve with the accumulation of the experience of initial trials, errors and experiments, it was suggested that the duty actually in force should be somewhat higher in the first seven years and lower in the next eight years, the average during the whole period remaining approximately equal to the calculated margin of difference between the import price and the 'fair selling price' of Indian sugar, i.e., Rs. 6–9 as. 3 pies per cwt. The rates proposed were Rs. 7–4 as. per cwt. for the first seven years, and Rs. 6–4 as. per cwt. for the succeeding eight years.

Additional Deferred Duty

The Tariff Board's estimate of the price of import was based upon the assumption that the International Sugar Conference (December, 1930, Brussels) would be successful and that the proposed export restriction scheme would be effective in stabilising sugar prices on a remunerative basis. But as the export restriction schemes of this kind had not always materialised or succeeded in the past, the Indian Tariff Board considered it safe to provide for the contingency of failure. Accordingly they recommended that the Sugar (Industry) Protection Act should vest a discretionary power in the Governor-General-in-Council to raise the protective duty by 6 annas per maund (i.e. 8 annas per cwt.),[1] should there arise any of the contingencies noted below:

(1) If the International negotiations for the stabilisation of sugar prices failed.[2]

[1] This deferred duty may be compared to the suspended duty of the Union of South Africa, where the basic rate of duty on Sugar in 1930–31 was 4s. 6d. per 100 lb., while there was also an additional suspended duty of 3s. 6d. per 100 lb., which is now in force.

[2] The International Sugar Convention (1931), known as the 'Chadbourne Export Restriction Scheme,' regulating the export of sugar over a period of five years, was signed at Brussels on May 9, 1931. The signatories are Java, Cuba, Czechoslovakia, Poland, Germany, Hungary and Belgium. Furthermore, under an earlier agreement concluded towards the close of 1930, Cuba, Hawaii, Philippines, Porto Rico and Louisiana have also agreed

(2) If the stabilisation scheme, though agreed to, failed to effect its purpose.[1]

(3) If prices as a result of a policy of price-cutting directed by any country against Indian manufacturers fell below the level of Rs. 4 a maund.

5. EXAMINATION OF THE AVOWED OBJECTS OF PROTECTION

The thesis that it is in the best interests of Indian Agriculture to ensure the maintenance of the area under sugar-cane is founded on insufficient facts and hasty and ill-considered arguments.

Those who are familiar with the arguments that are usually advanced in favour of the extension of the cultivation of sugar-beet in Europe and America under the stimulating tonic of protection cannot fail to perceive the strikingly close similarity of those arguments with the ones that are now put forward by the protagonists of sugar-cane cultivation in India. In both cases, it is claimed that the cultivation of the particular crop (cane or beet as the case may be) leads to the improvement in the quality of the soil in direct or indirect ways. In both cases, again, it is plausibly argued that since the cultivation of the sugar crop requires deep ploughing, careful preparation of the

to limit production and export. The three important sugar-exporting countries which remain outside the scheme are Russia, Peru and San Domingo (*The Economist*, January 10, January 17, and May 16, 1931).

[1] In well-informed quarters, it is expected that the sugar export restriction scheme is likely to meet with a large measure of success, and that for the following reasons:

(*a*) The Cuban Sugar Industry is largely in the hands of big American capitalists, and, therefore, effective restriction through combination is not a difficult thing to carry through.

(*b*) In Java, further increase of the area under cane is restricted by the Government in order to secure sufficient land for the production of food for the dense and growing population.

(*c*) In Europe, though the beet lands have completed the process of recuperation from the effects of the war and its aftermath, yet the encouragement of the Beet Sugar Industry by exaggerated protective tariffs has probably reached its limits.

(*d*) The bringing of new areas under cane cultivation is a comparatively lengthy process (*The Economist*, January 17, 1931).

soil, heavy manuring, and (in the case of cane) also irrigation, it leads to the promotion of intensive methods of agriculture and thus has an educative influence on the farmer. It is further pointed out that each one of these sugar crops is an important source of cattle food and thus serves to augment the stock-raising capacity of the farmer to a considerable extent.[1] Furthermore, in the case of Indian sugar-cane, the three-fold additional claim has also been urged that, firstly, it will relieve the agriculturist in his present distress; secondly, it will provide him and his cattle with occupation between the 'kharif' (autumn) and the 'rabi' (winter) harvests; and thirdly, it will enable the agriculturist to pay his land revenue and irrigation charges at a time when the prices of all other alternative cash crops like jute, cotton and wheat are rapidly declining.

Since, like the enthusiastic supporters of sugar-beet cultiva-

The widely held view that the cultivation of sugar-beet has a beneficial influence on agriculture has been also supported by Messrs. F. O. Licht of Magdenburg in their recent memorandum submitted to the Economic Committee of the League of Nations:

"From the strictly agricultural point of view, it is universally recognised that beet-growing ensures a good rotation of crops, clean fields, a richer yield of other crops following on beet and a general improvement of the soil.

"Not less important are the many uses of the residual by-products of the beet, such as slices or pulp, leaves and molasses, which enable the farmer to keep larger stocks of cattle and so increase the production of meat, milk, butter and cheese. Molasses are also increasingly used in many chemical processes. Sugar-beet culture, inclusive of leaves, slices and tops, yields on the average a far higher proportion of starch equivalent and proteins (76·70 and 3·51 metric quintals respectively) than any other crop.

"The labour problem in relation to the Sugar Industry must also be examined. Beet-growing, as a highly intensive form of cultivation, provides employment for a considerable portion of the rural population, whose number would be greatly reduced if this crop were discontinued; the sugar factories enable many field labourers to earn good wages during the winter months when they would otherwise be unemployed.

"In terms of men's working years, the number of hands employed in intensive farming on good soil without beet crops is 3 per 25 hectares (62 acres); in the same conditions, with 10 per cent beet crops, it is 5 per 25 hectares; with 20 per cent beet crops, 6 per 25 hectares; and with 30 per cent beet crops, 7·5 per 25 hectares."

[League of Nations, Economic and Financial Section, Sugar: Memoranda prepared for the Economic Committee by Dr. H. C. Prinsen Geerligs, Messrs. F. O. Licht and Dr. Gustav Mikusch (1929), p. 25.]

tion in Europe and America, the Central and the Provincial Departments of Agriculture in India as well as the Indian Tariff Board have laid great emphasis on the agricultural aspect of the case for protection to the Indian Sugar Industry, it would be instructive for us to analyse the basis as well as the meaning of these 'agricultural' arguments.

But before we turn to an examination of the specific agricultural arguments that have been advanced by the Tariff Board for the protection of the Sugar Industry, we should admit at the outset that the real importance of the cultivation of sugar-cane is that it gives a greater monetary return per acre than almost any other staple crop in India. This is certainly of great advantage to a densely populated country like India. This aspect of the case, though perhaps tacitly assumed, has not been sufficiently emphasised by the Tariff Board. It is, however, necessary for us to state clearly that the case for a protective tariff on sugar is examined in the following pages from two different but related points of view. In the first place, since there are many other valuable staple crops like jute, cotton, oilseeds, rice, etc., which are just as important to and suitable for wide geographical zones as sugar-cane is in its own specific areas, and since these other crops also undoubtedly require improvements in output, quality, and commercial organisation, it is debatable whether sugar-cane should be given more state help and encouragement than these other crops. For, unless we attempt such a balancing of the relative claims to state help of different crops that are suitable to different geographical areas, we are likely to do too much for some crops and too little for other crops in the matter of state assistance, thus distributing the benefit of governmental measures unequally as between different areas and different sections of the cultivating classes. In the second place, although sugar-cane undoubtedly requires great improvements in its agricultural and commercial aspects, there are excellent reasons for doubting whether a protective tariff on sugar is the most effective method of encouraging and promoting those improvements. It is from these two points of view that we offer the following criticisms on the 'agricultural' arguments used by the Tariff Board in making out the case for a protective tariff on sugar in India.

Sugar-cane Cultivation and Intensive Agriculture

(*a*) Sugar-cane is not the only crop where intensive agriculture is applicable.

The term 'intensive agriculture' is a very loosely defined but broad and comprehensive term used to denote all and sundry methods of effecting improvement in the productive capacity of the soil. Briefly defining intensive agriculture as that kind of agriculture where there is an increasing application of science to the problems of water-supply, plant diseases, manurial experiments, power supply, heavy-yielding and high-quality seeds, etc., we find that there is nothing either in the history of scientific experiments in agriculture in foreign countries or in the past experience and present conditions of India to show that the methods of cultivation loosely known under the name of intensive agriculture are applicable to sugar-cane alone, and not to other crops as well. Were that so, we should have expected the operations of the irrigation and agricultural departments in India to be confined only to this one particular crop—sugar-cane. But the agricultural statistics of India show that, considered from the point of view of the comparative scope for intensive agriculture, sugar-cane certainly does not occupy the most important position among the cultivated crops of India, as is attempted to be made out by the advocates of sugar protection in India. Take irrigation, for example. In 1928–29, the total area of irrigated crop in India was approximately 53·9 million acres. Of this, 33·6 per cent was under rice, 19·1 per cent under wheat, 6·5 per cent under cotton, and only 3 per cent under sugar-cane.[1] Although it is true that the percentage of the irrigated to the total area under sugar-cane is by far the highest among all the crops of India

[1] *Agricultural Statistics of British India*, 1928–29.

(being, in 1928–29, 62·3 per cent for sugar-cane against 22 per cent for rice and 41 per cent for wheat), it can never be contended that the scope for the extension of irrigation facilities for other crops has been even nearly exhausted by now. Let us turn to a second item of improvement—the introduction of improved variety. In 1927–28, the percentage of the area under improved varieties to the total area sown was 30·3 for jute, 22·3 for cotton, 14·6 for wheat, and only 9·3 for sugar-cane.[1] Here, again, the fact that in 1929–30 the percentage of the area under improved variety to the total area under sugar-cane reached high figures in the United Provinces (37 per cent for the whole province, and 20 to 79 per cent for individual districts), and Behar (24·4 per cent for the whole province)[2] can only mean that in those two provinces particular efforts have been made for the extension of the cultivation of superior canes, and can hardly be taken to imply that sugar-cane is the only crop which is capable of improved yield in India. As the recent comprehensive survey of Indian agriculture by the Royal Commission shows, the scope for the application of the principles of the physical and biological sciences to the improvement of crop-production and intensification of agricultural practice is almost unlimited in the case of practically every important crop in India.[3] Moreover, we should remember that the promotion of intensive agriculture demands, besides irrigation, manuring, deeper ploughing, and heavy-yielding seeds, also the aid of better implements, stronger draft animals, larger financial resources, efficient communications, skilled and organised marketing, and last, though not least, some measure of literacy on the part of the agriculturist so that he may understand, appreciate and apply the vast and rapidly increasing lessons of agricultural science and agricultural experience to his own problems. It is obvious that the combination of all or most of these factors for the purpose of intensive agriculture

[1] *Review of Agricultural Operations in India*, 1927 28.
[2] *Report of the Tariff Board on the Sugar Industry*, pp. 46–47.
[3] *Report of the Royal Commission on Indian Agriculture* (1927).

is applicable not only to sugar-cane, but also to everyone of the other major crops of India, such as rice, wheat, maize, cotton, jute, oilseeds and tobacco.

(*b*) Sugar-cane cultivation does not in any way make for special improvement in the quality of the soil or offer special scope for the provision of irrigation facilities.

It has also been suggested that if there were to be any substitution on an appreciable scale of rice or wheat or cotton or any other crop for sugar-cane, "on balance the agricultural system would be the poorer and the productivity of the soil less." In support of this claim, it is pointed out that in the United Provinces improved types of wheat grown after sugar-cane gave a yield of 30 maunds per acre as against 20 maunds when the same types are grown after other crops. It is also mentioned that the cultivation of sugar-cane in the same province has been responsible for the introduction of a large number of tube wells driven by oil engines, which would not be paying propositions without some form of intensive agriculture such as is involved in the cultivation of cane.[1] But we may well ask the question, do these facts in any way serve to support the claim that cane cultivation is of special importance to the agricultural economy of the country? It has not been proved either in India or in any other country that the rootlets of sugar-cane add to the valuable mineral constituents of the soil in the same way as crops like peas, beans, clover and alfalfa are known to do. If the cultivation of sugar-cane has been found to improve the yield of the next following crop in the rotation, that must be largely due to the heavy manuring and deeper ploughing of the field in the previous season of cane cultivation, and since a similar result might be obtained by deep ploughing and heavy manuring in the case of many other crops besides sugar-cane, no special merit need or can be attributed to the latter crop. Nor can the introduction of tube wells be regarded as depending in a special sense upon the cultivation of cane. As argued already, it is merely a question

[1] *Report of the Tariff Board on the Sugar Industry*, p. 39.

of general irrigation facilities which are required for many other crops as well as sugar-cane. These two additional pleas also, therefore, do not in the least degree strengthen the case that has been sought to be made out for the special promotion and encouragement of sugar-cane cultivation in India.

(*c*) Maintenance of a high price for sugar-cane through the artificial stimulation of demand is neither the only nor the most effective way of relieving agricultural distress and ensuring the collection of Government dues.

Another subtle but fallacious argument that has been advanced in support of the case for affording special indirect assistance to the cultivator of sugar-cane is that, since sugar-cane is the only one among the staple crops of India for which the demand can be stimulated and a high price maintained through governmental action, the protective tariff on sugar will also serve as a measure of public relief for agricultural distress. In this connection it is also contended that by strengthening the cash resources of the cultivator in a time of acute depression, the sugar tariff will also indirectly facilitate the collection of land revenue and irrigation charges and thereby considerably ease the budgetary position of the Administration in some of the provinces.[1] Here also the arguments used are exceedingly one-sided and ill-considered. In the first place, the argument that in a time of world depression sugar-cane is the only crop for which effective assistance can be given by the Government in the shape of a tariff on sugar makes the thoroughly unwarrantable assumption that there is no other way of assisting the agriculturist through a period of slump than by means of a protective tariff. For, since the present slump in the staple agricultural commodities is mainly due to a large increase of output in a period of reduced purchasing power among the consumers, the most direct and effective way of helping the farmer in his distress would be, firstly, to provide him with large and liberal credit so as to enable him to withhold his merchandise from a glutted market, and secondly, to persuade

[1] *Report of the Tariff Board on the Sugar Industry*, pp. 40–41.

him to reduce the area under particular crops for a number of years. While this is the method that has been pursued for some time past in the U.S.A. and Canada with regard to wheat, the principal sugar-exporting countries of the world have also recently decided to stabilize the price of sugar through the reduction of output and export. Similar methods of financial assistance combined with the limitation and regulation of the production of the principal crops might as well be adopted in India with a view to alleviating the acute economic distress among the agricultural population.[1] Moreover, the Provincial Administrations in the Punjab, the United Provinces, the Central Provinces, Bombay and Burma have also wisely decided in the current year (1931–32) to make large remissions of land revenue as a measure of relief to the agriculturists. When these direct methods of assistance and relief are not only available but also being actually applied over large areas, it is neither wise nor necessary to rely upon the doubtful efficacy of a tariff as a measure of relief to a very small section of the agricultural population. And lastly, since sugar-cane covers only 1 per cent of the total cropped area (2·7 million out of 262 million acres in 1928–29), and 3·4 per cent of the total irrigated cropped area (1·7 million out of 49·08 million acres in 1928–29) in British India,[2] it would be a gross exaggeration to state and a dangerous delusion to believe that the two tremendous problems of agricultural relief and revenue collection in a period of widespread economic distress and social and political unrest either could be or would be solved through the artificial maintenance of a comparatively high price for sugar-cane in the country.

(*d*) It is neither desirable, nor necessary, nor again possible, to safeguard the cultivation of sugar-cane in Southern India.

The ambitious and all-pervading scheme of sugar protection in India is intended not only to promote intensive agriculture,

[1] It may be noted that both the Government as well as the jute interests of Bengal are now planning to stabilise the price of jute through the reduction of its cultivation for a number of years.

[2] *Agricultural Statistics of British India*, 1928–29.

protect the cultivator of sugar-cane, and ensure the collection of Government land revenues and irrigation charges, but also to safeguard the cane-growers of the less favourably situated regions such as Bombay and Madras against the competition of the more advantageously placed cane-growers of the United Provinces and Behar. The costs of production of cane, and consequently also of gur, are, as has been noted above, appreciably higher in Bombay and Madras than in Northern India. The Departments of Agriculture in the United Provinces and Behar anticipate that the whole of the cane areas in those two provinces would be sown with superior variety of heavy-yielding canes in the course of the next three years, and that this would lead to an increase in the yield of sugar-cane by about 6 million tons. It is feared that if this anticipated increase in the output of cane in Northern India could not be absorbed by a rapidly expanding White Sugar Industry, an excessive production and large exportation of North Indian gur would create a slump in the gur markets of the South and thereby completely disorganise the agricultural life of the Southern provinces.[1] One of the avowed objects of the proposed protective tariff on sugar, therefore, is to stimulate the swift expansion of white sugar manufacture in Northern India and thereby safeguard the high-cost cane and gur of Southern India from the competition of the lower-cost cane and gur of the North.

The principle underlying the argument in this case has only to be clearly stated to be disapproved and condemned. The principal achievement of the British Government in India during the last 150 years has been the growth of a steadily increasing unification of diverse geographical and racial regions into one single closely-knit economic (and, of course, also political) unit, and it is through this unification that the people of India have been enabled to enjoy the advantages of division of labour and specialisation of production, which constitute the essence of modern economic progress. It is for the sake of the greater

[1] *Report of the Tariff Board on the Sugar Industry*, pp. 55–59.

good believed to be arising out of this ever-growing political and economic unity that the people of the predominantly agricultural provinces in the North and the East have gladly borne the burden of the protective duties on cotton manufactures, which have been so far a virtual monopoly of the Presidency of Bombay. If now at length, due to a temporary economic distress and a fear of further distress in the near future, the governing authorities and the public in the different provinces become so utterly short-sighted as to seek to obstruct the operation of those forces that make for political as well as economic unity, it would not be long before the separatist and disintegrating influences, violent, powerful, and always lying near the surface, but so long successfully held in check by a strong and efficient centralised administration, begin to undo the excellent work of economic unification that has been steadily going on for over a century and a half. Economic provincialism or regionalism, such as is indicated in the above argument, is a strong barrier to the promotion of national economic unity and would undoubtedly be a retrograde step. If the cane-growers of Bombay and Madras are unable to produce gur as cheaply as those of Northern India, the larger economic interests of India would demand that the cultivation of cane and the manufacture of gur should be concentrated in Northern India and gradually contracted in Southern India. Moreover, even if the competition of the Northern Indian gur should depress the price of gur in Southern India and thereby reduce the income of the cane-growers in Madras and Bombay, it would be a great benefit to the vast majority of the agricultural population in those two Presidencies, who are not cane-growers and to whom gur is the only luxury food available on any considerable scale. In 1928–29 the area under sugar-cane in Madras was only 0·3 per cent of the total cropped area, while in Bombay the corresponding figure was less than 0·2 per cent.[1] If we assume the numbers of agricultural population dependent on each different crop to be roughly proportional

[1] *Agricultural Statistics of India*, 1928–29, Vol. I.

to the acreage under that particular crop, then it would follow that in Bombay and Madras for every person that would suffer from a slight fall in the price of gur, there would be at least ninety-nine persons who would gain in the result. It is also worthy of note that the price of sugar, including gur, has fallen much less than that of every one of the staple crops of India in recent years. Thus, while the index number of Calcutta wholesale prices during 1930 was 100 for cereals, 119 for pulses, 114 for tea, 127 for oilseeds, 63 for raw jute, 91 for raw cotton, and 116 for all commodities together, the corresponding number for sugar was as high as 149. During the first quarter of 1931, again, while the index number was 86 for cereals, 82 for pulses, 114 for tea, 90 for oilseeds, 45 for raw jute, 80 for raw cotton, and 100 for all commodities together, the number for sugar was no less than 133.[1] It is, therefore, clear that it would undoubtedly be in the interest of the overwhelming majority of the agricultural population in Bombay and Madras as well as in the rest of India to allow the forces of competition to bring about a more rapid fall in the price of gur and sugar than has been the case so far.

Even if it were granted that it would be desirable to safeguard the stability of cane cultivation in Madras and Bombay on account of its supposed merits from the point of view of intensive agriculture, there are good grounds for believing that the proposed safeguarding measure would be either unnecessary or ineffective. On the one hand, it is exceedingly improbable that the far too sanguine expectation of the agricultural departments of the United Provinces and Behar that the entire cane area in those two provinces would be placed under heavy-yielding canes in so short a space of time as three years could be realised in practice, because, in view of the present depression and economic distress, neither the provincial administrations nor the cultivators are likely for some years to come to be in command of the large funds, which would be

[1] *The Indian Trade Journal*, April 30, 1931, p. 319. The datum line is July, 1914.

required for the necessary demonstration and propaganda, irrigation facilities and manuring, stronger bullocks, and better ploughs and implements. If under normal circumstances it has taken twenty years to bring only 37 per cent of the cane area in the United Provinces and 24 per cent of the cane area in Behar under heavy-yielding canes, where is the ground for the expectation that, in a period of extreme financial stringency both for the Government as well as the cultivator, the remaining 63 per cent of the cane area in the one province and 76 per cent of the area in the other will be placed under intensive agriculture and superior canes in so short a period of time as three years? Judging by past experience and considering the meagreness of the financial resources of the Government and the agriculturists at the present time, we would not perhaps be far out in our estimate if we put the minimum period for the spread of superior canes in Northern India at approximately ten years. In the light of these observations, therefore, it would seem that there is no legitimate ground for the fear that a rapid increase in the output of sugar-cane, unless absorbed by a quickly expanding White Sugar Industry, would produce a slump in the gur market of India and thereby bring about a crisis in the cane-growing areas of the South.

On the other hand, should the anticipated increase in the output of sugar-cane in the United Provinces and Behar by over 6 million tons actually take place in the course of three years, there would be little likelihood of the White Sugar Industry expanding so rapidly as to absorb the major portion of this increased supply of sugar-cane and thus prevent the over-production and slump in the gur market. At least 550,000 tons of sugar would have to be manufactured in order to absorb the anticipated increased supply of 6 million tons of cane.[1] Assuming the average factory to have an output capacity of 4,500 tons, this would require the establishment of over 120 new factories in the course of three years. In 1929–30 the number

[1] The percentage for average sugar extraction in India is at present approximately 9 per cent of the weight of the canes crushed.

of factories in India was only twenty-nine, and the output of white sugar only 89,800 tons, and this is the result of over two decades of development. Considering the state of great uncertainty and utter lack of confidence that have characterised the world of trade and industry during the last few years, and specially in view of the accentuated slump that has set in since the last quarter of 1930, there would be scarcely any legitimate basis for the expectation that the number of factories would expand by as much as 400 per cent, and the output of sugar by over 600 per cent in three or four years. The swift expansion of the White Sugar Industry in India at the rate and to the extent necessary for absorbing the large anticipated increase in the output of sugar-cane being thus improbable in the highest degree, the elaborate scheme for safeguarding the cane-growers of Southern India from the consequences of over-production in the North can hardly be calculated to be effective.

(*e*) If the cultivation of sugar-cane be really advantageous for agriculture and the agriculturist, no artificial stimulus or safeguard is necessary for its maintenance.

If, as is suggested by the protagonists of sugar-cane and sugar protection in India, the cultivator can in fact derive a greater net return, direct as well as indirect, from the cultivation of cane than from any other competing crop, it is exceedingly difficult to see why artificial protection should be necessary at all. Unlike the beet crop in Europe and America, sugar-cane has been known and cultivated in India for hundreds of years, and the cultivator is undoubtedly well acquainted with the comparative advantages and disadvantages of cane cultivation. Accordingly, the argument that is sometimes urged in Europe and America that the cultivator has to be encouraged and assisted for a number of years before he can understand and realise the advantages of beet culture can scarcely be applied to the case of sugar-cane in India. The motive of economic self-interest is strong even in the illiterate cultivator of India, and since through centuries of observation and experience he has learnt the comparative merits of different crops, he can safely be relied upon to grow that crop which is likely to give him the highest net return. Furthermore, we find that, in spite of great ups and downs in the price of sugar in the last twenty years, the acreage under sugar-cane in India has been steadily increasing, the figures (in thousands of acres) for the four quinquennia, 1909–10 to 1913–14, 1914–15 to 1918–19, 1919–20 to 1923–24, and 1924–25 to 1928–29, being 2,619, 2,695, 2,848 and 2,906 respectively.[1] It will be noticed that the percentage increase in the area under cane in each successive quinquennium over that of the previous one is 2·9, 5·6 and 2·0 respectively, while the acreage in the last quinquennium represents an increase of 10·5 per cent over that of the first. This would also indicate that as long as sugar-cane appears to the cultivator to be the most profitable among the competing crops, there is no reason to fear that the area under cane would decline or to assume that the cultivator needs any external and artificial stimulus to continue growing cane in preference to other competing crops.

If, on the other hand, due to a change in the relative levels of prices, the substitution of some other crop for sugar-cane gave a greater net advantage to the cultivator, there could be no sound reasons, economic or otherwise, why the operation of economic forces should be interfered with and the cultivation of cane bolstered up at the cost of the tax-payer.[2] That the cultivation of some other crop might be on the whole more profitable than that of sugar-cane in certain areas and over a period of years has been well illustrated in the case of jute cultivation in Bengal. While in the United Provinces, the Punjab, Bombay, Madras and some of the Indian states, there was a fairly steady increase in the area under cane during the twenty years, 1909–10 to 1928–29, the cane acreage in Bengal

[1] *Agricultural Statistics of British India and Native States.*

[2] This is also the comment recently made by the Economic Committee of the League of Nations on the artificial encouragement of beet-sugar cultivation. [*The World Sugar Situation:* Report by the Economic Committee of the League of Nations, 1929, p. 14.]

fell from 223,300 in 1911–12[1] to 196,000 in 1928–29, and the acreage under jute rose from 2·74 millions in 1911–12 to nearly 3 millions in 1927–28.[2] And the explanation for this change lies in the fact that the relative price-level of jute throughout the entire period remained much higher than that of any other staple article of export from India, and that, therefore, the Bengal cultivator derived a greater measure of material prosperity from the cultivation of jute than he would have done from any other substitute crop. The relative changes in the wholesale prices of the staple articles of export from India during the period 1910–29 are given in the table of Index Numbers (see p. 268).

These facts would seem to go far in supporting the thesis that while on the one hand the cultivation of sugar-cane in India does not need any artificial stimulus, on the other hand, there may be specific regions where over particular periods of time it would be a positive advantage to replace sugar-cane by some other crop if changes in the relative price-levels should indicate the profitableness of such a substitution.

6. A TARIFF IS NOT THE RIGHT INSTRUMENT FOR PROTECTING AND PROMOTING THE MANUFACTURE OF GUR IN INDIA

It is estimated that in 1928–29, out of a total cane output of 35·2 million tons, 25·45 million tons, or over 72 per cent, was turned into gur (jaggery).[3] Gur may be briefly defined as "cane juice in its natural state concentrated to solidifying point without having undergone any material process of purification other than the addition of a small amount of alkali or other clarifying ingredient and the removal of the scum." Whereas the sucrose content of modern white sugar is between 99 and 100 per cent, that of the Indian gur has been placed at between

[1] The Bengal figures for the earlier years include also those of Behar and Orissa and Assam, and hence cannot be separately ascertained.

[2] Due to the collapse of the jute market in the last two years, there is now a tendency to reduction of the area under jute in Bengal.

[3] *Report of the Tariff Board on the Sugar Industry*, p. 44.

INDEX NUMBERS OF WHOLESALE PRICES OF STAPLE ARTICLES OF EXPORT FROM INDIA, 1910–29.[1]

	2 Cotton, Broach (Bombay)	3 Rice, Ballam (Calcutta)	4 Wheat, Delhi, No 1 (Bombay)	5 Jute, Picked (Calcutta)	6 Linseed (Bombay)	7 Tea (Calcutta)	8 Sugar, Raw, Cane, Jaggery (Madras)
1873	100	100	100	100	100	100	100
1910–14 ..	123	223	106	338	196	116	65
1915–19 ..	171	282	150	364	161	167	66
1920–24 ..	195	352	178	491	232	286	94
1925–29 ..	142	362	158	501	184	279	120

[1] *Statistical Abstract for British India*, Eighth Issue, New Series (1919–20 to 1928–29), Table No. 296. The 1873 prices are those for March, and those for the other years are the prices for January.

65 and 75 per cent. In spite of this distinctly lower sucrose content of the gur, it has long been a highly prized article of consumption in India. In fact, gur is regarded as a kind of sweetmeat rather than sugar, and consumed as such by the vast majority of the agricultural population of the country. It should, however, be noted that the quality of gur varies from province to province, while its price depends not merely upon quality, but also and sometimes very largely upon the peculiarities of local tastes and prejudices. The result is that the market as well as the price for gur is usually independent of the market and the price for sugar. This is the reason that would explain the fact that the cultivation of cane and the manufacture of gur in India have remained fairly steady during the last twenty years in spite of a marked increase in the importation of white sugar from 526,000 tons in the triennium 1908–09 to 1910–11 to 940,000 tons in the year 1929–30.

Now, although owing to its age-old popularity with the people of India, gur has been so far well able to stand competition of white sugar, it should be noted that the present methods of gur manufacture in India are crude and wasteful in the extreme. In the first place, partly due to the weakness of the bullocks that run the crushing mills and partly due to the lightness of the wooden mills themselves, the extraction of juice from the cane is exceedingly inefficient. In the second place, largely on account of the careless way in which boiling is done, there is a considerable loss of sucrose in the process of boiling. It has been estimated that, on account of these leakages, the Indian gur-makers can recover only 52·4 per cent of the sucrose content of the cane as against a 86·4 per cent recovery attainable in a modern white sugar factory.[1] It will thus be seen that, owing to the inefficiency of the crude processes of crushing and boiling employed in the Indian Gur Industry, some 34 per cent of the sucrose content of the cane is entirely wasted. Assuming the average sucrose content of the Indian cane to be 12 per cent, the 25·50 million tons of cane used in the

[1] *The Report of the Indian Sugar Committee* (1920), pp. 262–63.

manufacture of gur in India in 1928–29 would contain over 3 million tons of sucrose, of which only 1,575,000 tons could be extracted under the present methods of sugar manufacture in the form of gur as against a possible extraction of 2,592,000 tons by thoroughly efficient methods of manufacture in the form of white sugar, thus involving a total loss of over 1 million tons of sucrose, and the waste being equivalent to more than the million tons of white sugar, which are imported at present.

This extravagant waste might, of course, be eliminated if the gur manufacture could be altogether replaced by white sugar factories. But, partly on account of the strong and traditional bias[1] in favour of gur among considerable sections of the people, and still more due to the fact that the cultivation of cane in small and scattered holdings is not conducive to the promotion of central sugar factories, it is not likely that the manufacture of sugar in the form of gur will decrease to an appreciable extent in the future. Nevertheless, much of the waste involved in the existing methods of manufacture could be prevented by the introduction of better and heavier crushing mills, preferably with iron rollers, and better furnaces and boiling apparatus so as to eliminate the present defects in boiling; by the substitution of oil or steam for bullocks; and last, though not least, by the general enlargement of the ability and strengthening of the position of the cultivator-producer[2] through education and organisation. If the gur manufacturer were thus gradually taught and trained to equip himself with these improved means and methods of production, there need be no doubt that the Indian Gur Industry, even at present securely entrenched through a pronouncedly conservative demand, could be placed on a stable and progressive basis in a decade or two. The problem, in the case of the Indian Gur Industry being largely one of reduction of waste, and not protection against foreign competition, it is clear that the solution lies primarily along these direct lines of instruction and

[1] The bias is in some cases also religious.

[2] The cultivator of cane is also the manufacturer of gur.

assistance, and scarcely, if at all, in the adoption of an indirect, uncertain and incalculable remedy like a protective tariff.

7. THE PROTECTION OF THE 'KHANDASARI' SUGAR INDUSTRY NOT DESIRABLE

The 'Khandasari' or the 'Bel' Sugar Industry of the United Provinces is an archaic and uneconomic method of sugar manufacture. Its survival is due to certain abnormal but transitory conditions. Its protection by means of a tariff is neither necessary, nor desirable, nor again likely to be effective in the long run.

The 'Khandasari' or the 'Bel' Sugar Industry is a wasteful process of sugar manufacture practically confined to the Rohilkhand Division of the United Provinces. A 'bel' is a "series of five pans which are placed in the form of a cascade over a furnace constructed to burn megasse and trash." Around the 'bel' are usually clustered ten or twelve crushing mills driven by bullocks. When the processes of boiling, clarifying, and solidifying have been carried out in the five pans, the final product which emerges is a kind of syrup called 'rab.' The hot 'rab' or 'massecuite' "is run into a series of small earthenware coolers in which it is kept in violent motion until crystallisation commences." The 'rab' is now poured into spherical earthenware vessels known as 'ghurrus,' each holding approximately 120 lb. of 'rab.' After being stored for two or three months, these are taken to the neighbouring markets and sold to the numerous small local refiners called 'khandasaris.' Ten years ago, the process followed in these refineries was exceedingly crude and primitive and was described as follows by the Indian Sugar Committee: "In the refineries the pots containing the massecuite are broken and their contents are transferred to bags. These are stacked in piles of twelve and are pressed down by the feet. The molasses exudes through the bags and runs off in small drains. This process lasts for about eight hours, after which the resulting product is removed from the bags to another room in the refinery where it is stacked to a depth of three or four feet on bamboos covered with reeds or cotton stalks. There it is covered with a layer of water-weed known as 'siwar,' which is renewed on alternate days. After a month's treatment in this way, the upper layer which has become bleached is scraped off. Further scrapings take place on alternate days, the renewals of water-weed continuing during the process. Each scraping is darker in colour than its predecessor. The sugar made by this process is known as 'khand.' "[1]

It was estimated in 1920 that this process of refining gave a sugar recovery which was only 4 per cent of the weight of the canes crushed as against the 9·5 per cent recovered by a thoroughly efficient modern factory. The Indian Sugar Committee, therefore, opined that this branch of the Sugar Industry had no future before it, and that, consequently, it did not deserve any encouragement.

In spite of this prediction of the Sugar Committee, however, it seems that the 'bel' Sugar Industry has so far been able to withstand the competition of white sugar to a considerable extent. The estimated output of 'bel' sugar in 1920 was about 250,000 tons. In 1929–30, the area under cane in the Rohilkand Division, which is the main centre of this branch of the Sugar Industry, was 300,000 acres, and on this basis the Tariff Board estimate that the present output of this class of sugar would be approximately 200,000 tons. This survival of the 'khandasari' Sugar Industry is in part due to the replacement of the crude and primitive process of refining described above by the use of centrifugals, which is said to have raised the percentage of sugar recovery from 4 to 5·25. The present extractive efficiency of a 'khandasari' as compared to that of a modern sugar factory has been stated to be as follows:[2]

	'Khandasari'	Factory
White sugar	5·25	9
Second-class gur	3·58	—
Molasses	2·64	4

[1] *The Report of the Indian Sugar Committee* (1920), pp. 266–68.
[2] *Report of the Tariff Board on the Sugar Industry*, p. 50.

Assuming a ton of second-class gur to be approximately equal to two-thirds of a ton of white sugar in value (according to the sucrose content), the percentage of sugar recovery in a 'bel' may be placed at about 7·63 per cent as against 9 per cent in a factory. The sugar recovery in a factory is thus 18 per cent greater than in a 'bel.' The total wastage on account of the low recovery efficiency of the 'bel' process may, therefore, on the present scale of output (200,000 tons), be placed at 36,000 tons of sugar. Despite the slight improvement in its extractive efficiency during the last ten years, it is thus clear that the process still remains undoubtedly wasteful. The real explanation for the survival of this industry must, therefore, be sought largely in other directions. In the first place, on account of the persistence of a semi-religious sentiment among the orthodox sections of the people in favour of 'bel' sugar, it commands a special market and often fetches a price that is considerably higher than that of factory sugar. Thus, for example, in the last week of March, 1925, when Java sugar was selling for Rs. 13½ per maund in Cawnpore, the price of 'khandasari' sugar in the same market was as high as Rs. 25 or 26. Again, in the last week of March, 1926, when the price of Java sugar in Cawnpore was Rs. 12½ per maund, the corresponding price for 'khandasari' sugar was between Rs. 18 and 23.[1] In the second place, the cultivator being permanently indebted to the 'khandasari' the price paid for the sugar-cane is generally less than the competitive fair price,[2] and this makes up to a great extent for the inefficiency in the process of refining. And lastly, the 'khandasari' can operate in the out-of-the-way parts of the country, where the lack of communications and the cultivation of canes in small and scattered holdings hinder the establishment of large central factories.

[1] Evidence of Mr. Wynny Sayer, Secretary, Indian Sugar Bureau, before the Royal Commission on Indian Agriculture (1927), *Minutes of Evidence*, Vol. I, Part II, p. 176.

[2] Evidence of Mr. G. Clarke, Director of Agriculture, United Provinces, before the Royal Commission on Indian Agriculture, *Minutes of Evidence*, Vol. VII, p. 38.

From the above description of the 'Bel' Sugar Industry, it is evident that its persistence is mainly due not to any efficiency in productive methods, but to the existence of a highly specialised and selective market on the one hand and the special advantage enjoyed by the 'khandasari' in the purchase of sugar-cane from the debt-ridden cultivator on the other. The United Provinces Government seem to hold the view that, since the area under sugar-cane in the Rohilkhand Division is between one-quarter and one-fifth of the whole cane area in the Province, the protection of the 'Khandasari' Sugar Industry is of great importance to the agricultural life of the Province as a whole. Despite this opinion of the United Provinces Administration, it is nevertheless a debatable question as to how far special protection at the expense of the general taxpayer is necessary or desirable for an industry whose survival is largely due to the entertainment of medieval sentiments and prejudices on the part of a special class of consumers. Since this process of sugar manufacture is in no way conducive to the growth of a stable and efficient Sugar Industry in India, it would, on the contrary, seem that a long-range policy, while concentrating on the encouragement of the more modern, efficient and progressive factory industry, should allow this archaic and wasteful branch of the indigenous sugar manufacture to linger on to its slow but inevitable death. And lastly, the 'Bel' Industry may very well be compared to a 'sweated' industry, in as much as the 'khandasari,' taking undue advantage of the economic weakness of the cultivators, can directly or indirectly compel them to sell their canes to him at considerably less than the fair market price. The prolongation of the life of this industry with public assistance, therefore, is in no way calculated either to aid the rapid promotion of an efficient Sugar Industry in India or to improve the economic position of the cultivators of sugar-cane.

8. A TARIFF IS NOT THE BEST METHOD OF PROMOTING THE WHITE SUGAR INDUSTRY

The problems of the White Sugar Industry in India are largely matters of scientific research and co-ordination of efforts. In solving these problems India can derive valuable guidance and fruitful suggestions from the brilliant examples of Java and Hawaii. On the other hand, since a protective tariff, even in an extreme form, has nowhere been able to place the Sugar Industry on an economically sound and independent basis, it is reasonable to conclude that the sugar tariff in India, while inflicting a considerable and long-period burden on the consumers, will by itself be ineffective in promoting the industry along healthy lines. It is suggested that a Central Sugar Board be constituted to plan, guide and co-ordinate policy and research in all the several branches of the Indian Sugar Industry.

White sugar is manufactured in India by two different methods. In the first place, we have a number of factories that manufacture sugar from gur or jaggery. Since there is already a considerable loss of sucrose in the manufacture of gur, this process of manufacturing sugar from gur is wasteful and uneconomical. It has been estimated that in Northern India 100 maunds of cane give only 10 maunds of gur, and since the sucrose content of gur varies between 60 and 75 per cent, out of which not more than 55 per cent can be recovered in the refinery, for every 100 maunds of cane crushed, the manufacture of sugar from gur gives a sugar return of 5½ maunds as against an average return of 9 maunds in direct manufacture from cane.[1] Moreover, since the price of gur does not usually bear any direct relation to the price of white sugar, the refining of sugar from gur necessarily becomes an extremely speculative business. For these reasons, those factories that merely refine sugar from gur have never had a healthy basis of growth, their out-turn having declined from 56,555 tons in 1923–24

[1] *Report of the Tariff Board on the Sugar Industry*, pp. 28–29.

to 31,000 tons in 1928–29. It would, therefore, seem that this method of sugar manufacture has no hopeful future before it and does not deserve any encouragement.

The second method of white sugar manufacture followed in India is the one that is practised in progressive cane-sugar-producing countries like Java, Hawaii and Cuba—the manufacture of sugar direct from cane in central factories. It is this branch of the industry that may properly be called the White Sugar Industry of India. Now, although the beginnings of this industry in India can be traced as far back as the nineties of the last century, its progress during the last forty years has been exceedingly slow and disappointing. In 1929–30 there were only twenty-nine factories in all India with an output of 89,800 tons of sugar. Of these twenty-nine, again, as many as twenty-four with an output of 80,000 tons of sugar were located in the United Provinces and Behar and Orissa as against only two in Bombay and three in Madras.

It will be noticed that the White Sugar Industry of India has been so far largely concentrated in Northern India, and that, therefore, its present conditions and future prospects are largely determined by the circumstances of sugar-cane production in that area. It should also be noted that the central sugar-cane belt of India is principally located in the United Provinces and extends into the contiguous districts of Behar and Orissa in the East and the Punjab in the West, the cane acreage in this central belt being 77 per cent of the total cane area in the whole of India in the quinquennium, 1924–25 to 1928–29. Now, this principal cane belt of India lying entirely outside the tropics, its climate is marked by great seasonal variations and wide extremes of temperature, which impose serious limitations on the yield and the quality of cane. Thus, we find that whereas the yield of sugar-cane per acre is as high as about 48 tons in Java and about 54 tons in Hawaii,[1] the corresponding figure for Northern India is as low as 10 tons. This climatic limitation will be still more apparent when we are

[1] Francis Maxwell, *Economics of Cane-sugar Production*, pp. 51–55.

reminded that the yield of cane under the tropical conditions of Bombay and Madras is no less than 30 tons an acre, although due to the competition of other crops and on account of the high cost of irrigation, the cane area in these two Presidencies has been comparatively small. The result of this low yield is that the radius of cane-supply for a sugar factory in Northern India has to be three or four times as big as that for a factory in the tropical regions. And since sugar-cane is a commodity that can neither bear a high freight without being unduly expensive nor stand a long journey without serious loss of quality, the sugar factories in Northern India suffer considerably both from the irregularity and insufficiency of supply as well as from the deterioration in the juice content of the sugar-canes they are able to obtain. This great difficulty in securing the regularity and maintaining the quality of sugar-cane is further multiplied by the fact that the cultivation of sugar-cane, as of every other crop, being carried on in India by numerous individuals in tiny and scattered holdings, very few factories can count upon the supply of cane from the same area or by the same persons in successive seasons. The cumulative effect of all these adverse factors upon the sugar factory is often to be found either in the smallness or in the partial operation of the plant, and the consequent inefficiency and high costs of production. In 1920, for example, it was found by the Indian Sugar Committee that, of the sugar factories then in existence, 50 per cent crushed only half the canes with which their mills were capable of dealing, 30 per cent from two-thirds to three-quarters, and the remaining 20 per cent about four-fifths. In the same year, while the average sugar output per factory was only 1,280 tons, the output of individual factories ranged all the way from 250 tons to 3,350 tons, thus showing the wide variations from factory to factory in points of size, efficiency, and ability to secure cane. Judging from the complaint made by the sugar manufacturers of Northern India as well as by the Secretary of the Indian Sugar Bureau before the Royal Commission on Indian Agriculture on the score of irregularity, insecurity and inadequacy of the supply of sugar-cane,[1] it would appear that the difficulties experienced by the sugar factories in respect of the supply of cane are still nearly as great as they were in 1920.

A second limitation imposed by the climatic factors is the comparatively inferior quality of the canes produced in Northern India. Due to the wide seasonal variations and extreme fluctuations of temperature, the type of cane that has been acclimatised in Northern India is the thin cane as contrasted with the thick and medium canes grown in the tropical regions. Whereas the average sucrose content of the tropical canes of Java is between 13 and 14 per cent, the corresponding figure for the canes of Northern India is only 11·5 per cent. Very largely on account of this inferior quality of the canes crushed, the average sugar recovery in the factories of Northern India is 8·95 per cent of the weight of canes crushed as against a corresponding percentage of 11·84 for Java.[2] This means that, for a given weight of canes crushed, the quantity of sugar obtained by the average Java factory is more than 30 per cent greater than that recovered by the average factory in Northern India, and that, consequently, this one factor alone is largely responsible for an increase in the costs of production of sugar in India by 30 per cent over those of Java.

These two serious limitations—low yield and inferior quality—of the sugar-canes are, as we have seen, largely imposed by climatic factors. Although the replacement of low-yielding sugar-canes by heavy-yielding ones has made considerable progress in India, much still remains to be done. The proper acclimatisation and economical production of thick tropical canes in the conditions of Northern India are still largely in the experimental stage. Considering the fact that centuries of adaptation have gone to the evolution of the thin varieties now grown under the unfavourable climatic conditions of

[1] Evidence of the Representatives of the Indian Sugar Producers' Association before the Royal Commission on Indian Agriculture (1927), *Minutes of Evidence*, Vol. VII, pp. 495–517; and also evidence of Mr. Wynne Sayer, Secretary, Sugar Bureau, ibid., Vol. I, Part II, pp. 170–77.

[2] *Report of the Tariff Board on the Sugar Industry*, pp. 64–65.

Northern India, it is extremely doubtful whether suitable types of thick and medium canes can be evolved and acclimatised in Northern India in a short period of time. Moreover, as shown by the history of cane cultivation in Java and Hawaii, successful evolution and introduction of heavy-yielding and high-quality canes has to be preceded by expensive drainage and irrigation works, elaborate analyses and experiments in soils and manures, pathological studies in plant diseases and the means of their control, and entomological investigations into the habits and life-history of sugar-cane insects.[1] When this vastness and complexity of the task of cane improvement in Northern India is realised, it would become clear that the principal problems facing the Sugar Industry are to be solved mainly by means of organised research on an elaborate scale and for a fairly long period of time.

Then, again, the problem of assuring a regular and adequate supply of canes to enable the sugar mills to be operated to their full capacity throughout the crushing season has yet to be solved. This problem can be solved either by the delimitation of the cane zone for each factory under a system of licensing, as in Java,[2] or by introducing a system of leasing the cane areas to the sugar factories for the cane season, or by encouraging and assisting the formation of cane-growers' associations through which effective and mutually beneficial contact can be established between the cane-growers and the sugar manufacturers. While approximate precedents for each one of these methods can be found in the progressive cane-sugar countries like Java and Hawaii, some one or other of these methods has also been successfully adopted by a few of the more enterprising and resourceful sugar factories in India.

[1] For a careful description of the work done along these lines in the Experiment stations of Java and Hawaii, see Maxwell's *Economics of Cane-sugar Production*, pp. 132–41; also an article named "The Experiment Station of the Java Sugar Industry," by Arthur H. Rosenfeld, in the *International Sugar Journal*, May, 1930.

[2] This was strongly advocated by Mr. Wynne Sayer, Secretary, Sugar Bureau, in his Note of Dissent to the *Report of the Indian Sugar Committee*; and again in his evidence before the Royal Commission on Indian Agriculture, 1927. (Vide *Minutes of Evidence*, Vol. I, Part II, pp. 190–94.)

And lastly, since modern sugar manufacture is a highly technical industry, it demands a large amount of organised research on the engineering as well as the chemical aspects of manufacture. Arrangements for handling the canes in the factory, the layout and construction of the mills, fuel consumption, mechanical balance and chemical control in the sugar house, systematic analysis of results and maintenance of records —in all these respects the average Indian factory is far behind the practice in Java.[1] Unlike Java, India has no scientific staff to advise the sugar factories with regard to improvements in the chemical and engineering aspects of manufacturing. Nor is there any organisation or arrangement in India for pooling the results of experiments and practice in the different factories, as is done through the experiment station in Java. At the manufacturing end of the Indian Sugar Industry also, therefore, while each individual factory can undoubtedly always effect some improvement in respect of internal equipment and control, the more fundamental problems of chemical control and engineering efficiency must be systematically studied for the industry as a whole, and for this purpose also there is needed an appropriate machinery for the conduct of scientific investigations, for collecting, recording and systematising the results of individual experiments and practices for the common benefit, and also for assisting the factories in the solution of problems of a technological character.

It would be clear from the above anlaysis of the more fundamental problems of the Indian Sugar Industry that a protective tariff can hardly be an appropriate or satisfactory machinery for their solution. And moreover, since even an extreme form of tariff protection, supplemented by various other direct and indirect concessions from the state, has so far failed to establish a healthy and independent Sugar Industry in the U.S.A., Australia[2] or South Africa, it would be the

[1] *Report of the Indian Sugar Committee* (1920), pp. 322–27.

[2] In no other country in the world has the protection of the Sugar Industry been so complete and absolute as in Australia. While there is an embargo

height of unwisdom for India to place any great reliance on the protective tariff as an effective instrument for promoting her Sugar Industry. The Indian Tariff Board, while marshalling forth a formidable array of hasty, ill-considered and inconclusive arguments in favour of a protective tariff, have been unable to record any single piece of evidence to show that the Indian Sugar Industry would be independent of the tariff assistance on the expiry of the proposed period of protection. On the contrary, the figures given by them for the estimated costs of production in India at the close of the fifteenth year would clearly indicate that the need for high tariff protection would still continue for an indefinite period. Thus, for instance, while the landed c.i.f. price of Java sugar in India at the present time is approximately Rs. 4 per maund, the estimated costs of production of Indian sugar at the end of the protective period would remain as high as Rs. 7¾ per maund.[1] Even on the most favourable assumption that the productive efficiency of the Java factory would remain at its present level during the next fifteen years, while the Indian factory would be able to effect all the economies and improvements anticipated by the Board, the Indian costs of production in 1945–46 would still be as much as 90 per cent greater than those of Java.

The evidence of history as well as the data of comparative costs would thus strongly indicate that the protective tariff is neither the most effective nor the most expeditious instrument for the development of the Sugar Industry in India. On the other hand, as is so well shown by the examples of Java and Hawaii, an appropriate organisation for guiding, controlling and co-ordinating extensive and continuous research

on the importation of foreign sugar, the prices of the Australian sugar itself, as also the wages of the labourers at the sugar works, are fixed by the Government. See N. Skene Smith, *The Australian Tariff*, p. 20; also Francis Maxwell, *Economics of Cane-sugar Production*, p. 9. The authors of *The Australian Tariff—An Economic Enquiry* draw attention to the significant fact that in 1928–29 the Australian consumer was paying £27 per ton for raw sugar (Australian) in order that other countries might buy it at £10 or £12 a ton (*Report*, p. 85).

[1] *Report of the Tariff Board on the Sugar Industry*, pp. 69, 77.

and experiments on the different phases of the agriculture and the manufacture of the Sugar Industry will undoubtedly function as a much more efficient and trustworthy machine for achieving the desired development. It is more than a decade ago that the Indian Sugar Committee outlined a well-devised scheme for the organisation of a representative Sugar Board, which would promote and co-ordinate research, experiments and technological training through a Sugar Research Institute and a Sugar School. It may also be mentioned that the Sugar Committee's outline scheme was based upon the accumulated experience of the principal cane-sugar-producing countries of the world. That scheme has been so long held in abeyance largely no doubt on account of the lack of necessary funds. But since it has now been decided to accelerate the growth of the Sugar Industry through a large measure of public assistance, and since that assistance can be rendered more effectively for the industry concerned and more economically for the tax-payers of the country at large, through the proper functioning of an organisation like the Sugar Board than by means of a protective tariff, there is at present a much stronger case for the establishment of the Sugar Board with the Associated Research Institute and School than there was ten years ago.

CHAPTER IX

CONCLUSION

THE detailed analysis of the conditions of three of the major industries of India, which we have given in the seven preceding chapters, serves clearly to show that the competitive weakness of Indian industries is largely traceable to grave defects in the principles and structure of business organisation, inadequate and unsatisfactory technical equipment both in personnel and machinery, the failure to adopt modern methods of marketing, and last, but by no means least, over-capitalisation and the consequent excessive burden of fixed charges. Since these deficiencies are obviously, in a large measure, the inevitable result of the lethargy, thoughtlessness and mistakes and miscalculations of those who are individually and collectively responsible for the management of industrial enterprises in India, it is hardly necessary to labour the point that the application of the principal remedies must also be initiated and carried out by them. These remedies, as has been indicated in connection with each one of the three industries examined in the previous chapters, are largely matters of intelligent planning and effective co-ordination in respect of production and distribution both for the individual units of an industry as well as for the industry as a whole. In fact, it is necessary for the industrial leaders of India to replan and reconstruct wholesale the industrial structure of India by adopting, in full measure, the new technique of business organisation, known as 'rationalisation,' which was unanimously recommended by the leading business and economic experts of the world at the International Economic Conference of 1927, and which is being applied with increasing success by the ablest and foremost business organisers in the U.S.A., Germany, and Great Britain, and also by the state in the U.S.S.R.

It should be mentioned, however, that this principle of

business 'planning' or 'rationalisation' is not a hard-and-fast rule, precise, definite, and universally applicable, but only a technique to be adapted to the well-ascertained necessities of each individual case. As a recent writer forcibly puts it, 'planning' or 'rationalisation' implies the "substitution of research, foresight and control for ignorance, guess and particularist chaos. Scientific management is its name when applied to individual enterprises. It implies a continuous working process of co-ordination, of discovering the necessities of a given situation and meeting them. It means applying intelligent management as a substitute for haphazardness."[1]

Now, while the internal replanning and reconstruction of each individual unit of an industry must generally be left to itself, the rationalisation of the industry as a whole, involving as it does the co-ordination of the activities of many separate, and sometimes geographically isolated, industrial units, may occasionally call for the interference of the governmental authority, either by way of initiation of group discussions so as to form a collective opinion as to the need, means and method of rationalisation, or in the shape of permissive or compulsive legislation.[2] Again, although the organisation of the necessary scientific services should, as a rule, be undertaken by each separate industry for itself,[3] there may be cases such as that of the Indian Sugar Industry, where the organisation and financing of those services may be initially undertaken by the state, but to be gradually transferred to the financial support and control of the industry concerned.

In all cases of basic world industries, as well as those that are of considerable importance in the scale of national production, however, the principal function of the state is and must remain the provision of precise, complete and up-to-date information concerning raw material supplies, output, stocks, prices, wages,

[1] *The New Republic*, New York, September 16, 1931.

[2] Cf. The British Coal Mines Act of 1930.

[3] This is the most characteristic feature of the German Metallurgical Industries. (See Walter Meakin, *The New Industrial Revolution*.)

employment, etc., so that production may be effectively co-ordinated and supply adjusted to demand, both from the national as well as from the international point of view. It is equally important that the Economic Intelligence Service of the state should keep every considerable industry in the country fully and accurately informed of the best methods employed and the most conclusive results obtained in other countries in the application of the principles of rationalisation, as well as of the broader changes which take place in the general industrial activity of the world.[1]

As has been argued at considerable length in Chapter I, both from the point of view of a fair distribution of the burden of protection as well as from that of a rational allocation of the public funds to the promotion of development in different departments of national, economic and social life, bounties are distinctly preferable to customs duties as a method of protection for industries. The administration of bounties may be organised on the same lines as that of spending departments like education and public health, and this would only involve the adaptation and application of the ordinary principles of financial administration to a new department.

The raising of a disproportionately large amount of the revenues in India through the consumption taxes on the necessaries of life and means of production makes the Indian tax system as a whole highly regressive in character. This marked regressiveness, which runs directly counter to the modern ideal of progressive taxation, is further aggravated in the case of protective import duties on these two classes of commodities, because they usually result in a transfer of incomes, through the mechanism of prices, from the general mass of consumers, the overwhelming majority of whom in India live on a bare and precarious margin of subsistence, to a limited and favoured group of financiers, entrepreneurs and wage-earners, thus widening the existing inequalities of wealth in the country.

[1] Cf. *Final Report of the World Economic Conference*, May, 1927, pp. 40 et seq.

A second and still more serious objection to these protective import duties on the necessaries of life and means of production is that they severely handicap the unsheltered industries in the domestic market and the export industries in the foreign markets, primarily by raising their cost of production. This has tended very materially to affect the financial position of the Indian agriculturist in the recent years of acute agricultural depression. Thus, while on the one hand the price he receives for his products in the world markets has appreciably fallen, on the other hand the price he has to pay for many of his necessaries of life and means of production has continued comparatively high, and what is most serious of all, the real burden of his debts, very heavy even in normal times owing to the usurious rates of interest, has become considerably higher. The result has been the spread of grave agrarian unrest throughout the whole of India, which has shown itself in a growing movement for the non-payment of rent to the landlords and of interest and principal to the moneylenders, and even in sporadic outbreaks of violence against the zamindars and the creditors in the countryside of Northern India.

The Indian Tariff Board, in practically every important case where they have recommended protection, do not seem to have sufficiently realised the cumulative effect of protective import duties in their reaction on the agricultural and export industries of the country. In recommending a series of protective tariffs in the last seven years, while they have been at considerable pains in each case to argue that the burden of the tariff in question on the average individual is comparatively small, they have never examined the cumulative burden of all the protective tariffs on the agricultural and export industries of the country, nor paused to consider whether these industries were in a condition to bear that burden in the recent years of falling prices, shrinking exports, and increasing weight of interest and debts. This would seem to indicate clearly the grave dangers of hasty and ill-considered procedure in tariff-making, and to point to the need for a more thorough and adequate economic analysis than has been done by the Board in the past.

In order to minimise the unfavourable reactions of protective import duties on the redistribution of the national dividend as well as on the competitive strength of the basic agricultural and export industries of the country, it is necessary that the principle of discrimination in protection, so insistently urged by the Indian Fiscal Commission, should not merely remain as a largely empty phrase as hitherto, but be accepted as an active principle in the selection of industries and also in fixing the rate and limiting the duration of the duty to be granted. The existing practice and procedure of tariff-making in India, which we have examined in detail in connection with the protection of the Cotton, the Steel and the Sugar Industries of India, would appear to be characterised by a large failure to observe the principle of discrimination, partly because of the effect of political propaganda, partly due to the lack of full and precise data, and partly also on account of an inadequate analysis of the data that are available. While even the guiding principles of tariff policy are open to debate, the technique of tariff administration is also still in an imperfect state of development. The validity of the principles can be properly tested, and the technique of administration refined and elaborated, only in the light of fuller and more precise and reliable data than have been so far available to the Tariff Board. The enunciation of rational principles and the execution of a wisely conceived policy must be based upon a continuous collection, classification and interpretation of the data regarding the relative importance and comparative costs of domestic industries, the variety, volume and trend of imports, as well as unfair trade practices.[1]

In the absence of such relevant data as well as their proper analysis and interpretation, tariff-making in India will tend to become less and less rational, and more and more dominated by organised vested interests. There is considerable danger that the existing practice and procedure may lead to unnecessary,

[1] Cf. T. W. Page, *Making the Tariff in the United States*.

wasteful and ineffective extensions of the protective tariff of the country. To safeguard against these real dangers of an unwise extension of the tariff, it is necessary to considerably strengthen the Statistical and Commercial Intelligence machinery of India so as to obtain the basic statistical and other facts, both domestic and foreign, a thorough examination of which is indispensable to the making of rational decisions on tariffs as on other current economic problems of the nation.

And lastly, since industrial development is only one, though undoubtedly an important one, among the broader avenues of national economic and social progress, the cost and the benefit of industrial development should be compared and weighed in the balance against the relative cost and benefit of other departments of economic development, such as agriculture, mining, transport, banking and foreign trade, as also against those of urgent items of social development, such as universal education, improvement of public health and insurance against unemployment, sickness, accidents and old age. It is clear that the formulation of a wise policy of national, economic and social development, which should have sufficient regard for the maintenance of a due balance and harmony among the different departments of progress, and which must itself be based upon a correct interpretation of full, precise and up-to-date economic and other facts, can be successfully undertaken only by a representative Economic Advisory Council, which has now become an increasingly important adjunct to the regular machinery of government throughout the greater part of Europe. It is, therefore, necessary and desirable that the Government of India should take early steps to establish such an institution in India, preferably on the well-considered lines indicated in his recent Report[1] by Sir Arthur Salter, late Director of the Economic and Financial Section of the League of Nations.

[1] Sir Arthur Salter, *A Scheme for an Economic Advisory Organisation in India* (1931).

SELECT BIBLIOGRAPHY

[*In the case of books which have passed through several editions, the date given is that of the latest edition.*]

I. TARIFFS: THEORY AND PRACTICE

(*a*) BOOKS

ASHLEY, Percy. Modern Tariff History, London, 1920.

ASHLEY, W. J. The Tariff Problem, London, 1903.

BASTABLE, C. F. The Commerce of Nations, London, 1923.

Theory of International Trade, London, 1903. A good exposition of the Theory of International Trade.

BASTIAT, FREDERICK. Economic Sophisms. Translated by P. J. Sterling. Edinburgh, 1873. Shows up the absurdities of protectionism with irresistible logic and sallies of wit and humour.

BERNHARDT, JOSHUA. The Tariff Commission, Its History, Activities and Organisation, 1922, John Hopkins.

BEVERIDGE, SIR WILLIAM, and Others. Tariffs: The Case Examined. A stimulating treatment of the advantages of Free Trade and criticism of the arguments and proposals of the Neo-Protectionists. A valuable contribution to public judgment on Free Trade versus Tariffs as a political issue of the day in the United Kingdom. London, October, 1931.

BROWN, H. G. International Trade and Exchange, New York, 1914.

CULBERTSON, WILLIAM SMITH. Commercial Policy in War Time and After, 1919, New York.

DELLE DONNE, O. European Tariff Policies since the World War, New York, 1928.

GREGORY, T. E. G. Tariffs: A Study in Method, London, 1921. An authoritative treatise on the technique of tariff administration.

GROTKOP, WILHELM. Breaking Down Tariff Walls. Translated by Eric Shadow, London, 1930. Contains suggestions for tariff reductions with a view to a European Customs Union.

GRUNZEL, JOSEPH. Economic Protectionism, Oxford, 1916. An objective study of the Genesis, Directions and Effects of Protectionism.

HIGGINSON, J. H. Tariffs at Work, London, 1913. An interesting and suggestive little book on the technical problems of tariff administration.

HIRST, F. W. Safeguarding and Protection, London, 1927. Brilliant criticism of the theory and practice of safeguarding in the United Kingdom.

HOBSON, J. A. International Trade, London, 1904.

The New Protectionism, London, 1916. A vigorous criticism of the neo-protectionist movement.

LIST, FRIEDRICH. The National System of Political Economy. Translated by S. S. Lloyd, London, 1885. May be regarded as the Bible of the Protectionist Movement.

MARSHALL, ALFRED. Memorandum on the Fiscal Policy of International Trade, London, 1903.

MCKINLEY, WILLIAM. Tariff: A Review of Tariff Legislation, 1896–1912, New York, 1916.

MORRISON-BELL, SIR CLIVE. Tariff Walls, London, 1930. A picturesque description of the tariff walls of Europe, with a plea for a tariff holiday.

PAGE, THOMAS WALKER. Making the Tariff in the United States, New York, 1924. The author was the first Chairman of the U.S.A. Tariff Commission, and makes an authoritative and suggestive review of the tariff administration of the U.S.A.

PATTEN, SIMON N. Economic Basis of Protection. Advocates extreme protectionism. Philadelphia, 1895.

PIERCE, G. M., and FISK, P. S. International Commercial Policies, New York, 1923.

PIGOU, A. C. The Riddle of the Tariff, London, 1903.

Protective and Preferential Import Duties, London, 1903. Analytical Study of the Effect on the National Dividend and Welfare.

RAMSAY, ALEXANDER. The Economics of Safeguarding, London, 1930. Defends the policy of safeguarding in the United Kingdom.

ROBERTSON, RT. HON. J. M. The Political Economy of Free Trade, London, 1928. A stimulating exposition of Free Trade Theory and brilliant defence of Free Trade Policy in the United Kingdom.

SCHMOLLER, GUSTAV. The Mercantile System, London, 1896.

SMITH, N. SKENE. The Australian Tariff, London, 1929. The Structure and Working of the Australian Tariff with particular reference to Empire Marketing.

STANWOOD, E. American Tariff Controversies of the Nineteenth Century, Westminster, 1903.

TAUSSIG, F. W. International Trade, New York, 1927.

Selected Readings in International Trade and Tariff Problems, Boston, 1921.

Some Aspects of the Tariff Question, 1915. A realistic study of American tariffs in relation to specific industries, Cambridge, Mass.

Free Trade, The Tariff and Reciprocity, New York, 1920.

State Papers and Speeches on the Tariff, U.S.A., 1892, Cambridge, Mass.

The Tariff History of the U.S.A., New York, 1924.

VINER, JACOB. Dumping: A Problem in International Trade, Chicago, 1923.
Articles on "The Tariff Question and the Economist" in the *Nation and Athenæum*, February 7 and 14, 1931.
WRIGHT, P. G. Sugar in Relation to the Tariff, New York, 1924. A realistic study.

(*b*) OFFICIAL PUBLICATIONS AND REPORTS

Australian Tariff Board. Annual Report.
The Australian Tariff: An Economic Enquiry, Melbourne, 1929.
Report of the Commissioners of His Majesty's Customs and Excise, London. Annual.
U.S.A. Bureau of Foreign and Domestic Commerce. Tariff Systems of South American Countries. Tariff Series No. 34.
European Commercial Policies Since the War. Trade Information Bulletin No. 228.
U.S.A. Tariff Commission. Annual Report.
Dictionary of Tariff Information, 1924. A useful book of reference on the history, theory and practice of tariffs in different countries.
Colonial Tariff Policies, 1922.

II. TAXATION AND TARIFFS IN INDIA

GENERAL AND HISTORICAL

(*a*) BOOKS

BANERJEE, PRAMATHANATH. Fiscal Policy in India, Calcutta, 1922. Historical and critical.
A History of Indian Taxation, London, 1930.
LEES-SMITH, H. B. India and the Tariff Problem, London, 1909.
SHAH, N. J. History of Indian Tariffs, Bombay, 1924.
SHAH, K. T. Trade, Tariffs and Transport in India, London, 1923.
Sixty Years of Indian Finance, London, 1927.
Wealth and Taxable Capacity of India, London, 1924.
SHIRRAS, G. F. The Science of Public Finance, London, 1924. With special reference to India.
VAKIL, C. N. Financial Developments in Modern India, London, 1924.
Our Fiscal Policy, London, 1922.

(*b*) OFFICIAL PUBLICATIONS AND REPORTS

Financial Statement of the Government of India. Annual.
Government of India's Despatch on Proposals for Constitutional Reform, 1930, Sections on Commerce and Taxation, London.
Indian Council of State and Legislative Assembly Debates on the Annual Finance Bills.

Report of the Indian Statutory Commission, London, 1930, Vol. I, Part V, and Vol. II, Part VIII (Finance).
Report of the Indian Taxation Enquiry Committee, Calcutta, 1926, 7 vols., including evidence.

III. INDIAN INDUSTRIES IN RELATION TO TARIFFS

Policy and Administration

(a) books

Amalsad, D. M. Hand-loom Weaving in Madras Presidency, Madras, 1924.
Burnett-Hurst, A. R. Labour and Housing in Bombay, London, 1925. A study of the economic conditions of the wage-earning classes in Bombay.
Coubrough, A. C. Notes on Indian Piece-goods Trade, Calcutta, 1921. Statistical Analysis.
Coyajee, Sir J. C. The Indian Fiscal Problem, Patna, 1924. The author was a member of the Fiscal Commission and signed the Majority Report. The book is in large part an able defence of that Report.
Gandhi, M. P. The Indian Cotton Textile Industry, Calcutta, 1930.
Hardy, G. S. Report on the Import Tariff on Cotton Piece-goods and on External Competition in Cotton Piece-goods Trade, Calcutta, 1930. An authoritative statistical analysis.
Harris, F. R. Life of J. N. Tata, London, 1925. An account of the early history of the Steel Industry in India.
Maxwell, Francis. Economic Aspects of Cane-sugar Production, London, 1927. With reference to Java, India and other tropical countries.
Pearse, A. S. The Cotton Industry of India, Manchester, 1930. Present condition.
The Cotton Industry of Japan and China, Manchester, 1929. Present condition.
Rao, K. S. A Note on Hand-loom Weaving in India, Patna, 1924. Bulletin Nos. 2 and 11 of the Department of Industries, Behar and Orissa.
Rutnagur, S. M. Bombay Industries: The Cotton Mills, Bombay, 1927. Contains important data regarding the Managing Agents.
Solomon, F. G. Protection of Indian Steel, Calcutta, 1924.
Utley, Freda. Lancashire and the Far East, London, 1931. A study of the Cotton Industry of Japan as compared to that of Lancashire.

(*b*) OFFICIAL REPORTS AND PUBLICATIONS

P.P. 56 H.C. 1876. London. Correspondence and Council discussion relating to the Indian Tariff Act of 1875; also the Report of the Tariff Committee of 1875.

P.P. cmd. 8078 of 1896, London. Indian Tariff Act, 1896, and the Cotton Duties Act, 1896. Correspondence, Council Proceedings and Representations.

Debates in the Governor-General's Legislative Council (up to 1920), Legislative Assembly and Council of State on Tariff Bills.

Reports of the Director of Industries in each Province in India. Annual.

Report of the Indian Fiscal Commission, 1922, with three volumes of evidence, Calcutta.

Records of the Geological Survey of India: Reports on Mineral Production, Calcutta.

Report of the Indian Trade Mission to the Near East and Africa, Bombay, 1928.

League of Nations. The World Sugar Situation: Report of the Economic Committee of the League of Nations, Geneva, 1929.

Sugar: Memoranda prepared for the Economic Committee by Dr. H. C. Prinsen Geerligs, Messrs. F. O. Licht and Dr. Gustav Mikusch, Geneva, 1929. An authoritative survey of the present position of the Cane and Beet Sugar Industries, and of state policy in relation to sugar, throughout the world.

Indian Munitions Board Handbook, Calcutta, 1919.

Monthly Statistics of Cotton Spinning and Weaving in India, Calcutta.

Report of the Indian Sugar Committee, Calcutta, 1920. An authoritative survey of the Indian Sugar Industry, with proposals for improvements.

Report of the Bombay Strike Enquiry Committee, Bombay, 1929.

Report of the Court of Enquiry (on industrial disputes in the Cotton Textile Industry of Bombay), Bombay, 1929.

Indian Tariff Acts and Tariff Schedules, Calcutta.

Report on an Enquiry into Wages and Hours of Labour in the Cotton-mill Industry in 1921, 1923 and 1926. Bombay.

The Indian Tariff Board. Report regarding the grant of Protection to the Steel Industry, 1924, with three volumes of evidence, Calcutta.

Report regarding the Increase of Duties on Steel, 1924, Calcutta.

Report regarding the Grant of Supplementary Protection to the Steel Industry, 1925, Calcutta.

Statutory Enquiry on the Protection of the Steel Industry, 1927, 8 volumes.

Report on Steel Rails, 1931.

Report on Additional Protection for Galvanised Sheets, 1931.

Report on the Grant of Protection to the Wire and Wire-nail Industry, 1926.
Report on the Sugar Industry, 1931.
Report on the Salt Industry, 1930, with two volumes of evidence.
Report on the Ship-building Industry, 1926.
Report on the Spelter and Galvanised Hardware, 1926.
Report on the Cement Industry, 1925, with two volumes of evidence.
Report on Camel Hair, Cotton and Canvas Ply Belting, 1928.
Report on Heavy Chemical Industries, 1929, with two volumes of evidence.
Report on the Coal Industry, 1926.
Report on the Cotton Textile Industry, 1927, with three volumes of evidence.
Report on Electric Wires and Cables, 1928.
Report on the Magnesium Chloride Industry, 1925 and 1929.
Report on Manila Rope, 1929.
Report on the Match Industry, 1928, with four volumes of evidence.
Report on the Mineral Oil Industry, 1928, with two volumes of evidence.
Report on Paper and Paper Pulp Industries, with two volumes of evidence.
Report on the Plywood and Tea-chest Industry, 1927, with one volume of evidence.
Report on Printers' Ink Industry, 1925.

(*c*) OTHER ANNUAL AND PERIODICAL PUBLICATIONS

Report of the Ahmedabad Mill-owners' Association, Ahmedabad. Annual.
Report of the Bombay Mill-owners' Association, Bombay. Annual.
The Investor's India Year-Book, Calcutta, from 1911 onwards. An indispensable volume for the study of the movements in the market for securities, and the general financial position of principal banks, railways, mining companies, large industrial establishments, etc.

IV. MISCELLANEOUS

(*a*) BOOKS

MEAKIN, WALTER. The New Industrial Revolution, London, 1928. A study for the general reader of rationalisation and post-war tendencies of capitalism and labour.
SALTER, SIR ARTHUR. A scheme for an Economic Advisory Organisation in India, Delhi, 1931.
URWICK, L. The Meaning of Rationalisation, London, 1929. A clear statement of the purpose, principles and methods of rationalisation.

(*b*) OFFICIAL REPORTS AND PUBLICATIONS

Report of the Indian Economic Enquiry Committee, Calcutta, 1925, 2 vols., including evidence. An examination of the existing sources of economic and statistical data in India, with suggestions for improvements.

League of Nations. The World Economic Conference, Final Report, Geneva, 1927. An objective general survey of post-war commerce, industry and agriculture.

Memoranda on production and trade, 1913 and 1923–27, and 1923–28–29, Geneva, 1929, 1930.

Report of the Committee on Finance and Industry, United Kingdom, London, 1931. An authoritative exposition of the operation of the mechanism of the gold standard in the United Kingdom, with reference to its influence on banking, finance and credit, and with proposals for improvements.

The Committee on Industry and Trade, United Kingdom, Final Report, London, 1929.

Factors in Industrial and Commercial Efficiency, 1927.

Further Factors in Industrial and Commercial Efficiency, 1928.

Survey of Metal Industries, 1928.

Survey of Textile Industries, 1928.

INDEX